Building an Import/Export Business

Building an Import/ Export Business

Third Edition

Kenneth D. Weiss

John Wiley & Sons, Inc.

New York

Copyright © 2002 by Kenneth D. Weiss. All rights reserved.

Published by John Wiley & Sons, Inc., New York
Published simultaneously in Canada

This publication is designed to provide accurate and authoritative
information in regard to the subject matter covered. It is sold with the
understanding that the publisher is not engaged in rendering professional services. If professional advice or other expert assistance is
required, the services of a competent professional person should be
sought.

Library of Congress Cataloging-in-Publication Data
Weiss, Kenneth D. (Kenneth Duane).
    Building an import/export business / Kenneth D. Weiss.—3rd ed.
        p.   cm.
    Includes bibliographical references and index.
    ISBN   0-471-20249-5 (pbk. : alk. paper)
    1. Trading companies.   2. Export marketing.   3. International
trade.   I. Title.
HF1416.W43 2002   2001046734
658.8—dc21

Printed in the United States of America

10 9 8 7 6 5 4 3 2 1

This is the fourth dedication I have written for the book, *Building an Import/Export Business*.

The first edition was dedicated to one Mr. Peter Gaffney, who in 1965 helped me escape from retailing and enter the world of international development and trade. Since then I haven't seen or heard from Peter, but I hope he is doing well.

The first revision of this book was dedicated to the World Trade Institute (WTI) which was then an activity of the Port Authority of New York and New Jersey and was housed in One World Trade Center. Its activities included organizing and conducting training courses in international trade for U.S. and foreign importers and exporters. A few years ago the WTI was purchased by Pace University, which kept it in the World Trade Center until the disastrous events of September 11, 2001.

The second edition was dedicated to my wife, Beatriz, whom I met in Bogota, Colombia in 1966. I am happy to report that we recently celebrated thirty-four years of marriage. One daughter lives an hour to the northeast of us and the other an hour to the southwest, and we have a granddaughter who can sing "Happy Birthday" in English, Spanish, and Polish.

I am dedicating this new and updated version of my book to you, the reader. I speak of all my readers—past, present, and future—and especially those who have given the book five stars on Amazon.com, those who have contacted me with questions and comments, and of course those who have founded growing importing or exporting companies. I wish each one the best of health, happiness, and success in business. Most of us dream of being our own bosses, enjoying what we do, and making money at it. I can't claim that this is easy in importing or exporting, but many have succeeded and many more will do so in the future. Reading this book cannot guarantee you success, but it can definitely help you achieve it.

Contents

Illustrations

Figure

Acknowledgments

In this updated edition of *Building an Import/Export Business* I would like to, once again, acknowledge some people who helped with the first edition: George Haber of Information Services in Jericho, New York; Bill Laraque of the Standard Chartered Bank in Melville, New York; Bill Maron of Maron International Shipping Corporation in New York City; Arnold Ceglia of Sky-Sea Forwarding Corporation in Valley Stream, New York; Sherry Singer of Soller, Singer & Horn (attorneys at law) in New York City; and Charles Cardile of C & S Laboratory Consultants in New York City.

Thanks are due also to Pam Michel and Sue Harris, who helped with this edition, and to the many readers who have written to tell me of their import-export ambitions, plans, and activities.

Finally, acknowledgment is due to our dynamic world, which keeps the theater of trade interesting by continually changing the scenery, the script, and the actors. Events swiftly outdated the first and second editions of this book, setting the stage for this updated one.

Introduction

John T. Hyatt, president of the Irwin Brown Company and the International Freight Forwarders and Customs Brokers Association of New Orleans, tells me that the number of importers in the United States has doubled in the past ten years, to about 40,000. The number of exporters today is probably smaller but has increased as well. International trade is a highly popular kind of business. Yet it is changing rapidly.

The World Wide Web, Global Positioning Systems, ISO 9000, and NAFTA. Only ten years ago, none of these things existed, but today they are having decisive impacts on the way the world does business. When this book was first written in 1987, it was done on a typewriter and the only computer I owned was a Commodore Vic 20. Now world traders are able to get information, communicate, and close deals with a few keystrokes. Therefore, this book *had* to be brought up to date.

This third edition is still true to the objectives of the first— to help readers decide whether to start small-scale import and/or export businesses and then to show them how to get started and avoid the pitfalls. While I haven't included information useful mainly to large corporations, this book does assume that the reader has a fair understanding of the world in general and the business world in particular. Unlike some other books of this type, it tries not to make building an import or export business sound either harder or easier than it actually is.

In the first edition there was a chapter based on the question, "What comes first, the product or the market?" This question is no longer as important as it was then because it is now clear that, for a small-scale international trader, the answer is "neither." What comes first is a *buyer*. If you find someone who wants to buy something from you, in the United States or abroad, you can probably find a supplier and work out the procedural details. There are exceptions, of course. Governments prohibit some trade, such as imports of endangered species and exports of products that may be used by armies that are hostile to them. Also, there are many brand-name products whose manufacturers won't supply them to independent exporters. Beyond that, there are not many limits.

In the year 2000, total global trade came to $6.23 trillion (in goods only, not including services). The United States' share of this was approximately $1.7 *trillion*. This includes, on what is known as the *census* basis, $1,025 billion in imports and $696 billion in exports. The huge amount of imports provided jobs for millions of Americans involved in importing and distributing imported goods, while the exports provided millions of jobs for manufacturers of finished products and their components, parts, and ingredients. Businesses in the United States traded in thousands of different products and with nearly every nation on earth. This is a gigantic undertaking, with room for both old hands and newcomers.

So, come along on a tour of this exciting business, which thousands of people think about when they travel and see product or market opportunities. We'll begin with a couple of get-your-feet-wet scenarios.

Building an Import/Export Business

CHAPTER 1

Jumping into the Water: Simple Scenarios

Greetings, and welcome to Guatemala City. You have just discovered some beautiful hand-woven wool jackets and are *sure* you can sell them in Toronto and Montreal. You have found what seems to be a reliable supplier and have gotten information on import regulations from the Canadian consulate. Now you are looking for a Guatemalan firm that can make bilingual labels for you in French and English. You wonder what else you will have to do to get your business started.

Greetings, and welcome to Washington, D.C. You are a recently retired diplomat with excellent contacts in West Africa. One of your contacts is setting up a cable TV business and would like you to supply all the equipment, including the cable to "wire up" hundreds of homes. This sounds like a fabulous business opportunity. Is it as good as it sounds, or do the pitfalls exceed the potential?

Let's think about these business ideas.

IMPORTING THE WOOL JACKETS

The product may look lovely to you but, remember, you cannot make money unless you can get the jackets out of Guatemala and into Canada and sell them for a profit. The supplier may seem reliable, but quality often tends to decrease gradually, especially with handmade products.

You will be moving the jackets in small quantities, which will give you high costs per unit for transportation and insurance. Also, there will be marking regulations and the cost of getting the goods out of Canadian customs. There probably will not be Canadian customs duties, as is common for a handmade product from a developing country.

Next you will have to get the product into retail distribution channels in order to move a significant quantity. The designs may not look good to buyers who have never traveled in Guatemala. And the prices . . . you will probably find that the jackets must retail for at least *four times* your cost in Central America.

When you evaluate these problems and calculate the number of jackets you will have to sell to earn a living, you may see the venture as a hobby but not as a business.

EXPORTING THE CABLE TV EQUIPMENT

As a retired diplomat, you may not be inclined to get involved in all the details of an export business. Yet, your experience will make it easier for you than for most other people.

The *Thomas Register of American Manufacturers* in any library will give you suppliers of cable TV equipment, and they will probably be pleased to hear from you. Their prices will be reasonable by world standards, and because of your background they may agree to sell to you on credit.

Because the equipment involved is not considered "sensitive," there should be no difficulty with U.S. export control regulations, and the quantities will be sufficient to let you ship in full container loads. Best of all, there will be no marketing problems because you already have the customer.

Your major challenges will be (1) making sure you send exactly what the customer wants, (2) making sure you get paid, and (3) keeping the business going after the needs of your one customer have been satisfied. If you can meet these challenges, dive in!

Now let's look at two somewhat more complex examples.

THE "WORLD CLOCK"

Suppose you are looking through an export promotion magazine from Taiwan and see a small clock that tells the time in major world cities. You ask for a catalog and price list and receive them immediately. You show the catalog to several people, being careful to not reveal the supplier's name and address to potential competitors.

Everyone thinks you have a good product, so you buy an international money order from your bank and send it with a letter, asking for samples. You might have been able to get them for free but didn't want to risk having the supplier delay shipment if he asked for and waited to receive your money.

While you are waiting for the samples, you phone the nearest U.S. Customs office and speak with a product specialist. She gives you the applicable tariff numbers, rates of duty, and marking requirements. Each battery, clock movement, and case should be marked indelibly "Made in Taiwan," and the country of origin should be on the packages as well.

Also while waiting, you think about who might want to buy your product—a world time clock. After reviewing several potential market segments, you finally decide that the best will be business executives who travel internationally. They will probably not buy clocks for themselves but will receive them as gifts from relatives or from firms they do business with. There-fore, you tentatively decide to sell the clocks through giftware channels.

Soon the samples arrive, by airmail. They come to your house marked "Samples. No commercial value," and no customs duty is charged on them. You like their appearance but not the packag-ing or the way the instructions are written. You plan, tentatively, to sell for about double your cost of $6.50 per unit.

From the yellow pages in the telephone directory you identify gift shops in what appear to be "good" sections of the nearest major city. You phone them, ask who does the buying, and try to make appointments to show them "a new product that (you) may be adding to (your) line of imported merchandise." After 15 calls to 8 gift shops, you have 5 appointments.

The buyers generally like your merchandise but are not thrilled with it. They have no criticisms of the clocks but point out that the country-of-origin marking isn't legally correct and the pack-aging isn't very attractive. They think the item is "a $20 retail," which may be too low for the business to be viable at your $6.50 purchase price.

With this doubtful outcome in mind, you decide to try a dif-ferent marketing channel and approach advertising specialty or corporate gift houses, which you also identify from the telephone directory. Their buyers tell you that the product is interesting but the price will have to be lower and should include imprinting with the name and address of the company that will be giving the clocks to its customers. No one will make a promise to buy from you.

Not easily discouraged, you decide to place a sample order to sell through giftware channels. You write the supplier asking to purchase 2 cartons of 60 clocks each at a unit price of $5.50, shipped to you by air, "freight collect." That way you don't have to worry about terms of shipment, such as "f.o.b." (see chapter 8), or about who will pay the shipping cost. You offer to pay 50 per-cent of the money in advance and the remaining 50 percent 30 days after the shipment arrives. Thus, you and the exporter will each be trusting the other for half of the small amount of money. You explain the U.S. marking requirements and ask for the order to be shipped immediately.

A few days later the supplier calls you by phone in the late afternoon, when it is early morning in Asia. He agrees to all your terms except the price, saying that he cannot sell for less than $6.50 on such a small order. You give in and tell him to pack the clocks and wait for your order and payment. You consider asking the supplier for his bank and trade references but are afraid that, if you do, he might ask for yours!

Then you buy an international money order for $390 ($6.50 × 120/2) and send it by airmail, with an order form that you have bought at a stationery store or created on your computer. Meanwhile, you register your business and order stationery and cards (see chapter 3). You also contact other potential buyers.

Just 10 days later you receive a call from Jumping Air Freight. You decide to pick up the shipment yourself to save the cost of a customs broker, which you can do because (1) the value is low, (2) shipment was by air, and (3) the goods are not under quota. You have to pay only $272 for air freight (34 kilograms at $8), $26 for airline collect charges, and $79 for "estimated" customs duties (see chapter 10). The shipment came uninsured; forgot about insurance, didn't you?

Your total cost is $780 for the clocks, $298 for shipping, and $79 for duties, or $1,157. Adding in the approximate cost of your money orders, trip to the airport, and so forth, you reach a total cost of about $1,200. There are 120 clocks, so you paid $10 each. You note that the supplier did not improve the packaging, marking, or instructions, but you think that this could be due to your request for urgent shipment.

Now you go back to the gift stores and offer the clocks for $156 a dozen ($13 per clock), with a 5 percent discount if they pay on delivery. You are successful! You sell some clocks. You deliver from stock (the trunk of your car) and offer to set up a small display in each store, unboxing a clock of each color and setting it to the correct time. Then you go back periodically to see how they are priced and whether they are selling.

If you sell the 120 clocks in a month and net $12 each ($13 minus discounts, your selling costs, and maybe a bad debt), your profit will be $240 (120 × $2). This won't make you rich but it may encourage you to try to expand the business.

You can't spend all your time visiting small stores, so you'll have to start selling through either wholesalers or "manufacturer's representatives." You choose the manufacturer's representative route (see chapter 6), finding them by advertising in *Gifts and Decorative Accessories* magazine. Also, you cannot make a living just on world time clocks, so you keep watching publications for other products to add to your line of merchandise.

Suppose you can move from 120 to 1,200 items a month and get the cost down so your gross profit is $3.00 a unit, or $3,600. This should pay office and other expenses and give you a little part-time income.

ROLLS OF PAPER

Now that you have started importing, you read on an Internet bulletin board that a firm in Nigeria wants to import rolls of paper for bank accounting machines. You write (or phone, fax, or e-mail) the buyer to ask exactly what he wants, how many, by when, and by which means of transportation. You also ask how he plans to pay and request bank and trade references.

The buyer gets back to you immediately with the information you requested. He also sends a piece from a roll of paper so you can see exactly what he is asking for. What he doesn't say is how much he expects to pay or how many other potential suppliers he is in contact with. He asks that you provide samples and prices immediately.

You contact the Nigerian consulate about regulations on shipping paper rolls to that country but are not sure that you are given reliable information. You also call the Nigeria desk officer of the U.S. Department of Commerce (USDC) in Washington, D.C., and go to a library and read the applicable pages of the Dun & Bradstreet *Exporters' Encyclopedia*. A "foreign freight forwarder" would have been able to save you some of this work (see chapter 8) but, because you are just starting, you do it yourself to learn how. You send fax or e-mail messages to the importer's trade references and ask your bank to check his bank reference. So far, it all sounds good.

Then you consult directories of manufacturers and find several that supply rolls of paper. You phone them and are happy to learn that most are pleased to sell to you for shipment to Nigeria. Some are willing to give you credit, if your rating is good, but they definitely want to collect *from you*. This means you can't work as an agent on this deal; you have to buy and resell. Three firms agree to send you sample rolls and price quotations.

Because the samples and information that arrive from the three manufacturers are almost identical, you select a supplier who seems pleasant to deal with and is located not far from a U.S. east coast seaport. You take that supplier's sample and contact a foreign freight forwarder, who helps you put together a quotation for 40 cartons of paper rolls. Each carton will cost you $95.60 at the factory, weighs 48 pounds, and measures 1.6 cubic feet.

Your cost calculation is as follows:

40 cartons of paper @ $95.60	$3,824
Inland freight	154
Forwarding and related charges	219
Ocean freight on 1,920 pounds	1,073
Marine insurance	323
Banking and miscellaneous charges	198
TOTAL	$5,791

There is one more important detail—profit. You doubt that big companies are interested in this small order, but there are probably other small suppliers in the United States, England, or Canada; therefore you decide to add just 15 percent for profit. Maybe later you can increase your earnings by negotiating a lower price from your supplier.

You prepare a quotation, "c.i.f. Lagos" (see chapter 8), for $6,659.65 ($5,791 + 15 percent) and suggest seafreight and "letter of credit" terms (see chapter 7). The same day you fax this quotation to Lagos you receive a fax in return. It asks for a "pro forma invoice" (see chapter 9) for 28 cartons by airfreight, showing "f.o.b." and "c.i.f." prices (see chapter 8). The customer needs this to obtain an import permit and to open a letter of credit.

You call the supplier to ask for the same carton price on just 28 cartons, and she agrees. She also agrees to 5/30 terms, which means you can take a 5 percent discount if you pay within 30 days of the date of the invoice. Your forwarder gives you an airfreight quotation, which is much higher than the ocean freight, but forwarding and insurance charges are somewhat less. You prepare an invoice, write "Pro Forma" across the top, and fax it to Nigeria.

The customer immediately faxes back that the airfreight charge is too high and suggests that you contact a firm called Pandair. With a lovely British accent, a representative of this company quotes $2,871, plus $53 for insurance and processing charges. You send a new pro forma and, lo and behold, receive the order by return fax.

You start to dial your freight forwarder's number to ask him to reserve space on a plane but, wait, there is something missing—the letter of credit. You call the firm in Nigeria and are assured that this has been taken care of. About a week later you receive a call from a bank in New York advising you that a letter of credit has been opened in your favor by the ICON Merchant Bank in Lagos. A copy comes in the mail. You check it and find that all its terms are consistent with your agreement to supply the rolls of paper. You consider having it confirmed (guaranteed) by a U.S. bank but are told that this should not be necessary. The "advising" bank assures you that the ICON Bank exists and the letter of credit is authentic.

At this point, you order the paper from the supplier, to be addressed to the Nigerian customer and shipped to Pandair at John F. Kennedy International Airport in New York. You also have to buy and sign a special form, "Invoice and Declaration of Value Required for Shipments to Nigeria." You send your documents and a letter of instructions to the freight forwarder, who prepares a "shipper's export declaration" (see chapter 9), makes sure the 28 boxes get on the plane, and sends you a copy of the "airway bill" (see chapter 9). With that, you can go to the advising bank and start the process of collecting on the letter of credit.

You could have made this shipment without using a freight forwarder, but his advice might have saved you from making some mistake that would invalidate the letter of credit. Also, you may need him in the future. You fax the airway bill number to the customer, take the discount and pay your supplier, and have dinner at a Nigerian restaurant to celebrate.

As in the import example, your task now is to turn an initial success into an ongoing business. Look for other items you can sell to the same customer or for other customers who will buy rolls of paper. Build slowly and steadily, and always be careful of how you do business and whom you do it with. That first valid letter of credit may be followed by a couple of others, but the fourth one might be counterfeit.

Now let's look at some personal characteristics that can make the difference between success and failure, some questions you should find answers to before you go into business, and some financial examples.

CHAPTER 2

Is This Business for You?

Everyone who reads this book is presumably thinking about starting an import and/or export business, but the business isn't for everyone. To help you decide whether the business is right for you, let's discuss some of the key criteria for success.

CONTACTS WITH BUYERS (OR THE ABILITY TO MAKE THEM)

Although it is possible to start in this business with an interesting product and then go looking for buyers, a far greater percentage of people who have *started* with buyers have been successful. Sometimes it's as simple as putting one and one together. A Chinese-American living in Maryland hears of people in China who want to buy industrial air filters because of growing air pollution there. He also knows people who sell the same kind of filters in the United States. He contacts their supplier and easily begins his business. He is likely to be successful as long as he can please the buyers and keep ahead of the competition, because the demand is high and the product is readily available.

BUSINESS KNOW-HOW AND EXPERIENCE

Importing and exporting are, of course, kinds of *businesses*, so people who already know how to run businesses are more likely to be successful. There's a wonderful nonprofit organization head-quartered in New York City, the National Foundation for Teaching Entrepreneurship, that helps inner-city youth start their own businesses. The young entrepreneurs' motto is "buy low, sell high, keep good records." While this may be the essence of running a successful business, it isn't easy to do, especially across national boundaries. Of course, there are individuals, organizations, courses, books, and computer software that can help you make up defi-ciencies in selling, accounting, or other aspects of running a busi-ness, but these will cost you valuable time and/or money. The more skills you already possess, the better.

MONEY (AT LEAST A LITTLE)

You can buy books about how to do this and that "on a shoe-string," but in most cases shoestrings aren't good for much besides tying shoes. There are people who dream of starting businesses in their houses, with their personal computers and postage stamps, and making big money "brokering deals" (arranging business trans-actions). I have a friend from Brazil who does this, and is success-ful because he knows people in Brazil who say they are in the market for specific products. Even so, he needs money to find and communicate with suppliers in the United States and other coun-tries, to communicate with his Brazilian buyers, and to follow up to see whether the goods were shipped and received. He could also have legal fees for writing contracts to make sure he is paid the commissions that are due.

On the import side, it's very hard to go into business as a broker without start-up money. It's a business in which you almost *have* to buy in order to sell, and you usually have to pay for goods before you get paid for them. You may be able to buy on credit, but, as you probably already know, it's much easier to get credit if you already have money in the bank. Before starting this kind of business on a part-time basis, you will need at least about $20,000 that you can afford to invest. To supply yourself with a full-time income, the figure is probably closer to $100,000.

ATTENTION TO DETAIL

In international trade, as with any business, you have to give the buyer *exactly* what he or she asks for. Before the days of computers, I received an export order for rolls of paper for calculators and adding machines. We found a supplier, made all necessary arrangements, and shipped the product. All would have been fine except that someone had typed "3/8 inch" instead of "5/8 inch" for the diameter of the cores. The rolls reached the buyer, but they couldn't be used.

Details can be especially critical when they relate to payment. Suppose you're exporting electric motors and getting paid with a letter of credit that calls for 100 boxes each containing 10 motors. If you accidentally ship 10 boxes each containing 100 motors, you will technically be in violation of the terms of the credit and your payment may be delayed.

KNOWLEDGE OF INTERNATIONAL ECONOMICS AND POLITICS

To do business in the world, it helps to know a good deal about it and most of us don't know nearly enough. Suppose you are buying computer parts from South Korea and paying in U.S. dollars, and suddenly the Korean won is devalued. This means that, for every dollar you pay, the Korean exporter will get more won. Don't expect the Korean exporter to lower the price to you in dollars unless you understand what is happening and request a price decrease.

Or suppose there are riots at Youngsei University over possible unification with North Korea, and you have ordered goods from a company that is located near the university campus. In this case, you would want to ask whether your shipment might be delayed because of transportation or other problems. Remember that if your supplier misses the boat *you* might miss a delivery date to your most important customer.

If your knowledge is weak in this area, it would be a good idea to subscribe to a major newspaper such as the *New York Times* or the *International Herald Tribune* to get yourself up to speed. It would also be helpful to watch *BBC World News* if it is available where you live.

FAMILIARITY WITH FOREIGN LANGUAGE AND CULTURE

This particular part of this book was written on the campus of the Instituto Superior de Agricultura in Santiago, Dominican Republic. While most of the students were Dominican and spoke Spanish, several were from Haiti and were French and Creole, and about ten were from English-speaking Caribbean islands. The idea was that they could learn each other's cultures and languages and later help Caribbean countries interact more with each other.

Perhaps the most obvious difference among peoples of different nations is their language, and even though international business people often speak English, there can be misunderstandings. Ask for a "boot" in England, for example, and you'll get the trunk of a car. Cultures go far deeper than language. There are entire books written about cultural blunders that even major companies have committed, such as giving white flowers to a dinner hostess in a country where white is the color for death. Such a simple blunder as receiving a business card in Japan and not paying proper attention to what it says can hurt your chances of successfully completing a transaction.

The more you know about language and culture, the better.

Take courses, read books, travel, eat in ethnic restaurants, and, above all, have dinner now and then and talk about culture with people from the countries you're dealing with.

PERSISTENCE, TEMPERED WITH JUDGMENT

How long does it take for a business to become successful? It varies, but most new firms lose money for at least the first year. One reason is that you can only make money if you *sell* something, and if you don't start with a buyer then the first several sales calls are likely to leave you empty-handed.

You have to be persistent. For how long, though? It's hard to say. Perhaps for a year *after* friends and relatives start saying you should quit. Many small business ventures end when the entrepreneur gets an engrossing full-time job. Others are over when there's no more money to invest. Perhaps a better approach is to sit down near the end of each year and prepare a plan for the following year, including a pro forma income and expense statement. If after a year or more you can't prepare a *realistic* plan that shows enough income to meet your needs, it's time to consider ending the venture.

TWENTY ESSENTIAL QUESTIONS

It's already time to stop and do a little self-analysis. I strongly suggest that you read the following questions and try to answer them. This exercise will be useful as you continue with the rest of the book.

1. **Why are you thinking of starting a business? What are your objectives?**

   If your answer is "to make money," you should spend extra time on good planning with emphasis on realistic financial projections. You should also be prepared to invest some serious time in the business. If you basically want to try your hand at being a trader and perhaps deduct some travel expenses from your income for tax purposes, you're at a lower level of commitment and you don't have to do as much advance planning. If you're unemployed and thinking of starting a business because you don't want to look for a job, please think more carefully. Some people *do* move from unemployment to being their own bosses, but many who try would be better off getting more work experience, even at a relatively low salary, before striking out on their own.

2. What do you have going for you?

Do you have good contacts? Business experience? A great business idea? Enough money? My guess is that, for every 100 persons who think of starting import/export businesses, 20 or 30 begin, 10 or so succeed more or less, and 1 or 2 are very successful. To end up in that little group of big winners, you'll want to start from the strongest position you can.

3. Do you plan to import, export, or both?

In general, it's not a good idea to start importing and exporting at the same time. Either one will give you enough to think about. I believe importing is the easier one for most people to start with because when you import the *selling*, the hardest part of the business, is done in your country, where you know the turf and can more easily identify, investigate, and contact potential buyers.

4. Do you plan to work as a merchant, an agent, a broker, or some combination of the three?

An international broker can make money by arranging sales between unrelated parties, but it is very hard for a newcomer to establish contacts and confidence and to make deals. In terms of the amount of capital needed, the cheapest way is to start as an import agent for a foreign firm. The next cheapest way is to be an export agent, then an import merchant, and finally an export merchant. Higher investment usually goes with higher profit potential.

5. **When you start, will you be working full-time or part-time?**

Full-time is better *if* you plan to start a business rather than a hobby and *if* you have enough cash to last until the profit is adequate. One person I know got laid off by his company (a bank) with a "golden parachute"—a year at full pay. He could afford to give full time to his new business. Another friend decided to give his all to a new import business but soon found that both he and his wife had to find part-time jobs to keep their bills paid.

6. **Who, if anyone, can help you with the work in the beginning?**

Working alone gets tiresome, and most people aren't good at everything. For example, do you like both selling and accounting? They are both essential but very different in nature. It helps to have a helper or an associate whose skills complement yours.

One acquaintance had a simple plan—to import children's clothing from the Caribbean and open a small store in which his wife would sell the products. Unfortunately, the wife very quickly tired of waiting on customers, dusting shelves, keeping records, and so on, and the business failed. Perhaps if he and his wife had honestly evaluated the tasks involved, they could have foreseen the outcome and planned accordingly.

7. **What is your target market?**

Of the millions of people in the United States—or overseas if you're exporting—what are the characteristics of the people you will sell to? Is there a market segment that you know well enough to pick as your target market? I once wasted several hours trying to supply cosmetics manufacturers with natural bath salts from Jordan before learning that the manufacturers made their bath salts chemically. They leave the natural products to the natural health industry.

8. How do you plan to sell to customers in the target market?

If you can't answer this question, you probably shouldn't start a business. If you have a monopoly on one of life's essentials, the buyers will beat a path to your door. Almost any other product will have to be *sold*, by you or by people whom you identify, hire or contract with, supervise, and pay. There's a lot of truth to the old saying, "Nothing happens until somebody sells something."

9. Which type(s) of product(s) do you plan to trade?

This is one of the most important questions. If possible, let your customers tell you what they want to buy. Otherwise, look for a product that you like and know something about, that can be obtained in sufficient quantity and consistent quality, and that can be transported to and entered into market countries. The item that excites you in a foreign country may be a total dud in the market. It may be that people who go to the country will buy it there and people who don't go to the country will have no interest in it.

10. What will be your sources of supply—countries and/or companies?

Normally, your supplier should be a competent, reliable firm in a stable country. If you get that big order, and your goods arrive too late or are not of good quality, you will lose your profit, your time and expenses, and your reputation. It's easier, for example, to buy from companies in Canada or Taiwan than from those in Burundi or Albania.

11. What means of international transport do you plan to use?

In general, you'll want to use airmail or courier for small shipments, and these methods have become more versatile and efficient in recent years. You'll want to use air cargo for larger shipments, seafreight for still larger shipments, and usually road or rail for trade with Canada and Mexico (chapter 8 includes information about these shipping options).

12. What will be the shipping terms?

There are several standard shipping terms, such as f.o.b. (free on board) and c.i.f. (cost, insurance, and freight), that you must know about and understand thoroughly. Small importers often begin buying c.i.f. by airfreight whereas small exporters often begin shipping f.o.b./vessel or f.o.b./airport (chapter 8 includes information about these terms).

13. Which method of international payment do you plan to use?

What you would like and what you can get are often quite different. As an importer you would like easy credit terms, while as an exporter you would like to be paid before you ship. The people or firms on the other side of the transaction will also be looking out for themselves.

I once heard of a small businessman in Taiwan who received an order from the United States for live birds. The Taiwanese invested all his capital in purchasing and shipping the feathery creatures, did not get paid, and was out of business almost before he started. There are ways to prevent this from happening to you.

14. Which U.S. and/or foreign government regulations will concern you?

Both importers and exporters are subject to the laws of all the jurisdictions they deal with. These include national, state, and local governments of both the importing and exporting countries.

For example, nearly all products are now free of duty in the U.S.–Canada–Mexico trade, but only if they meet the applicable rules of origin. This book will help you learn how to find out which rules your business is subject to.

15. What will be your company's name and form of organization?

Should your business bear your name or a trade name you create? Should you incorporate? If so, which kind of corporation should you organize? If not, which legal form should your business take? Your answers to these questions have important implications, especially for liability and taxation. Fortunately, you can change, within limits, from one form to another.

16. What will you do for an office, office equipment, and supplies?

The biggest advantage of working in your own home is saving money, but there are several disadvantages. For example, during working hours, you may not want to be that close to your spouse and kids, the refrigerator, or the garden tools.

Acquiring equipment for the home office has become more fun but more complicated than it used to be. This book will give you guidance about what you must have and what you really don't need to begin with. In general, you should open a "real" office only if it will help you earn enough additional profit to cover all related costs.

17. How will you communicate with the outside world?

This is related to Question 16 but involves the various ways you can get postal and electronic mail (e-mail) addresses and phone and fax numbers. In general, they are not expensive.

When the first edition of this book was written, the word "fax" was rarely mentioned and e-mail was unheard of, and that was only 15 years ago.

18. Which service companies will you need, and how will you select them?

You'll certainly need a long-distance telephone company and a bank and perhaps a customs broker, freight forwarder, attorney, accountant, insurance company, courier, and others. This book will tell you how each can help you and how you can locate them.

Did you know, for example, that there are numerous low-cost courier services that operate between the United States and just one other country? Such a service may be able to deliver a small package for much less than what a major courier would charge.

19. Where will you get information and help as your business develops?

Throughout this book, and especially in the last chapter, there are numerous ideas about where to get information and assistance, including information from the Internet. There is not as much low-cost help available to importers as there is for exporters, but sometimes it is wise to get assistance, no matter what the cost.

Suppose, for example, that customs says your Christmas merchandise cannot be released because it isn't properly marked. A good customs broker can probably get the goods released to you, under bond. Then, if you can get them marked in a hurry, you can still deliver before Santa Claus stops working for the year.

20. How much will you invest, and how much will you earn?

You will surely need to invest quite a bit of time and money in your business. This book will help you understand how much money will be needed and where you might obtain it.

To attract partners or investors, or even to make the go-ahead decision yourself, you should have a business plan that includes pro forma financial statements. It's time now to start finding out how to prepare these statements and how they can help you.

Let's now examine some financial examples and then move

on and begin getting detailed answers to the 20 questions just asked.

SOME FINANCIAL EXAMPLES

Let's look at two financial examples to see how money can be made in international trade. I've created two small businesses, an import merchant and an export agent.

The import merchant buys merchandise overseas, takes title to and possession of it, and resells it to stores in the United States. She sells through manufacturer's representatives and pays them 15 percent on their sales. She works from her home or in a small rented office and keeps costs to a minimum. Summarized operating results, after several months in business, are as follows:

Import Merchant

Planned sales for month	$20,000	
Less cost of merchandise	−12,000	(60%)
	8,000	
Less sales commissions	−3,000	(15%)
	5,000	
Less operating expenses	−2,000	(10%)
Profit before tax and owner's salary	$3,000	(15%)

Note that all figures are given as a percentage of sales. Note also that monthly sales of $20,000 have produced a nice part-time, but not a full-time, income.

The export agent books orders from foreign buyers for products of U.S. manufacturing firms. He probably has five or six principals who produce related goods so as to be able to offer a wide range of, for example, industrial lighting fixtures. This agent receives commissions from his principals that average 14 percent, but he pays 6 percent to his own agents in foreign markets. He is working from a small rented office and trying to hold down expenses. The financial summaries are as follows:

Export Agent

Planned sales for month	$100,000	
Times average commission earned	×0.14	(14%)
	14,000	
Less foreign agents' commissions	−6,000	(6%)
	8,000	
Less operating expenses	−3,000	(3%)
Profit before tax and owner's salary	$5,000	(5%)

Note that the agent must sell *much* more than the merchant to make as much profit. This is because the agent is performing fewer functions and taking very little risk. He may be able to get orders without having his own agents abroad but would then have to spend more time and money on communications and travel.

CHAPTER **3**

Setting up Your Business

Strangely enough, I've seen people who speak of going into importing and/or exporting but don't stop to think that these are kinds of businesses. To *do* business you have to *have* a business, and there are several factors to consider. Fortunately, you can find many good books on the subject that go into more detail than I can in this chapter. Just be glad you're not in one of the many developing countries where setting up a legal business is so burdensome that many people operate informally or give up entirely.

FORM OF ORGANIZATION

The form of organization to set up is an issue that new business owners should consider carefully. There are four basic options:

1. Sole proprietorship
2. Partnership
3. Corporation
4. Limited liability company

State laws on forms of organization vary somewhat, but they are basically the same throughout the United States.

Sole Proprietorship

A sole proprietorship is the quickest, easiest kind of business to establish. Normally you can just purchase a "Doing business as . . ." form from a stationery store, fill it out, and send it to the appropriate office in your county or state. Depending on the locality, you may have to send more than one copy and/or have your signature notarized. You'll have to send a small amount of money, which in some localities must be in the form of a cashier's check or money order.

The main purpose of this registration is to enable interested persons to identify people who do business under names that aren't their own personal names. You will make all the decisions and be personally liable for any problems that might be caused by operations of the business. At the end of the year, your personal income will be increased or decreased for tax purposes by the business's profit or loss. You can deduct business losses for a maximum of three consecutive years.

You can also deduct legitimate business expenses, including the cost of an office in your home. Deducting for an office at home does not increase your chances of being audited as it reportedly used to do, but it may be more trouble than it's worth to you. This is a decision to be considered carefully.

In general you can use a sole proprietorship if you don't plan to share ownership with anyone else, if your income and expense will be small, and if you will deal only with products that are unlikely to cause any sort of illness, injury, or damage, because as a sole proprietor you bear full legal responsibility for the consequences of your business decisions.

Partnership

A partnership is as easy to start as a sole proprietorship; you simply buy the appropriate "Doing business as . . ." form from the stationery store and write in more than one name. You can have a single partner or multiple partners and can decide among yourselves what each will contribute to the business. There are both full and limited partnerships. A full partner will normally share the ownership, work, and liability, while a limited partner will not participate in management decisions and will not be liable for problems that are caused by decisions the managers make. As you can imagine, the specifics of such a relationship should be set forth in a written document, with the assistance of a lawyer, and signed by all partners.

Most business advisors do not recommend partnerships. They can turn out worse than rocky marriages. The kind of person who wants to own his or her own business usually does not want to share decision making with anyone else. Also, a partnership usually must be dissolved if one or more of the partners formally leave the business (by dying, for example).

In this form of business, each partner's share of profit or loss is reflected on his or her personal tax return. As with a sole proprietorship, legitimate losses can be deducted.

Corporation

A corporation is a more formal kind of organization. It makes your business a separate legal entity, or corpus, which can theoretically go on even if its owners cease to exist. It allows you to attempt to raise capital by selling shares of stock, and it helps protect your personal assets from legal judgments. This can, for example, keep you from having to sell your house to pay the medical bills of the young man who falls when a wheel breaks on a roller skate that you imported (even if he *was* skating on gravel at 90 miles per hour). Incorporating, however, will not protect your personal assets if, for example, a jury decides that you *knowingly* handled a dangerous product and incorporated specifically for your own protection.

A corporation must be registered with your state government. The fee varies but is normally around $300 if you prepare all the forms yourself and a few hundred dollars more if you ask a lawyer or accountant to do it for you. It's the age-old trade-off of your time or your money. There are companies that advertise in magazines for entrepreneurs that will sell you books or software on how to incorporate, or that will do the job for you.

You can incorporate your business in any state; some advisers will recommend that you incorporate in a state such as Delaware, because of more favorable laws. However, incorporating in a state other than the state you do business in is not always worthwhile for new, small firms. The advantages are not usually very important, and you are required to register and report in your own state as an agent of a "foreign" corporation. You are not likely to come out ahead.

The corporation will have to pay taxes on its net profit. It can retain some earnings for use in the future and pay some profits as dividends to the stockholders. It can save you money, if the corporation is profitable, by treating part of your Social Security tax as a business expense. The losses of corporations cannot be deducted from their owners' earnings for tax purposes but they can be carried forward to future years in the financial records.

Import/export businesses should be incorporated from the beginning if they deal with products that are taken internally or applied to the skin or that can cause harm in any way. This applies especially to products that are used by children, and it applies more to importers than to exporters. An importer is closer to the parties who might be injured and is therefore more likely to be sued. Owners of businesses that do not fit this description can usually wait to see how well they do before spending money on incorporation.

One variation you may want to look into is an S corporation (S for "small"). This option involves restrictions to the number of owners, public stock offerings, and other aspects of the business, but it gives protection against liability and still lets you pay taxes as an individual. To form an S corporation, you must first incorporate and then file a separate form to choose the S option.

Limited Liability Company

The limited liability company is a relatively new form of organization that exists in most states but *is not the same* in every state. It usually lets you pay taxes as an individual and gives you some protection from liability, except in states that do not recognize this form of company. In most states, there must be at least two owners. The limited liability company is a potential alternative to limited partnerships and S corporations, but it should not be set up without careful consideration of its advantages and disadvantages in each state.

YOUR TRADE NAME AND LOGO

What's in a name? Plenty, if it has high recognition like Exxon or IBM. Several years ago I saw a store in Laredo, Texas, named Shirt on You. I would never go in there; I hated the name. By contrast, a store in Guatemala City was named Q Kiss. I think that's a fabulous name. To see why, pronounce Q and Kiss as in Spanish: "coo-kice."

If you want to do business in your own name as a sole proprietorship, technically you won't even have to register as a business with your state or local government (at least in some states). Most people, however, prefer to use trade names. You'll probably find that some of the more obvious choices, like International Traders, are already in use in your area. To begin checking on this, just look in area telephone directories.

If you plan to import and to sell nationwide, you could get into trouble if your company name is already being used by a similar firm *anywhere* you do business. Thinking of advertising on the Internet? Then you will *virtually* be doing business worldwide. There is a company called Trademark Express that offers reasonably priced statewide and nationwide searches for trade names, trademarks, logos, and product names (phone 1-800-776-0530, e-mail info@tmexpress.com).

It's often a good idea to pick a name that says what you do, such as Eurasian Traders if you plan to do business with Turkey, for instance (you could call it Turkey Traders, but that could be confusing and would limit your scope). Try not to pick a name that is vulgar or demeaning in the language of any country you might want to deal with, and do pick a name that translates easily. My company name, Plans and Solutions Inc., is very descriptive and is almost the same in most Romance languages.

Names with three letters are popular because it looks like you had a business with a long name and lopped off all but the initials. If you plan to be a used-clothing exporter, for example, call the business U.C.E. International. Sounds important, doesn't it?

You will probably want to pick a symbol or logo that reinforces your company name and creates an image in the minds of people who will see your letterhead and business card. I suggest not using a plane, a ship, or a globe. They have been overused and will mark you as an amateur. Printers, including mail-order stationery houses, have stock logos that you can choose from, or you can find a friend who's an artist and ask him or her to design a creative logo for you. Also, clip art software for computers provides a huge selection of potential logos, and you are not likely to run into any legal problems because by purchasing the software you are also purchasing the right to use them.

OPENING A BANK ACCOUNT

Why have a section in this book on something as simple as opening a bank account? Because choosing a suitable bank is vital to your success. In general, you want one that is trying to attract small-business accounts, is small enough to want your business, and is large enough to have a Letter of Credit Department. If it doesn't have the latter, then it doesn't do much international business and will have trouble helping with international credit and payment.

For example, I was once contacted by officials of a small bank in the New York area who said they would like me to teach them the basics of international trade because some of their clients were beginning to import and export. Until I worked with them on the ins and outs of trade finance, they weren't prepared to handle the businesses of their importing/exporting clients.

If you are forming a sole proprietorship or a partnership, just go to the bank with identification and a copy of the business certificate that was returned by your county or state registrar. If you have a corporation, take your employer identification number and a corporate resolution that says you are entitled to open a bank account for the firm. In some states, you have to take proof of incorporation and/or the corporate seal. Once your account is open, try to build a good banking relationship by occasionally speaking with an officer and by never writing a check for which you don't have sufficient funds. Unfortunately, the large international banks are usually reluctant to open accounts for small, new importers or exporters. You may not be approved by Citi or Chase until you have a nice volume of business.

ESTABLISHING YOUR OFFICE

Until recent years, there was quite a stigma against running a business in your home. While this is no longer the case, some localities impose restrictions on home-based businesses, including stipulations against having more than one employee, keeping stocks of merchandise, or receiving significant numbers of visitors. It's a good idea to check your local laws.

As a home-based business, you may have trouble getting approval to accept credit cards, but this too is changing. Also, there's an alternative to dealing directly with VISA and the others; there are specialized companies, such as National Bancard Systems in Austin, Texas (phone 1-800-550-7892), that will arrange for you to be able to accept any major credit card. Before entering into such an arrangement, you should be satisfied that the service firm you are dealing with charges reasonable fees.

Regarding insurance, homeowner's and tenant's policies do not usually cover business property or liability for business activities. You may want to add a rider to your insurance policy to protect that new computer or to help when your part-time secretary gets carpal tunnel syndrome and sues you for damages. A few companies now offer combined homeowner's and home-based business policies. You will also want to look into product liability insurance, especially if you are importing and/or dealing with products that can be hazardous in any way.

If you decide to set up an office outside your home, you may want to rent empty space from an existing firm or in a building that is set up to house small companies and provides photocopy and fax equipment, a conference room, and secretarial services. These are known as "office suites." Unless you plan to have a showroom on the premises, you don't need prime commercial space for an import/export business; you'll do just fine on top of the barber shop.

SETTING UP YOUR OFFICE

The computer revolution is having an enormous effect on small offices. If you're setting up, you may as well do it the modern way.

Your basic list of equipment might look something like the following:

- Desk and chair
- IBM-compatible computer with printer and modem
- Telephone with built-in answering machine and/or caller ID
- Fax/scanner/copier combination, unless you plan to make a lot of copies

- Filing cabinet and miscellaneous office furniture (computer table, lamp, etc.)

All this will cost you between $3,000 and $6,000, depending on the quality of your equipment and whether you buy new or used. Good used computers are available in most areas from Computer Renaissance franchises and other stores, but they have limitations. For example, AOL 7.0 doesn't work well on a Windows 95 operating system.

It's not a good idea to use your one personal phone line for business, especially if you have a spouse and teenagers in the house. You'll want a second line for the business phone and perhaps a third one for the computer. The fax can be connected to one of these.

There are so many telephone services available now that it is very hard to determine which has the best combination of service and cost. You should compare billing increments, such as every six seconds, as well as the cost of 1 + state-to-state calls, 1 + in-state calls, 1 + regional calls, and international calls.

It's also hard to decide on software, but here's a tip: Microsoft is trying to make itself *the* supplier for small businesses. Its Office 2000 is expensive but includes numerous features that will help you in your operations.

Also, in the international trade business your laptop or desktop computer is very likely to be exposed to viruses—corruption that travels from one electronic file to another that may infect your computer. You will probably want to inoculate it by installing antivirus software and keeping it updated. Also, don't download *anything* unless you know the sender.

STATIONERY AND PRINTING NEEDS

When you first get started, you'll probably only need stationery, envelopes, and business cards. For printing, Office Depot, part of a nationwide chain, has a good combination of speed, price, and quality. Photocopy chains like Kinko's and Sir Speedy are also options, although independent printers can often do as well for a bit less. Kinko's stores offer the advantage of being open nearly all the time, and their machines are usually in good working condition.

If you order stationery and cards from a mail-order house, try to get a firm commitment on the delivery date. I once had to wait six weeks for business cards (although I complained and got the price of the cards deducted from my bill).

Consider getting lightweight stationery and envelopes if you plan to do much international mailing. In fact, you can do without professionally printed stationery and envelopes if you want to simply create them on your computer. You can also design and print business cards on the computer, but you may find that this is more trouble than it's worth. However, if you want a small quantity printed on both sides, to give more information about your firm or to use two languages, doing it yourself is a good alternative. A commercial printer will take a few extra days and charge extra for printing the second side.

Business forms can be created on your computer, too, or you can buy stock forms and just type in your company's name and address. Hold off on getting forms printed until the business gets fairly big and well established; otherwise, they are a needless expense.

If you're working from home and don't want your home address on stationery or other materials, you can probably find a local mail box service or rent a post office box. You can make the mail box the first or last stop when you drive your car for business purposes. Because you can't deduct mileage from your home to the first stop, or from the last stop to your home, the stop for mail will let you deduct more miles.

On the other hand, mailbox services and post office boxes will cost some additional time and money. Also, using a post office box may lead some correspondents to think that your firm is trying to hide its street address and is therefore less than repu-table. Your image is very important in the import/export business.

ACCOUNTING AND TAXATION

Do you like accounting? Do accountants like accounting? Most people don't, but it is a necessity in business. You need financial statements in order to:

1. Know where your income is from
2. Know what you are spending money on
3. Know how much you are making (or losing)
4. Know whether your operating results and financial status are getting better or worse
5. Get a Dun & Bradstreet rating
6. Fill out your income tax statements
7. Apply for loans, etc.

At the outset, you can create your own simple accounting system, but I suggest going to a stationery store and buying a ready-made one such as the *Dome Monthly Record*. With this book, you can do your accounting in an hour or two a month. It uses a *cash* system, as opposed to an *accrual* system, which means you recog-nize income only when you receive money and expenses only when you pay out money. This can be a small advantage if you are working as a merchant and have to pay for merchandise before you get paid for it. Your cash accounting system will show the expense but not the income for some transactions. This will make your profit slightly lower at all times, including on December 31 or whenever your tax year ends. Note, however, that if your busi-ness is incorporated, the laws of your state may *require* the use of an accrual system.

When the business gets larger, you will want to use one of the many accounting software packages or have an accountant set up your bookkeeping and accounting systems and perhaps do the accounting for you. Good accountants charge $60 per hour or more, depending on the location and demand for their services, but they can often save you money on income tax. For example, suppose you are a sole proprietor and take a combined business–pleasure trip to Europe. You will probably be able to deduct part of the cost but not all of it. An experienced accountant will help you deduct the legal maximum and will then defend his decisions in case you happen to be chosen for an Internal Revenue Service (IRS) audit.

In the import/export business, as with any other business, business income is taxable and business expenses are deductible. As mentioned previously, with a sole proprietorship, a partnership, or an S corporation, you pay taxes as an individual on your share of the profits. You should pay estimated taxes quarterly, and the IRS will fine you if the estimated tax paid is not at least 90 percent of the final amount due. A corporation pays tax on its profits, and then the owners pay tax on the dividends they receive. There are also miscellaneous corporate tax reports, which vary from state to state. Even when no tax is due, you should always file on time.

The expense of an office at home is deductible on a square-foot basis. For example, if 15 percent of your residence is used as an office, you can deduct 15 percent of your rent. If you own your home, you can deduct 15 percent of what your house could be rented for. It is also permissible to take off the same percentage of your electricity, heating oil, and other utilities.

If you deduct for an office at home, the space can be used *only* for business purposes. A child's jack or marble on the floor technically cancels the deduction. If you sell your house and then buy another, thus avoiding the capital gains tax, you will still be liable for taxes on the capital gain on the space that was used as an office.

Business travel is a legitimate expense, but the rules on deducting for travel abroad were tightened a few years ago. Now a foreign business trip should be less than eight days or, if it is longer, at least 75 percent of the time must be spent on business in order for you to deduct the entire airfare. If you take a two-week trip to Budapest and only half the time is spent on business, you can deduct only half the airfare and half the living expenses.

I have a good friend who imported giftware from Europe and Asia for several years. He took a buying trip every winter to the country of his choice and a selling trip every summer, usually to beautiful Cape Cod. He kept detailed records of all business meetings and was able to deduct nearly all the expenses. Because his wife was active in the business, her travel expenses were deductible as well.

Of course, both individual and corporate profits are subject to state income taxes. Also, there are some cities that tax home offices and/or levy "unincorporated business taxes." The rates are not high, but with a new business every penny is important.

If you plan to hire employees, you will have to contact the IRS for an employee identification number. This is usually done in the process of incorporating. The number is free, and you can obtain it by mail. You will, however, be thrown into a jungle of payroll taxes and tax deductions. I suggest doing without formal employees for as long as possible.

If you plan to buy merchandise for resale in any state that has a retail sales tax, you will need to contact your state tax department for a sales tax number. For a sole proprietorship, this will probably be your social security number. Export merchants, and importers that make retail sales, must have sales tax numbers.

OBTAINING FINANCING

It is rarely easy to obtain financing for a new business of any kind. You probably have some personal savings and/or investments to draw on, and you may have friends or relatives who are willing to lend you money. If you have a well-conceived business idea, but banks are not willing to finance it, you may be able to get a loan from a Small Business Investment Corporation or a loan guarantee from the U.S. Small Business Administration. If your business is incorporated, you can try to sell stock through a private offering. A public stock sale is too expensive for most small firms to attempt.

If your financial rating is good, you can get some credit from suppliers. You may also persuade some customers to make partial payments with their orders.

In general, you should not finance a business by borrowing on credit cards or from finance companies; their interest rates are too high. Nor should you attempt to interest venture capital firms. They usually look for much higher growth in valuation than most import-export firms can provide.

Finally, it's usually a bad idea to start any business with 100 percent debt financing. Your equity should be at least half of the estimated funds needed until the business becomes profitable.

Now that your business is set up, let's go on to chapter 4 and talk about finding buyers.

Beginning with a Buyer

Starting with a buyer might sound pretty idealistic, but if you can do it you'll be miles ahead. Let's look at why someone would buy from you and then explore ways of starting with a buyer, as both an importer and an exporter.

WHY SOMEONE WOULD BUY FROM YOU

Everywhere in the world, people are more likely to buy from you if they know and trust you. This means that the quickest way to begin importing successfully is to have friends who buy for their businesses and will give you a chance to fill some of their needs. I remember meeting a person whose friend purchased gloves and other items for a manufacturing plant. After some discussion, the person I met began a search for the right kind and quality of gloves at the lowest price, delivered to a U.S. port. He settled on a supplier in Pakistan, got an initial order from his friend, and began building a business. By the way, industrial gloves are a good example of a product for which the key to sales is *lifetime costing*. Most buyers don't just get the cheapest. They look at the price of each product offered and how long it will last; if a certain brand costs 20 percent more than a similar one but lasts 30 percent longer, it will be preferred because its lifetime cost will be lower.

Beginning an export business by having friends who will buy from you is harder for most U.S. residents, but not for all. We'll explore this idea a few pages later.

Why would someone buy from you other than for friendship? Well, almost no one will if not convinced that you can offer a very good way (better than your competitors) to use their money. Assuming that you're selling to businesses, not individuals, you must keep in mind that a business has only so many dollars (or other currency) to spend on purchases. This is especially true of retail stores, whose buyers are periodically "open to buy" specific kinds of goods up to set dollar limits. If spending their dollars with you is the best for their profitability, you are likely to get the order.

What Profitability Means to Your Customer

To foreign importers and to wholesalers, retailers, and industrial distributors, profitability comes from volume multiplied by markup, with long payment terms and low risk, minus expenses. Volume comes from a "hot" item that buyers need or want. *Markup* is the margin of selling price over purchase cost and, for wholesalers, is usually calculated as a percentage of cost. For example, a wholesaler who buys an item for $100 and sells it for $130 will have a 30 percent markup. Actually, a more accurate word that is sometimes used in wholesaling is *markon*.

Business firms naturally like to delay paying their bills so that the cash they have on hand can be earning interest. This means that most importers have to be prepared to offer payment terms of 30 days or more. Exporters also are usually asked for favorable payment terms, which in the case of very expensive items can be quoted in years, not days.

Finally, to make yourself attractive to potential customers, you must minimize their risk. This means that you must be highly likely to deliver the right merchandise, in the quantity and quality ordered, on time. It also means that you must be able to deliver more stock quickly, in case your customer ordered too little, and accept returns in case he or she ordered too much.

Factors That Attract Customers

All this means that it helps greatly to have better products, prices, payment terms, advertising, delivery, and return policies than your competitors (and there are always competitors). Of course, you can't win on every count, so you must select a winning "marketing mix" (see chapter 6).

In August 1996, when Sony announced a new gadget that would allow people to connect to the Internet through their television sets, they seemed to have a superb product for people who would invest a few hundred dollars, but not a thousand or more, to try the Net. Competition came soon after from the "iOpener" and other products.

In the chicken business in the United States, the most lucrative market is for breasts and thighs. The other parts are almost surplus and so can be sold for very low *prices* in other countries. Of course, this is good for the market countries' consumers but not for their poultry producers or feed industries.

A very common kind of *advertising support* in international trade, although this is really a kind of "sales promotion," is to work jointly with your foreign partner to exhibit in trade shows. Major commercial exhibitions in the United States have importers sharing the time and expense of setting up and staffing booths with their foreign suppliers. Likewise, major exhibitions abroad have U.S. exporters cooperating with their importers who distribute in the country or region that the exhibition serves.

An acquaintance from Colombia wanted to sell coffee from his country in the Washington, D.C. area, but didn't know how to get into the market. Finally, he succeeded on the basis of *service* and *distribution*. He began importing coffee from Colombia and free-standing espresso machines from Italy and placed the machines in selected high-traffic locations.

Finally, a New York "rag trader" (someone in the textile or apparel business) wanted to change both his business and his lifestyle. He was able to do this by moving to La Paz, Bolivia, and setting up a showroom for men's suiting. "Just being there" put him in daily contact with a market where men's suits were often tailor-made and the production of suitable fabric was low, and he did quite well.

One tool that is sometimes used to get customers overseas is bribing buyers. I suggest avoiding this means of trying to influence buyers, especially if you are new to the import/export business. First, out-and-out bribery is illegal under U.S. law. Second, you probably won't know how it is done in a particular country or industry and will make mistakes. A major mistake is to pay a bribe to someone who talks a good game but is not actually in a position to throw the business your way. Small gifts and favors, by the way, are usually not considered bribes unless the recipient is a U.S. government employee, some of whom are so concerned about getting into trouble that they won't accept a free piece of candy from their neighborhood dry cleaner.

FINDING BUYERS AS AN IMPORTER

Before you even get your product and marketing plan together, you should find a specific person or company that might be willing to buy from you. There are several steps you can take. If you've ever gone through sales training with a direct marketing organization, one of the first documents thrust in your hand was probably a *Whom Do You Know* booklet. It would have guided you to think of the people you knew in all aspects of your life and to see each as a potential customer. Sometimes this approach can help you identify potential customers for imported or exported goods.

Another technique that can pay off is informal brainstorming with friends. If you go out to dinner and cocktail parties (where it's always wise to be armed with some interesting topics of conversation), why not pick people's brains for ideas of underserved markets? Most people will turn the question from markets to products and tell you which ones they think have good potential, and they'll name products in accord with their individual interests. Still, a good idea may turn up. Remember that one of the best-selling novelty items of all time, the Pet Rock, was supposedly thought of during casual conversation in a bar.

If you've ever bought anything by mail, your name and address are being sold from one mail-order house to another and you are probably receiving dozens of catalogs at this point. You can look at them for ideas and, at the same time, try to describe the characteristics of the *market segment* for each catalog. This will give you an idea of who is buying what. For example, the R. C. Steele catalog of wholesale pet equipment and kennel supplies includes dozens of items for pet owners, such as meat-flavored toothpaste, that are rarely found in stores. Perhaps you will see items advertised that you can import and offer to R. C. Steele, or perhaps you can work with them to set up distribution in a particular foreign market.

You can also wander through flea markets and stores, looking at products and trying to think of types of products that you know something about and that you might be able to find buyers for. Try to get guidance from your past work experience and your favorite activities.

Suppose, for example, that fishing is your passion and you especially enjoy tying flies. Then visit tackle shops. Look to see which items are imported and from which countries. Also, see how they compare with U.S.-made goods in regard to design, quality, packaging, and price. Finally, tell people who work in the store that you're thinking of importing fishing equipment and ask them whether they see potential in this idea, whether they can suggest any kinds of equipment and supplying countries for you to look at and, most important, whether they would be willing to comment on potential products when you have samples.

If you actually do import fishing equipment, you will probably not want to sell directly to each store; you will want to sell to chain stores, wholesalers who then sell to retailers, or directly to retailers through *manufacturers' representatives*. That means you should carry your research one step farther. Ask employees in the tackle shops who they buy from and try to visit some of these suppliers or at least speak with them on the phone. Basically, you want to find out whether they would be willing to speak with a new importer and possibly do business with him or her.

FINDING BUYERS AS AN EXPORTER

If you plan to export from the United States, there is a great deal of help available. Various federal, state, and local government agencies are at your service as well as private firms and associations. Several of these will be mentioned in this book.

Still, you have to have a starting point. Ideally, that point will be a specific foreign buyer or at least friends or relatives abroad who are in business. Friends or relatives abroad who are not in business may have good intentions of helping you but not know how to do so. There are other starting points for those of us without a friend in the business.

Look for Buyers in Periodicals

The *Journal of Commerce*, published in New York City by a company of the same name, is the newspaper of international trade and transportation. I recommend reading it before and while you are starting an import/export business. Suppose you regularly read the *Journal of Commerce*, which includes large numbers of export opportunities, and you notice over a month or so that there are several inquiries from Thailand for computer parts.

If you know enough about computers to correspond intelligently, you can send fax messages or e-mail to the Thais who are inquiring. Tell them that you may be able to supply some of their needs and ask for information about the types of parts they need, the quantities, and specific brand names preferred. Replies to the question about brand names will give you an idea of how sophisticated the buyers are, what quality/price level they might want, and which suppliers you should speak with initially. Your message must look and sound very professional because, realistically, it will be competing with similar messages from other potential suppliers.

If you receive two or three encouraging replies, you might conclude that there is in fact a market in Thailand for U.S. computer parts and that the market is also open to new vendors. You might find information, such as a report on the Thai market, in an import/export magazine or from the U.S. Department of Commerce, that will confirm your impression. A quick look at foreign trade statistics will also confirm this impression. Then you can begin looking for suppliers of computer parts (as described in chapter 5).

If you read serious newspapers and magazines, which a person in international business should do, you may get ideas that will lead you to potential markets. For example, a few years ago the *New York Times* carried a headline that read "London Stock Exchange Is Rocked by a Bombing." This told alert exporters that demand might increase in England for bomb detection devices. If you were subscribing to a British newspaper, you might have read about plans to increase airline security after the TWA disaster off Long Island, New York, in summer 1996. If Britain were your target market and you received trade publications from there, you might have found still more information that would have helped you identify potential clients for security equipment.

Check Trade Statistics

Finally, if you're the type who enjoys research with numbers, consider looking at international trade statistics to find trends that might lead you to potential markets. The main source of U.S.

foreign trade statistics is now the National Trade Data Bank (NTDB), which is available on-line or from the USDC in CD-ROM format. Many public libraries have this available, and some even have computers dedicated to it. Large libraries also have current foreign trade statistics from the European Union and Canada.

The best source of worldwide import or export statistics is the United Nations Statistics Office in New York. If interested, you can contact that office by sending an e-mail to tradestat@un.org.

When checking statistics, look at countries with which you might want to deal. Try to find kinds of products of which imports are increasing steadily. For example, statistics in 1996 showed that radio receivers were an important product moving from the United States to the Czech Republic and that this trade was increasing rapidly. If you know people there who can help you identify and make contact with the importers, it surely won't hurt to write them.

For another example, U.S. exports to Mexico of machinery for the poultry industry shot up (from a very low base) by about 3,000 percent from 1999 to the year 2000. This may be an aberration, or it may be the beginning of a trend that you can capitalize on. Perhaps the North American Free Trade Agreement (NAFTA) is reducing Mexico's duties on many types of animal husbandry products and is opening up a significant new market.

Okay, now that you've found a buyer, or even if you haven't but still want to press forward, let's look at how to locate products and select suppliers.

CHAPTER **5**

Choosing Products and Suppliers

If you don't have a buyer who leads you to a product line, you'll have to go the more traditional route of beginning with a product. Then you will need to identify, select, and begin relationships with one or more suppliers. Let's talk first about products to import and then look at the export side of the business.

FINDING IDEAS FOR PRODUCTS TO IMPORT

There are several easy sources of inspiration for ideas of products to import.

Traveling

Traveling is an excellent way to find product ideas. A few years ago, I was sitting in the lovely Hostal Los Alpes in Quito, Ecuador. That morning I had bought a fabulously beautiful wool sweater for 720 sucres, $8.37 at the then-current rate of exchange. Should I have brought back a hundred to sell in the United States? Should I have taken some to show to buyers in several stores so that, if I found a great deal of interest, I could return to purchase in quantity? Probably. As it turned out, hand-knitted sweaters from the Andean region have become a major product for many small-scale importers and street vendors, at least from October to March.

Specialized Publications and Web Sites

Another excellent way to find products to import is to look at specialized publications and web sites from foreign countries. Many of these are published by public- and private-sector export promotion organizations abroad. Most countries have export promotion offices in New York, Los Angeles, and other major U.S. cities, and if you call or visit them they can give you samples of useful publications. Some of these offices can also show you product samples, give you names and addresses of potential suppliers, and even publish your inquiries in their countries.

Unfortunately, these offices are not always easy to find, and some of them are not as helpful as they should be. One way to find them is to call the commercial office of the country's embassy in Washington, D.C. More and more of these offices are using voice mail, sometimes as an excuse to not answer their telephones, so be prepared to leave a message and wait to be called back.

There are also international publications from private companies that can help you identify products to import. Several are sold by De Paula Publishing in New York City, phone (212) 629-4541 and web site www.tradedirectories.com.

The number of such publications, however, is decreasing because the information they have provided is now on the Internet. There are two or three hundred (no one knows for sure how many) Internet trade bulletin boards and similar sites on which one can announce products for sale or products wanted for purchase. You can start searching by typing "trade bulletin boards" into any web browser and seeing what you come up with.

One interesting site on the Net is http://tradezone.com/busops.htm. This is on the site of the Mellinger company, which for many years has made money by helping people get into the

import/export business. You might want to back up to http://
tradezone.com and explore the rest of their site.

Then move on to www.asia.globalsources.com. Besides information about Asian suppliers and their products, there are names
and contact information here for freight service providers, banks,
and other organizations that will facilitate your trading activities.

Some other sites to include in your surfing are http://
trade.swissinfo.net, www.expoeuro.com, and www.bigex.com. The
first of these will tell you about products and suppliers from a
variety of countries (not just Switzerland). The second includes
products and suppliers from most European countries. The third
is an import-export bulletin board and trade information site.

Trade Statistics

You may already know which country or countries you want to
buy from but not what those countries produce and sell, or you
may know which product you want to import but not which
country exports it. In either case, trade statistics will help you.
You can consult United Nations statistics in a major library. Look
for the Food and Agricultural Organization production and trade
yearbooks, the U.S. Industrial Development Organization production yearbook, and the *United Nations Yearbook of International
Trade Statistics*. If you want to see what specific countries are selling to the United States, or from which countries the United
States imports specific products, consult the National Trade Data
Bank (mentioned in chapter 4).

Getting Samples for Testing

In the process of getting product ideas, you will have probably
found several potential foreign suppliers. Contact them, preferably by fax or e-mail, and ask for their catalogs and export price
lists. At this stage, you don't have to give information about
yourself or your company.

The catalogs you want may be available on the Internet or

may come by mail. When they arrive, examine them carefully and, if possible, show them to people who are in business and can give you good advice as to what will sell. Pick out a small number of items that you think you can (1) transport to the United States at a reasonable cost, (2) bring into the country with minimum difficulty, and (3) sell in sufficient quantities to be profitable. (Later chapters will explain these points in detail.) Then, ask for samples.

If the items are inexpensive and you want to try to get free samples, write a very professional letter on your new business stationery. Explain that you are an importer and that you have potential customers for products of the exporting firm. Then ask for a small number of samples, "for testing," and specify exactly which models you want and how many you want of each. If the package will be too valuable, bulky, or heavy to send by airmail, you should ask that it be shipped collect by courier or airfreight. This procedure will usually get you either the samples or a quick reply explaining that you will have to pay for them.

If the supplier says you must pay for the samples, follow this procedure: Take the lowest price quoted (which may be for a huge quantity), multiply it by the number of samples you want, add the approximate cost of insured airmail, and buy an international money order for the total amount. Send the money order, with your letter ordering samples, by registered airmail. Registry is available to most countries. Your samples should arrive in one and a half to six weeks, depending on how good mail service is in the country you are dealing with.

There is always a chance that the exporter won't reply and you will lose your money. Consider this another cost of starting your business. It isn't likely to happen if you select exporters that have attractive catalogs and that correspond with you in a professional way.

Testing Product Ideas

The sad fact is that most foreign products, as you receive them, will not be "right" for the U.S. market. They may not satisfy government regulations or consumer preferences, the price may be too high, or buyers may not be interested in them. Therefore, you should go through a testing process to find out whether the product will sell as is, will not sell at all, or (the most likely) will sell with modifications in its design, size, package, brand, price, or other characteristics.

First, try to determine the uses of your product and who would be the consumers (actual users) and the customers (buyers). Often the two are different. Then try to determine where (from which kinds of stores or other suppliers, including electronic merchants) the customers would buy the product. Identify several of these, make appointments to see their buyers, and show them the product. Try making appointments by saying that you are an importer of (type of product), you have a new item that you are considering adding to your line, and you would appreciate the buyer's opinion of the new item.

When you meet with buyers, ask them what they think of the product, whether they would recommend any changes in the product or its package, whether they would be likely to buy it from an importer (or from a foreign exporter through you as an agent), if so, how often they would order and in which season, how many they would order at a time, and *how much they would pay*. The question of price is critical, and you may have trouble getting honest answers. If you don't get information by asking "How much would you pay for this?" try asking the buyers about their estimated selling prices and percent markups, how much they are paying for similar products, or what price you would have to meet in order for them to buy from you.

You will soon find that each buyer with whom you speak has different opinions and ideas. This is because each one has his or her individual preferences as well as a unique group of customers to satisfy. You will have to analyze the various replies to your questions and draw conclusions about the viability of your product, modifications required, the target market, the channel of distribution, and the pricing structure.

You may find, as I did when dealing with an Egyptian manufacturer of candy, that the producing firm is not willing to modify its products as required by your buyers. The firm's managers may not think the extra profit would compensate for the cost of product modification.

As an example of this testing process, suppose you are offered some very nice rag dolls made in Colombia. They represent storybook characters such as Little Red Riding Hood. They are actually several dolls in one—turn Red Riding Hood upside down and she becomes the grandmother; flip over the bonnet and grandmother becomes the big bad wolf. You now decide that the main customers for these dolls will not be children, or even parents who buy for their children, but grandmothers and others who purchase gifts for girls. That would make the product a gift item, not a toy. You might then decide it would sell best in high-quality gift shops. Your next step would be to identify several such stores, make appointments to see the buyers, and show them the dolls. You will be asked questions about the doll clothing (what it's made of and whether it is flame-resistant), the buttons (are they toxic and how many pounds of pressure will they resist before being pulled off), and the dolls themselves (what are they stuffed with and are they hand-sewn). You might be told that the labeling is inadequate, that the dolls are too big (or too little), that they are too expensive (or too cheap), that the clothing styles should be more modern, the cheeks rosier, the hair more curly, and so on. After several interviews, you will have a good idea whether the dolls would sell, how they should be modified, how they should be packaged and labeled, to what market they should be targeted, how they should be distributed, and what prices they would bring at the wholesale and retail levels.

FINDING FOREIGN SUPPLIERS

Let's suppose that one of the products you looked at has passed the market test with flying colors. You will probably be inclined to start doing business with the company you got samples from, but this is not necessarily the best option. You should explore other options in the same country and perhaps in other countries, as well.

In the process of finding products by traveling, reading specialized publications, attending trade shows, surfing the Net, and perhaps checking statistics, you will develop a list of potential suppliers. If you do not have such a list, you can look at foreign manufacturers' or exporters' directories, ask for help from the countries' trade promotion organizations, consult electronic trade opportunity services, contact import/export service firms, and/or travel abroad.

Foreign Business Directories.   Business directories from most countries can be found in their trade promotion offices or embassies in the United States and in major libraries. The *Kompass* directories, for example, give excellent information on substantial firms in most major countries. You should be somewhat wary of using directories of exporters from developing countries. I have seen cases where, in order to make the directory look good, it is padded by including tiny companies that have only dreamed of selling abroad.

Trade Promotion Organizations.   As mentioned before, many countries have public and/or private trade promotion offices in the United States that can help you find suppliers. Two countries that do this well are Brazil and South Korea. If you call Korea International Trade at (212) 421-8804 and say you want to import a specific product—for example, high-density plastic bags (an area I was actually involved in)—you will receive several offers over the next few months.

WTCA.   The World Trade Centers Association is an association of about 300 world trade centers in nearly 100 countries. You can search its web site for free (with on-line registration) and find import and export opportunities as well as on-line catalogs. You can *post* trade opportunities by paying $19.95 per month or joining any world trade center. There are also links to sources of information for world traders. The URL is www.wtca.org and the address is 60 East 42nd Street, Suite 1901, New York, NY 10165.

Import/Export Service Companies.   Import/export service firms also can help you find potential suppliers, with the obvious purpose of getting your business. Many international banks and airlines routinely contact their foreign offices on behalf of their customers and ask these offices to suggest potential business partners. Some noteworthy examples have historically been the Hong Kong and Shanghai Banking Corporation and KLM Royal Dutch Airlines.

Traveling Abroad.   Finally, you can identify potential suppliers by traveling abroad. Suppose you want to import leather goods and you get off a plane in Tegucigalpa, Honduras. Check in at the Hotel Maya, or wherever you plan to stay, and then visit the Promotion Department of the Directorate General of Foreign Trade, of the Ministry of Economy, to get a list of exporters. Call them to make appointments. If you need an interpreter, the American Chamber of Commerce (AMCHAM) can help you find one to hire. There is an AMCHAM in almost every country, and the U.S. embassy can direct you to it. You can also get their address from the U.S. Chamber of Commerce in Washington, D.C., phone (202) 659-6000.

In some cases, you can plan your trip to coincide with a trade exhibit. Want to import Brazilian cookies? Then why not visit Brazil during the next International Bakery Fair? If you have a large communications budget, call Congresos e Ferias at 011-55-11-253-2133 for more information.

SELECTING FOREIGN SUPPLIERS

Basics of Supplier Selection

Your next challenge will be to choose among the potential suppliers, who may be located in different countries on different continents. In general, it is better to buy from a country that is politically stable, that has good transportation to the United States, and whose products can enter the country at the lowest duty. (These points will be discussed in more detail in later chapters.) Some U.S. importers have switched their sources from the Far East to the Caribbean and Central America (C/CA) because labor rates in the Far East are rising, changing currency values have made products from some Asian countries more expensive, freight rates from some C/CA countries to the United States have decreased, and nearly all C/CA products can enter the United States free of duty. More recently, importers have begun sourcing in Mexico because of NAFTA.

Next, you want to choose a supplier that is eager to work with you, competent, and honest. These three criteria create a contradiction in that the most competent and honest suppliers may be less eager to work with you. They will have a wider choice of customers or may have exclusive distribution already set up. Inquire about importing Waterford crystal from Ireland, for example, and you will receive a polite letter saying that the only authorized importer is the company-owned facility in Wall, New Jersey.

How Do They Respond to Communication?   You can assess whether a foreign exporter is eager to work with you by the way it responds to your communications. By the same means, you can get an idea of the exporter's competence. Does their letterhead show a street address and a fax number? Is the web site and/or catalog professionally done? When you ask for information, does the reply answer your questions or does it miss half of them?

Try *not* to judge the competence of a foreign firm by the correctness of the English used in its correspondence. A foreign executive may be first rate, except for his or her English, but may write to you in English to save you the trouble of finding a translator.

How Do They Respond to Requests?   Another way of assessing a foreign exporter's eagerness and competence is by the way he or she responds to requests, especially for product modifications. A friend of mine once tried to establish herself as an import agent for wooden toys from a firm in Central America. She asked for product modifications and found it took several months to receive a new sample with a slightly different design or a different color. She finally gave up on that exporter and sourced in Asia, instead.

How Is Their Credit?   Still another technique for evaluating potential suppliers is to obtain credit information about them. This vital topic will be discussed in chapter 7.

How Do They Look in Person?   Finally, you will want to visit a potential supplier before making a major financial commitment to it. This will cost time and money but may save you from a catastrophe like having your shipment of ski boots arrive in February or having a boot come apart on an expert slope. It is better to make appointments in advance to avoid arriving when the people you want to see are unavailable, even though that lets them prepare to make their company look better than it really is. Even then, unexpected circumstances like the death of the nation's president (or even an ex-president) can cause all appointments to be canceled.

When you do get to an exporter's place of business, try to meet with key personnel, look at their financial statements if you are given access to them, and tour the plant. Financial statements will not always help you because of differences in national accounting systems and dedication to accuracy (please read between the lines here). Touring a plant can tell you a lot if you understand the production process of the product you want to import.

Do They Use Formal Quality Management Systems?   The recently developed set of standards for quality assurance systems, International Organization for Standardization (ISO) 9000, is fast becoming a guide to the competency and reliability of many kinds of organizations. If your potential supplier is certified to standards in the ISO 9000 series, chances are good that your merchandise will be as you expect it to be. It is also a very good sign if the firm is certified to an ISO 14,000 standard, which will mean that it has in place a system to prevent or reduce any harmful effects of its operations on the environment. There are other environmental management certification systems in Europe, but they are likely to be replaced gradually by ISO 14,000.

Finally, if you are importing food products, you may want to ask whether the producing firm employs the Hazard Analysis at Critical Points system. This method for ensuring that food products are not harmful was first developed for foods that astronauts were to take into space. It is now required for seafood sold in the United States and may be extended to other products.

Middlemen Versus Manufacturers

In most cases, you will want to import directly from manufacturers rather than from exporting, or trading, companies. This is both to save money and to have direct contact with the producers of your goods. You can usually tell the difference between a manufacturer and a trader by the company name and the catalogs it sends to you. If, for example, the catalog pages have stickers with your exporter's name and address placed over some other name and address, your exporter is not the manufacturer.

While importing from the manufacturer is normally the best option, you may want to import from a trader under the following conditions:

- Your orders will be too small for a manufacturer to handle.
- You plan to order small quantities of several different items.
- You are buying from a country such as Japan in which exporting is normally done by trading companies.
- You will be dealing in handmade products. Most producers of hand crafts are too small and unsophisticated to do their own exporting.

FINDING IDEAS FOR PRODUCTS TO EXPORT

Let's suppose now that you want to begin exporting. You may have been inspired by federal and state departments of commerce or other organizations, which are constantly encouraging firms to export. Governments are eager to increase exports in order to create jobs and bring in hard currency. You may have products in mind, or you may have to do some research to find them.

Ad Hoc Deals

For both importing and exporting, I strongly recommend setting up ongoing, long-term business relationships. If, however, you want to begin with ad hoc deals, you might look at closeout, surplus, and liquidation products. Like everything else these days, you can find it on the web. Type "closeout merchandise" or a similar term in your browser's search engine and you will find several web sites that you can bring up and examine.

Your Own Company's Products

Suppose that you work for a company that makes screw convey-ors and lift conveyors to move ground coffee from one step in the manufacturing process to another. These pieces of industrial equip-ment are very efficient and are self-cleaning so that your firm can easily switch from making one coffee blend to making another.

How will you start? Your first step might be to use logic. Think about the characteristics of the product and of the countries in which it would be in demand. Basic consumer goods are needed everywhere but are produced in most countries, although U.S. brands can bring premium prices. Cigarettes are a prime example. Basic hard goods are produced in fewer countries, probably be-cause the market is much smaller; many bars of soap are sold for every soap dish. Very complex or very expensive items are pro-duced in still fewer countries but tend to be products of powerful manufacturing firms; you probably do not want to be competing with Daimler-Benz or Mitsubishi.

In the case of the conveyors for moving coffee, any large-scale producer of ground coffee would be a potential customer. These firms would be found mainly in developed but also developing countries, with large populations and the cultural habit of drinking coffee. Thus, there would be a finite, easily identifiable group of potential customers and probably not too many competitors. The market potential would be even greater if the conveyors had other uses, as well.

Your second step might be to call the U.S. Department of Commerce Trade Information Center at 1-800-USA-Trade or visit the nearest USDC field office. (See Appendix E for a list of them.) Ask the official there for the name and telephone number of the USDC industry analyst in Washington, D.C., who specializes in such products and plan to contact that person. Finally, ask for statistics that show U.S. exports of similar products by country of destination. The USDC field office may not have them but will be able to tell you where to get them.

You may find other experts to speak with in state or local export promotion organizations, trade associations, or export service firms. In the case of the conveyors, you might get ideas from the Society of Industrial Engineers or the editors of *Food Engineering* magazine. You could also try a direct approach to finding out whether you have an exportable product—call the production managers of coffee-grinding firms in a few countries whose languages you speak. You could request the companies' names and telephone numbers from the commercial offices in Washington, D.C., of your selected countries, or you might find them in directories on the World Wide Web or in a library.

Finding Products Via Research

Let us now assume that you know which country you want to sell to but not which product you intend to sell. If you have picked a country to sell to, you obviously had a reason for doing so. Hopefully this reason is, or at least includes, a good contact who is ready to buy from you.

In addition to speaking with friends, you can look at trade statistics to see which products your chosen country is buying from the United States. Check again with the NTDB. If you visit that country's commercial office or contact the Trade Statistics office of the United Nations in New York, you can also see what the country is importing from other parts of the world. If you see, for example, that The Netherlands is buying increasing quantities of medical and surgical devices from several countries, it may be a good market for such products from the United States. If the value of imports is increasing faster than the quantity, you can conclude that prices are rising. This is another good indicator of market potential.

Besides statistics, the easiest way to see what another country wants to buy from the United States is to read the "Global Commerce" insert in a Wednesday edition of the *Journal of Commerce* newspaper. I cannot overemphasize the usefulness of this publication.

You can also get information about foreign buyers' needs from the World Trade Center Association's web site and from U.S. Commerce and Agriculture Department Studies, many of which are also on the web. You can subscribe to publications of international organizations that describe opportunities to supply products for programs they finance. Such agencies include the U.S. Agency for International Development and The World Bank in Washington, D.C., and the African, Asian, Arab, Caribbean, European, and Latin American development banks. These publications describe mainly large deals, many of which are also in the *Journal of Commerce*.

Finally, you can often uncover export opportunities by reading national and international publications. In the late 1990s, the *Wall Street Journal* reported that both China and Singapore were restricting access to some sites on the Internet but that people with enough knowledge or money were able to circumvent the restrictions. To do this, they needed certain kinds of equipment and software. You could try advertising that software, perhaps in the *Straits Times* in Singapore, and shipping it by mail to those who respond.

A Quick Evaluation

If the product you are interested in is a consumer good, you may want to show it to U.S. residents who came from the countries in which you intend to sell. They can comment on the product's design, size, color, and other characteristics. Some products such as film sell with little modification in any countries, but others such as toothpaste must cater to local tastes and cultures. I once bought shaving cream in Argentina that smelled like wet wheat. It may have done well in Buenos Aires, but I wouldn't try to sell it in Boston.

Industrial goods can be described to people from a country in which you plan to sell to obtain comments on their specifications. You may be told, for example, that the conveyors should be smaller and made to metric sizes. If they are electrical, they will have to use 220- to 240-volt current in most countries.

Finally, you should not invest a great deal of money in trying to sell a product without doing research in the target market. The best way of studying a market is to go there, identify potential buyers, make appointments to see them, show them the product (or product catalogs), and ask a series of questions. The answers to these questions will help you determine whether the buyers are interested in the product; whether there is a chance they would buy your products from you; whether the product would have to be modified and if so, how; approximately how much the buyers would pay; who the competitors are; and how you should go about trying to make sales.

LINING UP SUPPLIERS

In the scenario we are now following, you will have to find and contact potential suppliers. I once saw a notice that read, "Frozen

Canned Avocado (New Zealand). Quantity; Refrigerated Containers—Quality Subject to Market Testing. Packaging; Canned. Delivery: Wants to Study Samples First. Quote: CIF Auckland [buyer's name and address]." Suppose you received this notice and thought you could make the sale. How would you go about it? Here's the best sequence of events to follow.

First, phone, e-mail, or fax the potential buyer. Tell her you are an exporter of frozen food products and have seen the notice. Then ask whether she is still looking for the product, whether she would like to receive a quotation from you, and whether she can give you some idea of the quantity needed. Also ask how she would like the merchandise shipped and how she normally pays for similar shipments.

If in this process you get an impression that the buyer is not interested in receiving your quotation, you probably should not spend much time on this supposed export opportunity. If, however, you receive satisfactory answers to all your questions and have a good impression of the prospective buyer, you may want to go to the next step.

In major libraries, you can find a three-volume set of books called the *Thomas Grocery Register* (although the name may change because the Thomas Publishing Company sold this publication in April 2001). A look in Volume 2 under "Avocados" will show firms supplying frozen avocados including Calavo Growers in California and Parman Kendall Corporation in Florida. Then look under "Frozen Foods: General List" and you will probably find others. For manufactured products in general, the best source is a much larger set of books called the *Thomas Register of American Manufacturers*.

If there are many potential suppliers and you have plenty of time, you can contact them by mail. Write letters to the export manager. Explain that you are an export merchant (or agent), that you have a potential customer ". . . in the Pacific area" for frozen canned avocado, and that you would like, for example, a quotation on a full container load, f.a.s./vessel, Port of Oakland. If you are not sure which of a manufacturer's products an importer will want, ask instead for a catalog and an export price list. Make sure to say "export" price list, because many firms have export prices that are lower than their domestic selling prices. Ask for two copies, in case you decide to send one to the customer. You should not reveal the buyer's name and often not even the country; this prevents the supplier from contacting the buyer directly and saving the cost of your commission or markup.

If there are only a few potential suppliers, or time is limited, it is better to phone or fax. Although telephone calls in the United States are no longer expensive, you can call 1-800-555-1212 to ask whether the firms you want to call have 800 telephone numbers. This is important if you have long conversations or have to call several times to speak with a person who can help you. Ask to speak with someone in the Export Sales Department or, if there is none, the Sales or Marketing Department. Then explain your position as described in the preceding paragraph.

Some manufacturers will not be interested in exporting. They may be willing to cooperate if you plan to work as a merchant and take care of the export procedures, but not if they have to assume these responsibilities. Other firms will not let you quote on their products at all or will let you handle only certain products or sell to only a few countries. For example, Lee and Levis are already represented in most of the world. Your quotations on their products may be limited to a few less developed countries in which it is very hard to sell and receive payment. In some cases, you may have to deal with a producer's exclusive export agent or even with a wholesaler in order to get the merchandise you need.

The manufacturer's quotation or export price list may already have your markup (if you are working as a merchant) or commission (if an agent) built in. If this is not the case, you will have to add it on. This involves difficult decisions; you have to add enough to make the transaction profitable but not so much that you lose the sale to a competitor. In some cases, you can increase your earnings by getting export prices with built-in markups and then charging your customers a bit extra. In effect, you will be paid double.

The manufacturer's prices may be f.o.b./factory or they may include transportation to a port or an airport. In either case, you will probably have to add all costs to the destination (Auckland for the frozen avocados) in order to deliver a quotation, usually in U.S. dollars, that will let the importer compare her cost from you with her cost from other suppliers around the world. Finally, you will need to send your quotation (and perhaps catalog pages) to the buyer along with an e-mail message or fax that explains how you can help her better than any other supplier in the world. Then follow up, follow up, follow up, and try to make the sale.

THE FORMAL SUPPLY AGREEMENT

Once you have found and selected a supplier, you may want a formal agreement as to how you will do business with that firm. This is to give both you and the supplier some security and to reduce the range of possible business disputes. This suggestion applies whether you plan to work as an agent or as a merchant.

A young man from Thailand who lived in California was acting, without a written agreement, as an agent for a spice exporter in his country. Apparently, he did a very good job because import brokers who were also handling the product complained to the Thai exporter. The exporter promptly told our young friend that he should not call on spice packers, the market segment he had done best with, but should confine his efforts to compounders. He already knew from experience that compounders would not buy from him because he could not make them better offers than their established suppliers, the brokers. He was literally put out of business.

By contrast, a neophyte export agent entered into a written agreement to be the exclusive U.S. agent for a new kind of art supply product from Japan. She spent an entire year contacting art supply dealers, wholesalers, importers, and manufacturers before making her first sale. That sale was to a manufacturer of similar products, who already had a distribution network and could easily place the item in stores throughout the country. After the first shipment was made, the agent learned later, her customer contacted the Japanese exporter and proposed that she (the agent) be cut out of the arrangement. Her services were probably no longer essential, but she had a signed agreement and the exporter honored it. Her commissions were safe for the term of her existing contract.

Supply agreements may be very brief or very long. Your supplier may have a standard agreement form that is acceptable to you (examine it carefully), or you can try to write one yourself using sample agreements in books on international commercial law. You may want to buy a copy of The *ICC Model Commercial Agency Contract* or *The ICC Model Distributorship Contract* from ICC Publishing SA in New York City. Look on the World Wide Web at www.iccbooks.com. If, however, the stakes are high, financially or in other ways, you should seriously consider using an attorney. Call your local bar association to find one with international business experience, or ask for a referral from your banker or the head of your local world trade club. The attorney's fees may be $2,000 or more.

The following are some topics that international trade agreements often include. Many of these are relevant to both foreign and domestic purchasing, as well as foreign and domestic selling, whether you plan to work as an agent or as a merchant.

- *The Products*. An agreement usually names the products you will handle. The supplier may, for example, give you her line of TV sets but not her computer monitors.
- *Competing Products*. Some suppliers will try to restrict you from handling other companies' products that compete with theirs. Others will want you to handle several lines, so the customers will go to you instead of to another agent or importer.

- *Sales Targets.* Suppliers often want to have sales targets or minimums written into agreements. A target tells you how much you are supposed to sell, tells the supplier how much you are likely to sell, and gives the supplier a way to void the agreement if you do not perform satisfactorily.

- *The Territory.* This is the geographical area in which you are authorized to sell the product and which you are supposed to cover. If you have exclusivity in the territory as a merchant, the supplier should not deal with any other importer who sells there. If you have exclusivity as an agent, you should receive a commission on every sale made to a customer in the area.

  As you can imagine, virtually every agent and importer would like an exclusive arrangement. Some suppliers will give it, because they feel it will encourage the agent or importer to spend time and money building up sales in the territory.

- *Prices, Markups, and Commissions.* The "principal" (the foreign or domestic supplier) usually sets the price at which his agents must sell. The agreement will specify the percentage of commission to be paid as well as when it will be paid. For example, a U.S. agent for heavy equipment from Germany might receive 5 percent of the f.o.b./vessel value of shipments, payable when the German supplier receives a letter of credit.

  It is common also to have the allowable markups for import merchants included in their contracts. This is because an importer may be able to earn more by selling a small quantity, for a large markup, than by selling a large quantity for a small markup. In such a case, however, the supplier will not do well.

- *Payment Terms.* International trade agreements usually say how the supplier wants to be paid, either by an agent's customers or by his importer. If the supplier agrees to sell on other than secure terms, orders will be subject to approval by his credit department.

- *Shipping Terms.* Agreements between exporters and importers usually state how the exporter intends to ship, that is, to which point in the journey he will make shipping arrangements, retain title to the merchandise, and be responsible for loss or damage. This kind of clause is often omitted in an agency agreement.

- *Level of Effort.* The exporter may want a clause that gives a minimum number of person-hours or sales calls that you must devote to selling the product. More often a vague term such as "best effort" is used, but if the supplier wants to cancel the contract and finds no other grounds for doing so, you may be accused of not putting forth your best effort.

- *Promotion.* There are often clauses in a contract that state how much promotion an importer will be responsible for and/or how much assistance the exporter will provide. For example, an importer of new canned food products may get thirteen cases for every twelve he orders in the first year. The extra case is for promotional use.

- *Service and Warranties.* Any product can be defective, and there should be contractual provisions that say what will happen in such instances. The exporter may agree to replace defective products at his expense, take them back for repair, or pay you for repairing them. The exporter will be very concerned about the warranty given to final buyers because, in most cases, he will end up paying the cost of repairs done under warranty.

- *Priority of Orders.* Export merchants or agents will always want their orders to be given priority over the supplier's domestic orders. This decreases the possibility that a customer tires of waiting and cancels his or her order.

- *Order Lead Times.* This is a clause, similar to the preceding one, that specifies how soon the supplier should ship after receiving an order from you. It may say, for example, that your orders will normally be shipped within 30 days of receipt by the exporter.

- *Reporting.* The supplier may want a clause that specifies how often you should send reports. These reports may cover your sales activities, sales results, and changes in the market country including the economy, government regulations, competition, and customers.

- *Patent and Trademark.* Foreign manufacturers' products may be patented or carry unique trade names or trademarks. In such a case, a manufacturer will usually apply for U.S. patents and/or register the names or marks in the United States, or ask you to do so *on their behalf*. Both registrations are with the Commissioner of Patents and Trademarks, Washington, DC 20231. Getting a patent is often time-consuming and expensive. Registering a trademark, if it is truly unique, is easier. It takes a few months and costs about $250.

  You may want to register your own trademark and have the supplier put it on the items you purchase. Then you will own it and can use it even if you change suppliers. As an option, you can have labels printed and send them to the foreign manufacturer. Under simplified rules that went into effect around 1996, you can register a U.S. trademark without having previously used it in interstate or international commerce.

  Trademarks and brand names can also be registered with the U.S. Customs Service. Then, customs will try to stop imports of counterfeit goods, such as fake Rolex watches. Customs, however, will not normally enforce business agreements. If you are the exclusive U.S. importer of "Beautiful You" cosmetics, and your supplier ships legitimate "Beautiful You" products to someone else in the United States, they will probably be allowed entry.

  If your suppliers hold U.S. patents or trademarks, they may ask you to watch for cases of infringement. What action you must take if you hear of infringement depends on your agreements with the suppliers.

- *Relabeling and Repackaging.* Sometimes manufacturers will want you to agree not to relabel or repackage their merchandise. In other cases, it will be better for them to ship in bulk and have you repackage, under their labels or yours. A tasty product of the maguey cactus, tequila, is an excellent example. Most of the U.S. supply is imported from Mexico in tank trucks and is bottled here.

- *Legal Agent.* Most supply agreements have simple statements that the agent or importer is not a legal agent of the supplier. That is, you cannot enter into commitments that the supplier will be obliged to fulfill.

- *Assignment.* There is usually a clause that says you cannot assign the agreement to anyone else without the supplier's approval. Without this clause, the supplier would have no control over who ended up representing him.

- *Duration and Termination.* There is usually a statement that sets forth the term of the contract, whether it will automatically be renewed if not canceled by either party, and how it can be canceled. Normally, the initial term of an agency or distributorship agreement should be for about two years. You don't want to work very hard for a year and have the agreement canceled just when you begin to write orders.

- *Disputes.* Finally, there is a clause that relates to the settlement of disputes. The agreement may say in which country disputes will be settled and which country's laws will apply. It is more common to specify arbitration, even though international arbitration proceedings are too expensive for small-scale importers and exporters.

    If, however, you choose your suppliers carefully and deal with them competently and honestly, you should be able to resolve any disputes with neither lawsuits nor arbitration. Ultimately, a long-term business arrangement will not benefit you if it does not benefit the other party. Throughout the world, business is fueled by profit, but it is oiled by friendship and trust.

PROTECTING YOUR INTEREST

I once worked for a small firm in the Boston area that acted as an import merchant for books from Africa and an export agent for U.S. books and school supplies. We received an inquiry from a company in Haiti about desks for schools. After contacting a number of potential suppliers, we chose to quote on products of a company named Adirondack Chair. This manufacturer agreed to pay us an agent's commission. We sent the manufacturer's catalogs and prices to Haiti and, after only a few phone calls and letters, the customer wrote an order to Adirondack Chair and mailed it to us. We forwarded it immediately and followed up by phone to make sure it was acceptable to the manufacturer. The goods were shipped, the importer paid, and the manufacturer promptly remitted our commission.

Unfortunately, not all export transactions go so smoothly. It is tempting for U.S. exporters and foreign importers to try to save money by eliminating the intermediary, especially if the transaction is large, and they don't know you.

It is very frustrating to be working on an export sale, have it fail to materialize, and then somehow find out that it was made without you. There are a few ways to protect yourself. First, try to deal with reputable companies. Second, obtain letters or other evidence that your commissions will be paid; when this is not possible, try to keep the exporter and the importer from identifying each other. Finally, try to make your services so valuable that they will be worth the money paid for them. Keeping the exporter and the importer from identifying each other usually works for only one transaction, because the importer can usually identify the exporter from information on documents or the merchandise itself. (This is a problem for international trade brokers on the Internet. They find it very hard to collect fees after the first transaction between two companies.)

There is a type of payment document, a back-to-back letter of credit, that lets an intermediary use his or her customer's credit to guarantee payment to the supplier but does not identify either of them to the other (see chapter 7). This kind of letter of credit can be arranged by banks that specialize in import/export finance, but it usually requires that the intermediary be experienced in international trade and have enough collateral to cover the amount of the letter of credit. In other words, if the deal you are arranging is much larger than your bank account, you just about have to try to work as a commission agent.

CHAPTER 6

Marketing in the United States and Abroad

However you start your business, with a buyer or with a product, long-term success depends very much on marketing. For import and export merchants the critical business functions are purchasing and marketing, and an agent's work is almost entirely marketing.

SO, WHAT IS MARKETING?

Traditionally, marketing is described as the composite of functions needed to move goods from producers to consumers to satisfy consumers' wants and needs. Consumers can be either individuals or "industrial" organizations, including wholesalers and retailers, manufacturing companies, hospitals, restaurants, and government organizations. The major functions—the Four P's—are product (the product and package and all their characteristics), price (pricing and credit strategies and activities), place (channels of distribution), and promotion, and the way they are combined is called the marketing mix. Each of these functions can be further subdivided. For example, the traditional elements of promotion are advertising, public relations, publicity, sales promotion, and personal selling. Then advertising can be subdivided into print, broadcast and other media, and so on.

A much newer concept of marketing, which applies very well to both import and export businesses, is set forth in a book and software package on marketing from Jian Software, in Mountain View, California. This guide to marketing planning has three major divisions: market analysis, marketing communications, and sales planning. Note the emphasis here on planning and promotion as opposed to questions of product, price, and place. There is a small fourth part on break-even analysis, competitive analysis, and related activities.

Market analysis includes analyzing markets, customers, and competitors; product development and positioning; pricing for the market; market segmentation; and analysis of risks and resources. Marketing communications includes communications objectives and strategies, budgets, sales literature, advertising, public relations, trade exhibits, and customer service. Sales planning covers sales forecasting, budgeting for sales, sales management, and channels of distribution.

As you go through this chapter, reflect back on this three-part description of the marketing process.

MARKETING IMPORTS

Marketing Imports as an Agent

If you decide to work as a selling agent in the United States for foreign products, you will have to find buyers who are willing and able to do the importing. Beyond that, they will have to place orders that are large enough to be shipped directly to them from overseas. An order does not generally have to be very large if the goods are small, light, and valuable enough to be transported by air.

For several years, there has been a respectable trade in Egyptian paintings on papyrus. In about 1985, the best-known supplier, Dr. Rageb's Papyrus Institute in Cairo, began by establishing an agent in the Midwest to be responsible for selling throughout the United States. Because Dr. Rageb's papyrus paintings were of the highest quality, this agent could contact stores that sold high-quality antiques and artworks. The number of such stores was not large, and they could be identified from trade sources or from telephone directories and yellow pages. The agent soon learned, however, that any art dealer or museum gift shop could be a buyer. Because of the nature of the product, it could be shipped in small quantities and imported by people who knew very little about importing. Later, other suppliers began selling to importers without using agents.

In contrast, two people who consulted me for advice decided to become import agents for a new kind of industrial floor sweeper made in northern Europe. This product could not be imported economically in small quantities. To be practical, several had to be brought in at a time, and each cost several thousand dollars. Because neither distributors nor the actual users were likely to buy several machines without seeing one in use, the importers had to bring in a sample, find a place to store it, and find a way to demonstrate it to potential buyers. They found an industrial equipment distributor to demonstrate the unit to potential users. They have since made some sales, but large orders will be hard to get until they become known in the industry.

The difficulty of being an agent comes from the fact that agents cannot make the decisions to buy or to sell but can only influence the importer and the exporter to make these decisions. Typically, a U.S. selling agent will sign an agreement with her foreign principal. Then the agent will try to obtain orders, which will be written to the principal but given to the agent. The agent will send them to the principal, who will usually accept them as long as the terms are satisfactory. The principal will ship directly to the customer, collect from the customer, and pay the agent a commission. The agent must follow up frequently to make sure the transaction is eventually made and then to collect the commission that is due.

After the agent selects a product and reaches agreement with a principal, she faces the daunting task of finding buyers and persuading them to buy. The best list of U.S. importers is the Journal of Commerce's annual *Directory of United States Importers/Exporters*. This book is available in major libraries and contains useful information on thousands of companies, and there is now an electronic version. Unfortunately, it omits many of the companies that import, especially manufacturers and retailers.

The Journal of Commerce also has an electronic service for reporting information on both imports and exports, taken from steamship manifests. Note that air, road, and rail shipments are not included. Called PIERS (Port Import and Export Reporting Service), this service is expensive but is a way to find out which firms are really importing (as opposed to *saying* they import) specific kinds of products. The telephone numbers for PIERS are 1-800-952-3839 and, for callers in New York City, 212-837-7051.

There are numerous other publications that either list importers or use codes to identify importing firms. These include directory issues of trade magazines, state and local industrial directories, and others such as the *Thomas Grocery Register*, mentioned in chapter 5. In some cases, however, you may have to find companies willing to import by telephoning or going to see them. There are also electronic directories of potential customers, such as DataShark, which sells directories of the following in various formats:

- *Food retailing and foodservice.* Chain restaurant operators, foodservice distributors, high-volume independent restaurants, single-unit supermarket operators, supermarket/grocery/convenience store chains, and wholesaler grocers

- *Mass merchandising*. Apparel specialty stores, department stores, discount and general merchandise stores, drug store and health and beauty chains, and high-volume independent drug stores
- *Specialty retailers and distributors*. Automotive aftermarket suppliers, computer and consumer electronics retailers, computer value-added retailer and systems integrators, home center operators and hardware chains, home furnishings retailers, and mail-order firms

I once assisted a company in Colombia that manufactured clothing for dolls. No directories showed U.S. importers of doll clothing, but I found that nearly every U.S. doll manufacturer was importing clothing, mostly from the Far East. I had no difficulty identifying manufacturers of dolls, making appointments with them, showing them samples of the clothing, and explaining that if they imported from South America they could save money on customs duties and forget about jet lag both during and after their buying trips. Several manufacturers gave me samples of products they were buying from Asia so the South American firm could examine them and prepare quotations.

Another Colombian firm wanted to export a canned or bottled fruit from the palm tree that is known in some countries as *chontaduros* and in others as *pejivalles*. This was a Latin American specialty food that would be retailed by small food stores that catered to an ethnic clientele, but the stores themselves would not be the importers. The technique used to identify importers was to go to Hispanic areas, find small food stores, and look at the imported products they were selling. On imported canned and bottled foods, the importers' names and locations (in this case, cities or boroughs of New York City) are identified. A few of the importers were small firms that were not listed in the telephone directory; in these cases, we got the telephone numbers from the retailers by simply asking and explaining why we needed the information.

Marketing Imports as a Merchant

As a merchant, you will actually import goods from overseas, take title to them and probably (but not necessarily) possession of them, and sell and deliver them to your customers. A merchant normally invests more money and performs more functions than an agent but has the potential to make a larger profit. Because a merchant loses if he or she cannot sell, or sells but cannot collect, there is also a potential for losing money.

In general, an import merchant will not sell to importers but to retailers, wholesalers, industrial users, and industrial distributors. The term *retailers* includes chain stores, independent stores, mail-order and Internet retailers, flea market operators, and other kinds of businesses that sell directly to individual consumers. The term *industrial users* includes business, government, and nonprofit organizations of all types. In general, *wholesalers* are merchant (buy and sell) firms that sell to retailers, and *industrial distributors* are merchant firms that sell to industrial users.

If you choose to sell directly to retailers, you can identify them from telephone directories or from specialized directories such as the *Salesman's Guide* series from the R. R. Bowker Company (phone 1-800-526-4902). There are similar books available from other companies. These directories list the names and telephone numbers of the buyers of each kind of merchandise in major stores and store chains.

In general, the larger the store or store chain, the harder it is to get in to see a buyer. When you phone for an appointment, you may be asked to send a catalog or prices and samples. If you agree to send a catalog and do not have one, you will find that the cost of creating a professional-looking catalog is around $500 per page (in color). You might try to do it on a computer, or you might choose to have a professional photographer take a good color picture for you. Twenty-five copies of one shot should cost about $200. Have the photograph printed on a full-size sheet of paper with the item number and name (and the dimensions and weight if relevant), and you have a catalog page. You can include the price on the same page or put it in your cover letter, or, if you have several models, you can prepare a separate list of prices. Your price list should mention your minimum order quantity, any discounts for large orders or prompt payment, and whether delivery charges are included.

A few retail stores have "open buying" days, when vendors can see buyers without having appointments. Some directories list these days, but you should call in advance to make sure they have not been changed. Then, be prepared to answer every possible question about your company and its product, including its material composition and how it is made. Buyers from big stores are very professional. They do not want to take time to educate you or to risk buying from you if they have any doubts about your ability to deliver.

The term *open buying* should not be confused with *open to buy*, which means that the buyer has money remaining in his or her current budget for the kind of merchandise you are selling. If you visit someone who is not open to buy, you will have very little chance of making an immediate sale.

Retail buyers know pretty well what will sell and what will not and at which price each kind and quality of merchandise can be bought. They negotiate prices and specify the quantities, delivery dates, and payment terms they want. They sometimes refuse to accept merchandise even after having ordered it, and they often take longer to pay than the terms agreed upon. A store that is given terms such as "2/10, Net 30" (2 percent discount if they pay within 10 days and payment due in any case within 30 days) will often pay in 20 or 25 days and take the discount anyway.

If you choose to sell to small independent stores, such as gift shops or boutiques, you will find it easier to see buyers. Sometimes you can even walk in unannounced, ask who does the buying, and show your samples. If the buyer likes the samples and prices, he or she may place a small order, ask for immediate delivery, and write a check or pay in cash. Cash payments may indicate that some of the retailer's transactions are "off the books."

You will not, however, have time to make enough sales calls in small stores to produce a profitable volume of business. A solution to this problem is to enlist the services of manufacturers' representatives. These are agents that will book orders for your products from retail stores and send the orders to you. When you accept an order, you will ship it to the customer, request payment from the customer, and send the agent his or her commission.

You can find manufacturers' representatives on the following web sites:

- Manufacturers Representatives of America, Inc., a national not-for-profit trade organization of multiple-line sales and marketing companies, www.mrareps.com/
- Manufacturers Agents National Association, with over 7,000 members and 23,000 representatives, www. manaonline.org/

There are other sites for representatives in specific industries, and there is a "play for pay" service called RepLocate Inc. that can help in your search. RepLocate is on the web at www.replocate.com.

Another approach is to ask retail buyers which agents they suggest you speak with. The buyers will probably give you the names of the agents they deal with the most. A manufacturers' representative (rep) will usually ask you for a 10 to 15 percent commission and perhaps to pay a share of his overhead expenses (office, and so forth). Also, you will need to supply him with catalogs or with product samples, price lists, and promotional literature. Thus, if you use ten reps and they have an average of five salespersons each, you will have to supply 50 copies of your catalog. However, in some industries, such as automotive parts, you may be able to get by with just an on-line catalog.

Wholesalers of most kinds of goods can be identified from the telephone directory or from directory issues of trade magazines. Wholesale buyers can be approached directly. They are generally very experienced and negotiate hard on prices and terms of sales. Wholesalers normally buy in quantity and pay their bills promptly, but do not invest heavily in promotion. It will be up to you to persuade retailers to buy your product from the wholesalers and perhaps even to persuade customers to buy it from the retailers.

The best way to persuade either manufacturers' reps or wholesalers to handle your product is to prove that retailers will buy it and can resell it. For example, a woman interested in importing high-quality wooden furniture from France began by locating a few stores that sold products similar to hers and persuading each one to stock a few pieces. Then she could import a container-load of furniture, place it in stores, and tell wholesalers that she knew the product *would* sell because it was already selling.

Many new importers plan to sell their products by mail order. This is usually not as easy as it sounds. There are essentially three ways to go about it.

First, you can identify your most likely target market, buy a specialized mailing list from one of the many list dealers such as Info USA in New Jersey (phone 1-800-551-1533), prepare your mailing, and send it out. You can buy names and addresses on lists, mailing labels, 3-by-5 cards, magnetic tape, diskettes, and sometimes CD-ROMs. Some now include credit ratings. You should get professional help in preparing your mailing pieces or at least read books on mail-order selling. You will learn techniques such as writing "Personal and Confidential" on your envelope, using a postscript in your sales letter to communicate an important point, and putting a real stamp on your reply envelope. People hate to throw away real stamps. For large mailings, you can save money by getting a bulk-mail permit, but many experts say the extra cost of using first-class mail is a good investment.

You should send a series of three mailings to the same addresses. Most people will throw away the first one because they have never heard of you. The second one may catch their attention, and the third time they may buy. The rates of response in mail order are very low. A major organization that markets seminars by mail is said to be satisfied with a rate of about 0.0025, or a quarter of 1 percent. Some reasons for this are that even the best mailing lists contain errors (wrong addresses, names of people who have moved, etc.) and that your tiny, unknown catalog must compete for attention with the likes of Spencer Gifts and Hanover House. You will be lucky to break even, especially when you consider the labor involved in sending the catalogs and processing the orders.

A second mail-order option is for you to advertise in newspapers or magazines (at least three issues of the same publication). You can ask respondents to order immediately or to contact you for more information. Advertising in general-interest publications is unlikely to pay off (although the *Wall Street Journal*, for example, carries ads over and over again for products that do not seem to be high-potential mail-order items, like the "poke boat"). But if you have a specialized product and can find a publication aimed at precisely your target market, this kind of marketing will work well. I once met an importer of Scottish bagpipe regalia who told me there was only one magazine written for bagpipe enthusiasts in the United States. He was receiving numerous orders from his advertisements in that publication.

A third mail-order option is to import products and try to persuade established mail-order houses to include them in their catalogs. Save all the catalogs that come to you and try to identify firms that sell products similar to yours. Also, you can look on the web at sites such as www.catalogsfroma-z.com/ (for online catalogs) and www.buyersindex.com/ (for hard-copy catalogs) to identify companies that might want to handle your products. Then contact them, preferably by phone. Describe your product and say that you feel it would sell very well in their catalogs. If the buyer you are speaking with is interested, he or she will probably ask for a sample and prices. Your sample will not be returned unless you provide a self-addressed label and offer to accept the shipment collect from a parcel service such as UPS, and sometimes even that will not be sufficient.

Professional mail-order firms place a high value on every square inch of every catalog page and are very selective about the products they include. Also, they keep their own inventories to a minimum. They won't want to take a chance on putting an item in a catalog and getting orders for it, only to find that you do not have the product. Therefore, they will probably insist that you invest in a substantial inventory in the United States. A few will send you mailing labels and ask you to "drop ship" directly to their customers, but this is becoming less common.

If you have an inexpensive, mass merchandise type of product, you may want to try selling it at craft shows or flea markets or, better yet, to flea market vendors or wholesalers. Flea markets in the United States are now an established industry with its own associations and publications, but they tend to go in and out of business quickly. Try going to flea markets in your area, speaking with dealers and asking them which wholesalers they buy from. These same wholesalers usually sell also to street vendors, house-party dealers, and other kinds of nonstore retailers.

Be warned, however, that the flea market industry works on low prices. People who shop at flea markets expect the dealers to sell cheaply. That means the dealers have to buy cheaply from the wholesalers, and the wholesalers have to buy cheaply from you. Some people consider flea marketing to be the method of selling of last resort.

Industrial users include manufacturers, wholesalers, retailers, schools, libraries, hospitals, government offices, military installations, and so on. They all have people or departments in charge of purchasing, and you can usually see them by appointment to do research on new products. It is harder to get through the door when you are actually selling something because they have established suppliers of known brands, and they don't have time to deal with numerous small manufacturers and importers. If you have a new and better paper clip, don't try to sell it to IBM. Sell it instead to a distributor that sells to IBM.

Industrial distributors are similar to wholesalers except that they buy from manufacturers or importers and sell to industrial users. To reach smaller users, there are often two levels of distributors. A familiar example is the automotive parts trade, in which numerous specialized companies make virtually all parts available to myriad repair facilities. Industrial distributors can usually be identified through telephone directories, state industrial directories, and directory issues of trade magazines or by asking industrial users which distributors they buy from. In general, they buy in good quantities, stock merchandise, pay their bills on time, sell and do some promotion, and deliver to their customers.

While I've never worked with paper clips, I did have a friend who was importing a new kind of stapler from Japan. It was small, light, inexpensive, durable, and effective. Unfortunately, my friend's business did not last long. He didn't do a good enough job of identifying his target market, selling to appropriate distributors, or promoting to potential users.

Of course, the modern way is to sell on the Internet. I recently read about people in a tiny Cambodian village who are selling handmade scarves to the world from a little computer, powered by a portable generator, and a satellite antenna to get them on the Net.

Unfortunately, the ease of selling on the Net created so much competition, so quickly, that here too it is better to sell through an established merchant. As an extreme example, how would you like to see your product in a "pop-up" ad on America Online? Every AOL user in the world would be exposed to it.

A Final Note on Marketing Imports

If it sounds too hard to start an import business, you might consider buying one. An excellent newsletter called *Relocatable Business* describes businesses that you can buy and move to wherever you want them. You can contact the publisher by phone at 1-800-927-1310, fax (516) 466-8672, e-mail (business@relocatable.com), or web site (www.relocatable.com).

Here's a typical description of a business you can buy from an issued published a few years ago:

The importer brings into the country an exclusive soft-goods product directly related to the drapery industry. The owners have exclusive rights to the design of their product, which they have manufactured in Europe and shipped to their location. The company then distributes the goods to their own accounts.

This business began as a home-based business in 1988. Since then, it has grown to require a 1,200 square foot facility. The seller says the business will soon require another 400 to 500 square feet.

The husband–wife team manage the company with one additional full-time employee and one part-time person. The sellers handle all administration, warehousing, and shipping from the Southeastern city where they prefer to live. The distribution network consists of about 60 independent sales representatives who sell to a group of approximately 3,000 dealers. The company repackages the product and ships nationally and into Canada, usually by UPS.

The business has realized an average gross profit of 65 percent over the last four years. The average gross sales since 1973 have been $298,000. Seller discretionary income has averaged $100,000 per year.

How much would it cost to purchase this business? The asking price was $250,000 for inventory and $245,000 for other assets. From these figures, I estimate a payback period of about six years, which is not bad at all.

MARKETING EXPORTS

Analysis

Export market analysis is complicated, but there is a lot of information to help you. For example, a firm in East Syracuse, New York, known as The PRS Group, publishes reports on conditions in numerous countries. An April 2001 report on the Philippines, read in part:

Despite some disorder surrounding the May elections, regional dissident violence, and residual support for President Estrada, Arroyo should be able to keep the disorder within tolerable bounds, and will move much more decisively to open the economy to competition and change.

The PRS Group publishes several different kinds of useful reports. They can be reached by phone (315) 431-0511 or fax (315) 431-0200. The web site is www.prsgroup.com.

In January 2000, the center to promote imports from developing countries in Holland, CBI, published a summary of the European market for tableware, kitchenware and household articles of wood, metals, glass, and plastic. The full survey report included the types of housewares, consumption in the European Union and each of its member countries, and trends in consumption with the reasons for those trends. It also included European production, imports with supplying countries, exports with market countries, and relevant import regulations.

This kind of market analysis does not guarantee you sales, but it can definitely help you start off on the right foot. You can do a lot of market analysis in the United States, in libraries and on the Internet. Also, you can buy market studies. Your Department of Commerce field office can guide you to some sources of published studies, although many of them are quite expensive. There are many sources on the World Wide Web. For example, the International Market Research Mall at www.imrmall.com lists market studies and other reports from a variety of publishers.

Communication

The analysis just described will help you develop your product line and pricing and decide with which kinds of potential buyers to communicate. Then you can communicate with a general audience by, for example, advertising in foreign trade magazines. Consult an international periodicals directory in your library to find a magazine that reaches buyers of the products you have selected in the markets you have selected or look at www.worldbizmedia.com. Want to sell U.S. apples in Europe? Then monthly advertising in *Eurofruit* would be a good choice.

A less costly alternative is to try advertising by direct mail. Select firms to mail to by looking in print or electronic sources. Perhaps the best source is Kompass, on line at www.kompass.com. Their site gives the names of 3.2 million executives, in 1.6 million companies in some 70 countries. For example, the following search:

"Building and civil engineering"
"Sanitary installations, plastic"
"Bidets, plastic"

brings up 67 companies. Information on 30 of them is available for free, and there is a large amount of data on each one. Kompass also has information on CD-ROMs and in hard copy, and there is an advertising service that you might want to utilize.

Another valuable service is Export Hotline, a pioneering organization in the field of trade facilitation that is now on the Web at www.exporthotline.com. There are contacts and research information for 50 industry sectors and 120 countries.

If you want help with international direct-mail advertising, it is available for a price. Your mailing pieces can be translated, overnight if necessary, by companies such as ASET in Arlington, Virginia (phone 1-800-787-8726, e-mail robert@asetquality.com). Their web site is www.asetquality.com. If you want to hire more help, there are local services everywhere that will help you prepare your mailings. You may want to save money on postage by sending in bulk overseas and having the mailing done locally, especially because it takes about three mailings of the same list to get results. Some of the international courier companies provide this service, or you can contact Deutsche Post GlobalMail, Ltd., in Sterling, Virginia (phone 1-800-545-8794, web site—www.global/mail.com).

You might also consider having your firm listed in directories such as the *American Export Register,* which is placed in U.S. embassies abroad. You can contact them in New York by phone at (212) 629-1130, or e-mail at info@aernet.com.

There are a huge number of fairs and exhibits abroad, and exhibiting in them can pay off well in market knowledge, exposure, contacts, and sales. Information on these is available from Department of Commerce field offices and in the *Journal of Commerce* and other publications. Unfortunately, the cost is usually quite high. The cost is much lower for "catalog exhibits," because you don't have to send either company products or personnel. There are some exhibits sponsored by the USDC and also by state and local export promotion organizations. The USDC also has an on-line catalog exhibit. See www.e-expousa.doc.gov/welcome.htm.

A large amount of foreign trade information and contacts are available from the Federation of International Trade Associations, on the web at http://fita.org. There are trade leads, trade information, trade events, and so forth. You might also look into the so-called "B2B trade portals" as a means of finding customers (and suppliers as well). These companies tend to come and go quickly. Some that show special promise are at www.worldbid.com, www.b2port.com, and www.bigex.com.

Let me end this section with a few words about translations. You can buy translation software or get this work done free on the Internet. Unfortunately (or fortunately), there is still no substitute for a human being. As a small test, I went to http://systran.aol.com and typed in Spanish the sentence: "Ayer hablé con mi vecina y me dijo que se sentía muy triste." In an instant, the following translation came back: "I spoke yesterday with my neighbor and it said to me that one felt very sad." This isn't bad, for a machine, but you wouldn't want to send it to a potential customer.

SELLING AS AN AGENT

Remember that, as an agent, your goal will be to find customers and make sales for your "principals." Once you have an order and your principal accepts it, your only job is to follow up now and then and make sure there are no problems. If you are exporting as a merchant, you will probably be responsible for international shipping and collection, as well.

A great deal of international selling is done by direct contact, which means that you would travel to see your potential customers and then follow up with them by phone, fax, and/or e-mail. My friend in Pennsylvania, who for many years made his living exporting construction equipment from the basement of his house, now considers himself retired, but he still travels once in a while and makes an occasional shipment. As you can imagine, you don't need to sell many "big-ticket" items to make the mortgage payments.

When you do travel abroad and have to take samples, you surely don't want to pay duty as you go from one country to another. The solution is an *ATA Carnet*, which is available from providers authorized by the U.S. Council for International Business. One such provider, for example, is Allegheny Brokerage in Dublin, Virginia, phone (888) 418-2219, e-mail—solutions@acustomsbroker.com.

WORKING WITH FOREIGN AGENTS

In many situations, especially in international trade, one can make more money by *lengthening* the distribution channel. This means locating agents or distributors overseas to sell for you. The USDA and most state governments can help you identify potential agents or distributors, and you can correspond with them and then visit them. Choose well because, if your representative doesn't sell, *you* won't do very well. If you select one who has a poor reputation in his country, your reputation will suffer. Also, if you pick the wrong one, local laws may make it nearly impossible for you to let him go. I once heard of a U.S. exporter who traveled to Saudi Arabia and fired his local agent; later, he was detained at the airport with the accusation that he had violated Saudi law.

Your main criterion for choosing foreign agents or distributors should be how well equipped they are to do the job you need done. If you are exporting electronic products that will need servicing, your distributor must have service facilities and trained personnel. If your product is a line of expensive clothing that will be sold to high-quality department stores, your agent needs good contacts among buyers for this kind of store.

When you have selected a foreign agent or distributor, enter into a contract with that person or firm. Make sure the key personnel thoroughly understand your products, by sending them literature and by training them either in the U.S. factory or in their own offices. Then keep in contact with them, both to motivate and to assist them. I once did a survey of how firms on Long Island, New York, treated their U.S. and their foreign sales representatives. The foreign reps did not receive nearly as much in the way of product information, advance notice of price changes, assistance with advertising, help exhibiting in trade shows, or personal visits. By comparison, they were being ignored.

CHAPTER **7**
_____

Money Matters

You're in the import business. You need to place an order, and your supplier in Zurich has asked for either cash in advance or payment "at sight" in Swiss francs by confirmed, irrevocable letter of credit with all charges for your account. Does this sound like a good deal, or will you negotiate?

Okay, now you're in the export business. You have an order from Tanzania, and the customer offers to pay in East African shillings and be billed on 60-day open account or shipped on 60-day SD/DA (sight draft, documents against acceptance) terms. Is this acceptable, or will you negotiate?

Now that you are both importing and exporting, a firm in Malaysia offers to trade $10,000 worth of beautiful cotton blouses for industrial sewing machines of the same value. "Don't worry about duties or quotas," the manager says. "They won't apply because this is a barter deal." Will you order the blouses and send the sewing machines?

This chapter will give you ideas about how to deal with these sorts of issues. If you don't know how to deal with them, and don't have a good banker to advise you, your business will be limited to the most routine transactions. Get involved in unique or complex deals without an understanding of how to deal with money matters, or a very good advisor, and you could lose your shirt, your trousers, and more.

CREDIT DECISIONS ON SUPPLIERS AND CUSTOMERS

Whether you plan to sell domestically or to export, as a merchant you will have to decide between taking the risk of selling on credit and losing sales by insisting on payment in cash. Your suppliers will face similar decisions about selling to you. If you work only as an agent, you will still be involved in credit decisions. You will negotiate sales for your principals and will then have to convince them that the terms of sale you have worked out with the customers are acceptable. In order to make credit decisions, you must know how to obtain and use credit information.

Bank and Trade References

The least expensive way to check on the credit-worthiness of a domestic or foreign firm is to ask for bank and trade references. A company that will not give you references is not likely to be a good paying customer.

To check a prospective customer's bank reference, give your bank (in writing) the company's name and address, its bank's name and address, and its account number. That information is not confidential; it is printed on checks. If you are checking on a foreign company and want the information quickly, ask your bank to communicate by e-mail or fax at your expense. You should receive a report that tells you how many years the company's account has been open, the approximate average balance, the amount of its credit line, and in general how satisfactory the account has been to the bank. This is not a great deal of data, but it will be helpful.

To check with trade references, send each a letter or fax that reads something like the one in Figure 7.1.

If you are checking on a potential supplier, the letter will be almost the same, but the questions will be something like the ones at the bottom of Figure 7.1.

Dear Sir or Madam:

The company named below has listed you as a credit reference. We will be very grateful if you will answer the questions at the bottom of this page and return this letter in the enclosed self-addressed, stamped envelope. Your prompt attention to this request will help us make an appropriate credit decision. We will be pleased to assist you in the same way if the occasion should ever arise. Thank you very much. Sincerely,

[your signature]

_____

Name and Address of Applicant: [you will fill this in] _____
_____
_____

[questions on potential customers]
Number of years you have sold to this company: _____
Highest recent balance: _____
Current outstanding balance: _____
Terms you extend this company: _____
Payment record: Discounts ( ) 30 days ( ) 60 days ( ) Over 60 ( )
Your rating of account: Excellent ( ) Good ( ) Fair ( ) Poor ( )
Additional comments: _____
_____
Your name: _____ Title: _____ Date: _____

[questions on potential suppliers]
Number of years you have dealt with this vendor: _____
Please comment on:
• Size of order supplier can fill: _____
• Adherence to shipping schedules: _____
• Accuracy in filling orders: _____
• Any problems experienced: _____
Other comments: _____
Your name: _____ Title: _____ Date: _____

Figure 7.1   Letter Requesting Credit References

Nearly all companies will answer this correspondence if it looks professional. If you send it by mail, it can help to enclose a stamped, self-addressed return envelope. Or you can give your fax number and offer the option of replying by fax.

Credit Reporting Services

How much is credit information worth to you? This depends on how much you stand to lose by making a wrong credit decision. If you make a $10,000 sale and don't get paid, a report that stops you from making the sale would be a good investment even if it cost $9,000. If you get paid, but a month late, at 12 percent interest, the report would be worth up to $100 ($10,000 × 0.12 × 12/360). If you stand to lose much, importing or exporting, you should consider using the services of a credit reporting agency.

The granddaddy of this business in the United States is the Dun & Bradstreet (D&B) company. Their services are numerous, and you can contact them by phone (800) 234-3867. Of course they are on the World Wide Web: www.dnb.com. There are D&B documents on credit and collections, supplier evaluation, global information, small business services, and other topics.

For firms in the United States, there are other options. There are small credit reporting agencies in most cities. I once called from Bolivia to such an agency in Miami, and the information they provided probably kept a Bolivian firm from losing both its merchandise and the shipping cost. Low-cost reports on U.S. companies are available from www.businesscreditusa.com, phone (650) 389-0700.

Finally, a visit to a potential vendor or customer can give you important information. If the tires on the trucks are too old, perhaps they can't afford new ones. If they still do their accounting manually, they must be too backward or too tight on money to buy accounting software and have an employee learn to use it. Finally, if they aren't willing to answer your questions or seem to be hiding something, perhaps they are.

METHODS OF PAYMENT IN INTERNATIONAL TRADE

In international trade there are several means of payment, each of which has its costs, advantages, and risks. The most important are the following:

- Open account
- Documents against acceptance
- Documents against payment
- Letter of credit
- Payment in advance

These means of payment are arrayed in order of risk, with open account being the riskiest for the exporter and payment in advance being the riskiest for the importer. Sometimes consignment is listed also as a payment term. It would go at the top of the list, because in consignment sales the risk is borne entirely by the exporter.

Terms of payment are a negotiable aspect of international trade transactions. Each party seeks a term that is favorable to him or her but that the other party might also accept. You need to understand the various methods; otherwise, you may accept a method of payment that is riskier or more expensive than can be justified by the profit on a transaction.

Open Account

How do you pay for water? It's simple: First you receive the product, and then the water company sends you a bill. Open account in international trade works the same way. First the exporters send the shipments, and then they send bills for the merchandise and related costs. The importer can pay in various ways, such as by sending a form of cashier's check or an international money order. Pitney Bowes (888-245-8741) now has an international payments system that is very easy to use.

This method is very inexpensive. It does not involve any risk for the importer, but the exporter runs the risk that the importer will not pay for the merchandise. The exporter's only protection is that of the underlying contract of sale and/or the importer's word and reputation.

It may surprise you to learn that open account is the most widely used method of payment in the import/export business. This is because the great majority of international trade (in terms of value, not number of transactions) is between affiliated companies or between large firms that know and trust each other. If Toyota/Japan ships auto parts to Toyota/U.S. or to General Motors, it will not bother with costly or complex terms of payment.

As a small importer, you are unlikely to get open account terms from foreign suppliers, but your steady purchases and reliable performance may earn you this reward in a few years. As a small exporter, you will almost certainly be asked to accept payment on open account. You will probably be reluctant to agree, but if your customer is a major firm or is well known to you, you may decide to take the risk. After all, why should a foreign importer buy from you with a risky or expensive method of payment if he can get open account terms from another exporter in the United States or a third country.

As an exporter, you will want to be careful of a little game that is played by a few importers. They may start paying you on secure terms and then request open account for a small order. If you agree, their orders on open account will become progressively larger, and they will pay right on time. Then you will ship the big order, and the money will not arrive. I once tried to help a Long Island company that had fallen for this scam. When the exporter traveled to the importing country, in West Africa, he found that most of the money had been invested in houses for the importer and his relatives.

Another problem with open account shipments is that even honest buyers can take a long time to pay—reportedly around 80 days in Greece or Italy, on the average.

Documentary Drafts for Collection—Against Acceptance and Against Payment

To "draft" a document is to write it. In international trade, a draft is an unconditional order in writing, signed by the seller and addressed to a foreign buyer. It orders the buyer to pay the amount specified in the draft, either when it is presented to him or on a specified date in the future. Drafts as methods of payment are used only in international trade, and you may have heard them referred to by names such as sight draft and documents against payment, among others.

In brief, a draft is a simple, inexpensive means of payment that is initiated by the exporter. It works like this: Suppose I agree to sell you 10 bags of coffee for $1,300. I have my bank, Citibank, prepare a document that looks something like a bank check. It says, "Pay Citibank $1,300." Citibank sends this draft to your bank, and the cashier either calls you to come or sends it to you. You have already received the coffee, and are an honest person, so you promptly sign the draft and return it to your bank. The cashier takes the money from your account and transfers it to Citibank for my account. Technically, we wouldn't even need a sales agreement. I could select your name from a directory, send you some merchandise, and have the draft sent to your bank. If you signed it, the merchandise would be yours and the money would be mine. To send merchandise without any previous agreement would, of course, be a terribly risky maneuver.

This kind of draft is also called a *bill of exchange*. A bill is a piece of paper that notifies you of something, and this kind of bill notifies you of an exchange of merchandise for money. The exporter's bank *cuts* the draft, and the importer's bank *presents* it to her. If the importer doesn't sign it upon *first presentation*, there will later be a second presentation, and so on. When the importer writes "accepted" on the draft and signs it, she has accepted her obligation to pay the money. If the importer is supposed to pay the draft upon presentation (as soon as she sees it), it is a *sight draft.* If the agreement is that she does not have to pay immediately, but sometime after seeing it, it will be called a *time draft* (even though it may say something like "60 days sight"). If payment is due by a certain date, it will be called a *date draft.*

This method of payment, as described so far, puts the risk entirely on the exporter. If the importer refuses to accept a draft for any reason, the exporter must sue the buyer to accept it, find a new buyer in the same or a different country, pay for return transportation of the goods to their point of origin, or abandon the shipment. All these options are time-consuming and expensive. If goods are abandoned, they are usually sold at customs auctions, and there is nothing to prevent the supposed importers from bidding on them. Beware of any foreign importer who wants essential parts of an item, such as axe handles and axe heads, in separate shipments with payments by sight draft. This importer is putting herself in a position to buy cheap at the customs auctions, because only she will know where both the handles and the heads can be found.

There is, however, a way for the exporter to use a sight draft and still control the merchandise. It involves using a *to order bill of lading.* (See chapter 9 for a discussion of documents in international trade). When the exporter places the goods on a ship or other vehicle for transportation, the ship's captain or his representative signs and gives the exporter a document called a *bill of lading* (an *airwaybill* if the shipment is by air). This document serves, among other purposes, as title to the merchandise. The person to whom the goods are "consigned" on the bill of lading can claim them. If the exporter wants the importer to receive the goods without regard to payment, as in an open account shipment, he uses a *straight* bill of lading. If, however, the exporter wants to impose conditions on delivery of the goods, he uses a *to order* bill of lading. It is usually "to order of shipper" (the exporter). Then the shipper can *order* that the goods be delivered only under certain conditions, as when the importer has accepted the draft. In practice, the shipper usually endorses the bill of lading *in blank* on the back and trusts the banking system to give it to the buyer, endorsed to him, only when he has accepted the draft. With a properly endorsed bill of lading, the buyer can receive the merchandise.

There are restrictions on to order bills of lading with airfreight because the goods can arrive before the documents, and airlines don't want their warehouses cluttered with incoming cargo. A solution that sometimes works is to make the airwaybill to order of a trusted bank in the importer's country and send the documents by courier.

With this system, the risk is not all on the exporter but is shared. If the payment document is a sight draft, the exporter still bears the risk that the importer will not pay and pick up the merchandise, but the importer bears the risk that the goods will not be as ordered. With a time or a date draft, the importer has the option of picking up the goods, examining them and, if they are faulty, instructing her bank not to pay the draft. Fortunately, this is not done often.

In summary, a documentary draft is a simple payment instrument, initiated by the exporter, that goes through banking channels but is not guaranteed by the banks. It can be used for transactions of any size but is often favored for those in the range of $500 to $3,000. There is always some risk for the exporter, and there is also risk for the importer when a sight draft is combined with a to order bill of lading, because he must pay before seeing the merchandise. The cost is usually about $100 for each party per transaction, and it is common for each party to pay his or her own charges.

Figure 7.2 illustrates a bill of exchange transaction with a to order bill of lading. Note that there are seven parties involved— the exporter, his bank, his freight forwarder, the ocean carrier (not shown), the importer, her bank, and her customs broker.

Figure 7.3 is a copy of a sight draft for a shipment exported from the United States. The exact appearance of this kind of document varies from bank to bank.

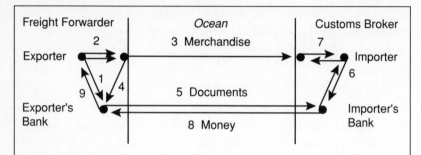

1. *Exporter* fills out form at his bank.
2. Exporter sends goods and documents to freight forwarder.
3. *Freight forwarder* sends merchandise and gets bill of lading signed by carrier.
4. Freight forwarder sends documents to exporter's bank.
5. *Bank* sends them to importer's bank.
6. *Importer* pays or accepts; gets documents.
7. Importer gives documents to carrier; gets merchandise.
8. Importer's bank transmits funds.
9. Exporter's bank credits his account.

Figure 7.2 Bill of Exchange Transaction

Letters of Credit

By now, or perhaps long before now, you have heard the words letter of credit (LC). There are various types of LCs, but the one we will discuss here is the commercial documentary letter of credit. The word *commercial* means it is used in a business transaction, and *documentary* means it is payable upon presentation of specified documents.

You can think of a letter of credit as a letter that is written by the importer's bank to the exporter and communicated to the exporter through banking channels. Your bank (you are the importer now) is telling the exporter that, when he presents specified documents containing specified information, he will be paid for a shipment.

Suppose an exporter in Somalia sells you flags from the civil war of 1991 for the sum of $40,000. The seller wants to be sure

United California Bank

601 South Figueroa Street
International Collections / W6-1
Los Angeles, CA 90017 U.S.A.

SWIFT: SANWUS66
FAX: 213-896-7779

TEL: 213-896-7483

DIRECT COLLECTION LETTER

Attach this copy to
Shipping Documents

Air/Express mail to
Collection Bank

SANWA BANK LIMITED
8 COTTONTREE DRIVE, CENTRAL
HONG KONG

DATE JULY 2, 2001

Refer to:

| United California Bank Coll. No. DX60 | 12345 |
| Drawer Ref. No. | INV385-A |

We enclose for collection draft and documents, subject to instructions marked below. Please handle for the account of UNITED CALIFORNIA BANK. Your acknowledgement of this item, all communications, and payments should be directed to the attention of **UNITED CALIFORNIA BANK'S International Collections, W6-1,** referencing this collection number.

Draft No.	Tenor	Drawee (Name and Address)	Amount
INV385-A	SIGHT	BUYERS IMPORT COMPANY	USD $28,000.00

THIS COLLECTION IS SUBJECT TO "UNIFORM RULES FOR COLLECTIONS" INTERNATIONAL CHAMBER OF COMMERCE, PUBLICATION CURRENTLY IN USE

Documents	B/L	Invoices	Packing List	Cert's of Origin	Insur. Certs	Insp. Certs	Weight Certs	Other Documents
No. of Docs	3/3	3	2	1	1/2			PHYTOSANITARY

Deliver documents against		Acceptance X	Payment X	Collect our charge of US $ 90.00
Advise by cable X		Non-Acceptance X	Non-Payment	All charges to be paid by us
Remit proceeds by cable X		Drawer's expense X	Drawee's expense X	Waive charges if refused
Remit proceeds by airmail		Drawer's expense	Drawee's expense	Do not waive charges
Protest		Non-Acceptance	Non-Acceptance	Hold for arrival of merchandise
Do not protest X				Waive interest if refused
Your charges including stamps, exchange taxes, etc. for drawer's account				Do not waive interest
Allow a discount of		if paid		
Interest to be collected at		% per annum based on a 365 day year from presentment date until date of payment.		

If U.S. dollar exchange is not immediately available at maturity (or on presentation if drawn at sight) and it is necessary to provisionally accept local currency pending availability of U.S. dollar exchange, the drawee shall remain liable for all exchange differences. At time of deposit of local currency obtain drawee's written undertaking to be responsible for any exchange differences. The draft must not be surrendered to drawee until payment for face amount in U.S. dollar exchange.

Other Instructions

In case of need refer to

| | And follow their instructions | | X | But do not alter terms without referring to our bank |

FROM: SELLERS EXPORT, INC.
45 SALES ROAD Drawer's Name

LONG BEACH, CA 93334
Address

Remit proceeds by wire through your USA correspondent for credit to United California Bank's account No. 122003516 with Federal Reserve Bank, Los Angeles, quoting United California Bank's reference number.

Authorized Signature

DATE JULY 2, 2001   NO. INV385-A

AT XXXXXXXXXXXXXXXXXXXXXXX _____ SIGHT of this SOLE BILL OF EXCHANGE

pay to THE ORDER OF **UNITED CALIFORNIA BANK** $ 28,000.00

TWENTY EIGHT THOUSAND AND NO/100

TO: BUYERS IMPORT COMPANY

8 STANLEY VILLAGE ROAD.

STANLEY, HONG KONG

U.S. DOLLARS

John G Seller

SELLERS EXPORT INC.

(DRAWEE)   (DRAWER)

Figure 7.3 Sight Draft (Reprinted with permission of United California Bank)

of being paid and therefore asks you for a letter of credit. If you agree, you must apply to your bank to open your LC, in favor of the exporter. This means that the bank is pledging to pay the exporter if he does exactly what the LC specifies. An LC normally specifies that an exporter provide "documentary evidence," that he or she has shipped the merchandise ordered, by the time and in the manner stated in the LC, including fulfilling any other specified obligations such as purchasing insurance.

The fact that you apply to your bank for a letter of credit does not mean you will get it. Your bank will not want to take the risk of paying the exporter and then not being able to collect from you. Therefore, it will look for strong evidence of your ability to pay—such as an account with an average balance that will easily cover the credit or other evidence of financial strength and stability. In some cases, a bank will allow you to pledge assets, such as a certificate of deposit, to guarantee payment on an LC. The "bottom line" is that it is very hard to get an LC for a larger sum than you are able to pay. That $40,000 deal will be hard to swing with only $400 in your bank account.

The importer's bank is known as the *opening bank*. When it agrees to write a letter of credit, it usually transmits it to its branch or correspondent nearest the exporter, which is known as the *advising bank* because it advises the exporter that a credit in his or her favor has been received. The banks' relationships serve, among other purposes, to protect the exporter because branches and correspondents can more easily ascertain that LCs are genuine. There have been instances, usually in developing countries, of importers using authentic looking counterfeit LCs and LCs of fictitious banks.

Importers *can* specify that their own banks be used as the advising bank. In other cases, importers use their own banks as intermediaries between themselves and the advising banks, although this increases the cost to them because more banks are involved.

When an exporter is advised of the letter of credit and receives a copy, he should study it carefully to make sure that each of its terms and conditions can be met. Otherwise, there will be a problem. For example, if the LC calls for 100 boxes each containing 400 civil war flags, and the shipping documents show that the cargo consisted of 400 boxes each containing 100 civil war flags, there will be a *discrepancy*. This will probably cause the payment to be delayed until the discrepancy is *waived* or otherwise resolved.

When the exporter ships and gives the required documentary evidence to the advising bank, with no discrepancies, payment is due. In some LCs, the advising bank is also the *paying bank* and can pay the exporter very quickly. In other LCs, where the opening bank is the paying bank, there will be a delay of a few days. Both importers and exporters often want the paying bank to be in their country because they feel it will look out more for their interests.

The letter of credit is an extremely flexible method of payment because the importer can ask her bank to make any legal stipulation. If an LC states that the exporter must personally load the baskets on the ship while wearing nothing but a civil war flag and that this must be tied around his ankles, payment will not be made unless he presents documentary evidence of having done exactly that.

Nearly all letters of credit are *irrevocable*, which means they cannot be changed or canceled without the consent of the beneficiary. In other words, once you open an LC and the exporter is advised of it, you can't back out unless the exporter agrees to let you.

If the exporter has any doubt that the opening bank is solvent, or that the country in which it is located will have hard (convertible) currency with which to pay, he can ask to have the LC *confirmed* by the advising bank or even by a different bank in the same or a third country. For example, LCs opened in some African and Middle Eastern countries are often confirmed in the United Kingdom. Confirmation means that, if the opening bank is obligated to pay and for some reason cannot do so, the confirming bank will pay. It usually costs the exporter less than 1 percent of the value of the LC, and gives him extra assurance of being paid. If you as an exporter receive an LC and no bank will confirm it, you should probably take this as a warning and run to the nearest exit.

There are numerous variations of letters of credit. Some operate like revolving lines of bank credit, and others permit partial payment for parts of an order. Still others allow a trading company to use its customer's credit to guarantee payment to its supplier. A good international banker can advise you on the appropriate kind for each situation.

Many exporters customarily ask for letters of credit on all transactions, but as an importer you do not have to accept the terms that are proposed to you. Come back with a counteroffer and negotiate. Better yet, be the first to propose the method of payment and propose one that is more to your advantage. Then the other party can accept your terms or make a counteroffer.

To summarize, a letter of credit is a formal payment document opened by the importer and communicated through banking channels. The party obligated to pay the exporter is the opening bank. The cost for this service to the importer is often a fixed fee plus a percentage or a percentage with a minimum, for example, 0.25 percent (a quarter of 1 percent), with a minimum commission of $120. The exporter will pay various costs that usually come to at least $300. The total is higher if an LC is not payable at sight, if more than two banks are involved, if there are amendments or discrepancies, or if the exporter wants the credit confirmed.

Figure 7.4 shows the steps in a typical letter of credit transaction. Note that some of the steps include more than one closely related activity.

Figure 7.5 is an example of an irrevocable documentary letter of credit for a shipment to the United States.

Most banks that issue letters of credit now have ways for their customers to apply for them electronically. At least one bank, First

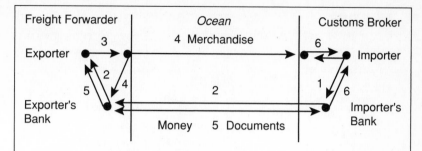

1. *Importer* applies for letter of credit.
2. *Opening bank* sends LC, through correspondent or branch, which advises exporter of receipt of LC.
3. *Exporter* sends goods and documents to freight forwarder.
4. *Freight forwarder* dispatches merchandise and provides documents to the advising bank.
5. *Advising bank* forwards documents to negotiating bank, which checks documents against LC, and authorizes payment if no discrepancies are found. The importer's account is debited.
6. *Importer's bank* gives him the documents with which he can claim the merchandise.

Figure 7.4   Letter of Credit Transaction

Union National, has its LC application on the Internet. Go to www.firstunion.com/international/tbon.html.

The ways that banks deal with the hundreds of potentially unique situations and disagreements relating to international payment instruments are specified in a series of procedures. These are agreed upon internationally and changed every few years. In the United States, they are published by ICC Publishing SA, in New York City (see chapter 12 for more information).

Letter of Credit–Like Instruments

There are variations on international payment that are intended to give exporters quicker payment on the letters of credit or to give them guarantees of payment without actually using LCs. One

UNITED CALIFORNIA BANK
INTERNATIONAL DEPARTMENT
601 S. FIGUEROA ST. 6TH FL.
LOS ANGELES, CA 90017

DATE: JULY 2, 2001

SAMPLE

ADVISING BANK:
SANWA BANK LIMITED
TOKYO, JAPAN

APPLICANT:
AMERICAN IMPORTER AND CO.
4587 TRADE WAY DRIVE
LONG BEACH, CA 93333

BENEFICIARY:
ASIAN EXPORTER LIMITED
4-23-65 HORIKARA
TOKYO, JAPAN

EXPIRY DATE: 25 JULY 2001 IN JAPAN
AMOUNT: USD 15,000.00
USD FIFTEEN THOUSAND AND N0/100 DOLLARS

WE HEREBY ISSUE IN BENEFICIARY'S FAVOR OUR IRREVOCABLE DOCUMENTARY CREDIT NO. MP6071666863 WHICH IS AVAILABLE WITH ANY BANK BY NEGOTIATION AGAINST PRESENT-ATION OF SIGHT DRAFTS FOR 100 % OF THE INVOICE VALUE DRAWN ON OURSELVES REFERENCING THIS CREDIT NUMBER AND ACCOMPANIED BY THE FOLLOWING DOCUMENTS.

1. SIGNED COMMERCIAL INVOICE IN TRIPLICATE
2. PACKING LIST IN DUPLICATE
3. FULL SET ORIGINAL CLEAN ONBOARD OCEAN BILLS OF LADING ISSUED TO ORDER OF SHIPPER, BLANK ENDORSED MARKED: "FREIGHT COLLECT" AND NOTIFY: APPLICANT AND IMPORT CUSTOMS BROKER, INC. 3458 HARBOR CIRCLE, LONG BEACH, CA 93333
4. BENEFICIARY'S CERTIFICATE CERTIFYING THAT EACH INDIVIDUAL ITEM HAS BEEN MARKED: "MADE IN JAPAN"

COVERING SHIPMENT OF: 1000 DOZEN MOUSE PADS PER PURCHASE ORDER 86A
TO BE INVOICED: FOB, TOKYO
SHIPMENT FROM: TOKYO   **TO:** LOS ANGELES
PARTIAL SHIPMENTS: PERMITTED   **TRANSSHIPMENT:** PROHIBITED

PRESENTATION PERIOD: WITHIN 21 DAYS AFTER SHIPMENT BUT WITHIN CREDIT VALIDITY

ADDITIONAL CONDITIONS:
- SHIPMENT MUST BE CONTAINERIZED AND SO EVIDENCED ON BILLS OF LADING
- FIVE PERCENT PLUS OR MINUS IN QUANTITY AND AMOUNT IS ALLOWED.
- ALL CHARGES OTHER THAN ISSUING BANK'S ARE FOR BENEFICIARY'S ACCOUNT.
- AMOUNTS NEGOTIATED MUST BE ENDORSED ON THE REVERSE HEREOF BY THE PRESENTING / NEGOTIATING BANK.
- IN REIMBURSEMENT WE SHALL REMIT PROCEEDS AS INSTRUCTED ON RECEIPT OF DOCUMENTS IN COMPLIANCE WITH THE TERMS OF THIS CREDIT.
- ALL DOCUMENTS TO BE FORWARDED TO US IN ONE LOT BY EXPRESS COURIER.

PLEASE ADVISE BENEFICIARY WITHOUT ADDING YOUR CONFIRMATION.

WE HEREBY ENGAGE WITH DRAWERS AND BONA FIDE HOLDERS THAT DRAFTS DRAWN UNDER AND IN COMPLIANCE WITH THE TERMS OF THIS CREDIT SHALL BE DULY HONORED ON PRESENTATION.

THIS LETTER OF CREDIT IS SUBJECT TO THE UNIFORM CUSTOMS AND PRACTICE FOR DOCUMENTARY CREDITS (1993 REVISION), INTERNATIONAL CHAMBER OF COMMERCE PUBLICATION NO. 500.

Figure 7.5   Irrevocable Documentary Credit (Reprinted with permission of United California Bank)

of these is the *back-to-back letter of credit,* which essentially lets a trader use an importer's LC to him as collateral for a bank's LC to the supplier. This is a sophisticated and risky instrument and is best left alone for the first few years.

Another variation is *factoring,* which means selling export receivables to a firm that will be responsible for collecting them. If the sale is *without recourse,* nonpayment means that the factor will lose and not the exporter. Of course, factors charge enough to cover their costs, profit, risks, and interest if they pay the exporter before receiving funds from the importer. Also, they like to approve the importer *before* a sale is made.

There is a similar but more complex system called *forfaiting.* This involves bank guarantees and long-term credit to the buyer, usually on sales of a quarter of a million dollars and up.

The company Danzas (phone (212) 383-2330, fax (212) 908-1111) has a system called cash forwarding, which involves credit insurance supplied by them and is a less expensive alternative to letters of credit. The steps involved are:

1. An approved customer (importer) submits an open-account purchase order to a participating Danzas client (exporter).

2. The client submits shipping instructions to Danzas and requests financing.

3. Danzas handles the shipment, assuring delivery to the customer.

4. Upon shipment, Danzas insures the transaction and instructs the lender to advance funds to the client.

5. The lender transfers funds (most of what is due) to the client's account by wire.

6. The customer pays the lender when payment is due.

7. The lender takes out its fees and transfers any remaining funds to the client.

There is more information about this on the web at this address: www.danzas.com/portal.cfm?page=general/contact.cfm.

There are some banks that have followed the lead of export finance companies and are offering international receivables management services, which you can investigate at the web site, www.barrettwells.co.uk. The challenge for readers of this book is to get big enough to use these kinds of services and then to carefully consider the costs and the benefits of each one.

Payment in Advance

Suppose you make a small sale to an importer in Africa, who has no doubts about your honesty or ability to ship. The importer may have trouble getting foreign exchange in his country but have a bank account in London or Paris. He may ask you to quote in British pounds or French francs and then send you a check.

This importer's sister in the Caribbean may ask you to find some parts that are urgently needed to keep machines in her factory running. She can't afford to have you hold up the shipment until you get paid and so may simply send a check on her Miami bank account. If the importer wants you to ship without waiting for the check to clear, she can have it certified. She would prefer to send a check drawn on a bank in her country, but such a check can take several weeks to clear and many foreign currencies are not readily convertible to U.S. dollars.

As an importer, you may be asked for cash in advance in some cases. If you order a suit from Hong Kong, your supplier will probably ask for half the amount in advance. If you order a small quantity of samples, the easiest way to pay is to simply buy an international money order from your bank. Of course, this means that you are taking all the risk. It is possible that the foreign exporter will simply pocket your money and not respond to your frantic phone calls and faxes.

Credit cards are being used now in several countries as a means of paying for small international purchases. This system seems to be working well, and I would classify it as a variation of payment in advance. You might go to www.cytronec.com on the World Wide Web. They offer to process international credit card sales, up to $500, for 3.9 percent. The Exim Corporation has special trade finance credit cards. They are in Richmond, Virginia at (804) 282-5052.

Consignment

Consignment is not actually a form of payment but a type of agency arrangement in which the buyer takes possession of goods but does not take title to them. Suppose, for example, that you buy a $1,000 dress, wear it once at a party, and then decide you do not want it anymore. You may take it to a high-quality used clothing shop and leave it there, on consignment. You might agree with the store owner to pay you 75 percent of what she sells it for, but not less than $250. If and when the dress is sold, you will receive your 75 percent of the revenue. If it is not sold within a set period of time, you may reclaim it or the store owner may ask you to take it back. If it is somehow lost or damaged, you will be paid the $250 minimum.

Consignment in international trade works much the same way. It is often used for U.S. imports, especially of fresh produce and works of art. If you decide to import fresh asparagus, for example, you cannot be sure how much of what you import will be of excellent quality or what the market will pay when your shipment is through customs and ready for sale. You will probably respond by seeking to import on consignment. When a shipment is about to arrive, you will make contacts to try to sell it. When it actually arrives, you will inspect it and, assuming it is of the expected condition and quality, deliver it and collect from your customers. Then you will deduct your actual expenses and perhaps a 15 percent commission and remit the remainder of the proceeds to your supplier. If you have to destroy part of the shipment because it cannot be sold, or if part of it is seized by U.S. regulatory agencies because of illegal pesticide residues or infestations, you will inform the exporter and will not pay for that part of the shipment. The exporter must trust you completely or must pay to have someone in the port of arrival verify your report of the condition and quality of the goods and the price at which they are sold.

I once heard of a Brazilian exporter of baler twine who used consignment selling to make sure he sold all his production every year. He shipped to a distributor in the midwestern United States, on consignment, for the entire haying season. His instructions to the distributor were to keep reducing the price until every roll was sold. The distributor, by pricing to maximize his own profit, automatically maximized the profit to the exporter.

In the U.S. export trade, the main use of consignment is to help foreign distributors of heavy machinery and equipment. If a manufacturer of construction equipment wants to sell in Jamaica, its distributor there will need floor models and demonstrators as well as an inventory of equipment for sale. Part or all of this may be shipped to Jamaica on consignment. If and when it is sold, the distributor will pay the manufacturer.

This system of paying for merchandise definitely favors the importer. In the worst case—for example, a shipment of fresh strawberries that cannot be sold because the plane that was carrying them had mechanical problems and the berries all spoiled— the exporter will lose both his produce and the money he paid for transportation. If the shipment is not insured, the exporter may not recover any money at all.

EXPORT CREDIT AND CREDIT INSURANCE

Whenever the importer does not have to pay for merchandise upon receiving it, he or she is buying on credit. Credit terms can be even more important to an importer than the actual selling price. Why should an importer in Brazil pay cash to you when an exporter in Japan will sell equally good merchandise on three months' terms, especially when the cost of money (the interest rate) in Brazil is high?

Exporters who provide financing normally do so from company funds or with bank loans. Eximbank, the U.S. export/import bank in Washington, D.C., has a variety of programs for helping U.S. exporters obtain working capital and loans and insure their export receivables. For information on these programs, log onto www.exim.gov or call 1-800-565-3946 and follow the instructions. You can order fact sheets about their services for small businesses; however a small business in Eximbank terms does not include a home-based exporter's shipment worth a thousand dollars or so. If you get up to shipments around $10,000, this organization is a possibility.

There are also several U.S. states and even some cities that can assist with financing and insurance of export shipments. Information on these is available from an Eximbank marketing specialist, who can be reached by phone (202) 565-3900 or fax (202) 565-3931. Also, you may want to speak with the U.S. Small Business Administration about their Working Capital, Loan Guarantee, and International Trade Loan Guarantee programs. The general information number is an easy one to remember— 1-800-U-Ask-SBA, and you can listen in English or Spanish.

Finally, there are private insurance companies that write export credit insurance. Euler American Credit Indemnity (ACI), for example, says that such a policy gives you the safety of a letter of credit at 50 to 75 percent less cost. This lets you sell on open-account terms to more buyers, and they will do the credit checks for you. Just make sure you can get the insurance before you sign a contract with the customer. Euler ACI is on the web at www.eulergroup.com/aci, and their telephone number is (877) 909-3224.

There is, of course, a significant cost involved in export credit insurance. There are some countries and many potential importers who can't be insured, and you cannot get full coverage. It is common to find insurance that covers 100 percent of loss due to political problems but only 90 to 95 percent of loss due to commercial problems.

FOREIGN CURRENCY TRANSACTIONS

Most international transactions are paid for with currency, and the U.S. dollar is used far more than any other nation's currency. Many Japanese and other exporters, however, prefer to be paid in the money of their countries. This has become the case in Europe as the European currency unit has become more firmly established.

As a U.S. importer, you can nearly always pay in dollars. If a foreign exporter insists on receiving some other currency, you have several choices. The best is probably to stand your ground and pay in U.S. dollars; if the exporter wants the sale, he will have to concur. A second option is to agree to pay in a foreign currency, such as Swiss francs, but to get a somewhat lower price to compensate you for the risk of having to pay more dollars than you expected for the stated amount in francs. The further in the future you will be paying, the greatly the likelihood that your cost in dollars will vary significantly one way or the other.

For larger amounts, you may be able to use the foreign exchange forward market. This means entering into an agreement now, with your bank, to buy the foreign currency you will need at a predetermined rate on a specified date in the future. This is a form of *hedging*. The more the market expects the foreign currency to rise against the dollar, the more you will have to pay for your hedge.

Large companies that have exposure in foreign currencies use other hedging techniques, such as playing the futures market. This involves buying contracts, for fixed amounts and fixed time periods, through foreign currency exchanges. International finance managers that are professionals at this earn very good salaries.

On the export side, it is very common to be asked to take payment in foreign currencies. This can be dangerous, because many developing countries have currency that is not convertible or whose actual value is much less than its official value.

If you are asked to take payment in foreign currency, check with your banker to find out the strength of the currency in question. Also, newspapers such as the *Wall Street Journal* report both current exchange rates and the values of futures contracts so you can see whether the market expects the currency in question to rise, or fall, against the dollar. If the currency in question is not quoted in the *Wall Street Journal,* you probably don't want to take it. The web site www.oanda.com\cgi-bin\ncc provides exchange rates and does the conversions for you.

If it looks as if your transaction is risky, you may be able to negotiate other terms, such as more time to pay but with payment by a letter of credit in U.S. dollars. Or perhaps you can agree to accept the foreign currency but at a rate that gives you a certain amount in dollars. That way the importer can pay in his or her currency but may have to pay more to give you the number of dollars agreed upon. Finally, it may be worthwhile for you to use one of the hedging techniques mentioned earlier.

In brief, try to avoid dealing in foreign currencies. For importers, this is usually not a problem. Exporters, however, may lose sales if they are not somewhat flexible. Also, there's often a chance that you will profit from the exchange rate fluctuation. If you agree to take payment in Danish kroner three months in the future, and during those three months this currency rises 10 percent against the dollar, you will receive 10 percent more in dollars. This may dramatically increase your profit on the transaction.

COUNTERTRADE

The term *countertrade* refers to international shipments that are not paid for entirely in cash. There are several variations, known as barter, compensation trade, buyback, counterpurchase, and offset. No one knows for sure the percentage of international transactions in which countertrade is involved, but most estimates are in the range of 10 to 25 percent.

Businesses often try to pay for merchandise with countertrade when they are in countries that are short of hard currency. This has been the case with most Eastern European and developing countries. Colombia, Malaysia, and other nations have passed laws that regulate countertrade transactions.

Suppose, for example, that you agree with a Peruvian businessperson that you will exchange outboard (boat) motors for alpaca sweaters. After considerable discussion, you determine how many motors, of which brand and horsepower, you will ship and how many sweaters, of which quality and sizes, your Peruvian counterpart will ship. Then you agree to when and how each commodity will be shipped and who will pay for the transportation.

To put this deal in motion, the Peruvian may have to obtain government permission to ship the sweaters without receiving hard currency for them. She may also need approval to import the outboard motors. Then there will be two shipments of merchandise, either of which could confront problems of loss, damage, poor quality, and so on. Finally, you will have to sell the sweaters for more than your total cost, including what you paid for the motors, in order to make a profit.

The transaction just described is an example of simple barter. More often, there is a monetary value placed on each shipment, such as $20,000 worth of motors in exchange for $20,000 worth of sweaters (or $15,000 in sweaters and $5,000 in currency, etc.). Sometimes more than one country is involved in a countertrade deal—for example, engines from the United States to Peru, sweaters from Peru to Canada, and cash from Canada to the United States. This kind of triangular deal is both more expensive and more difficult to arrange. There are specialized companies, mostly in Europe but some in the United States, as well, that specialize in arranging countertrade transactions.

With regard to the hypothetical situation at the beginning of this chapter, the fact that you pay for goods with other goods instead of with cash is of little interest to the U.S. Customs Service. All restrictions on importation will still apply.

I once met a New York businessman who was exporting cigarettes to Rumania and receiving clothing in return. His explanation for this was that the cigarettes were so valuable in Rumania that he was able to make more profit than if he paid for the clothing in cash. Still, countertrade has so many pitfalls that I definitely do not recommend it for a beginner. Remember that even a simple barter deal is really two transactions instead of just one. That means there are twice as many chances for something to go seriously wrong.

CHAPTER 8

Packing, Shipping, and Insurance

A large containership used in many transatlantic voyages was caught unexpectedly in a raging storm. Fortunately, the crew and ship were able to ride out the storm and reach port safely. In the height of the storm, however, more than thirty containers were released off one side of the vessel and more than seventy off the other side. Was your shipment among them?

International transportation, moving goods from one country to another, can make or break each transaction and its profitability. Importers and exporters are inevitably involved in such transportation functions as packing, shipping, and insurance. If these functions are not handled properly, your goods can arrive too late, in poor condition, or not at all. The cost of shipping can sometimes be even more than the cost of the products. There are commercial organizations, like customs brokers and freight forwarders, ready and able to help you, but of course their charges become your costs.

PACKING FOR INTERNATIONAL SHIPMENT

You may not ever have to pack goods for shipment abroad. If you work as an import or export agent, your principal will do the packing and, if you work as an import or export merchant, your suppliers will perform this function.

You may, however, buy from U.S. suppliers who are unable or unwilling to pack for export. Or you may import goods in large quantities and have to repack them in smaller units for your domestic customers. If the quantities are small, you can do the packing yourself, or you can hire a specialized firm to do it for you. Even if your principals or suppliers do the packing, you should know how they do it and you may want to give them instructions. If the packing is inadequate to protect the goods, your risks of loss and damage will be greatly increased; if the packing is grossly inadequate, the insurance company may cite that as justification for not paying a claim. At the other extreme, excessive packing will add weight and bulk to the shipment and thus increase your transportation costs. Finally, if your customer asks for a certain kind of packing and your principal or supplier does it differently, the shipment may be rejected and you will lose your commission or markup.

Insurance companies can often provide information on how specific kinds of goods are normally packed. Various kinds of export packs and their specifications are highlighted in a free video entitled *To Better World Trade*, available to serious entrepreneurs from the ACE USA insurance carrier. You can contact the Ocean Marine Department, phone (215) 640-2006, fax (215) 640-2594.

Kinds of Packing

Until a few decades ago, most products moved overseas in individual boxes or barrels. This was known as *break bulk* shipping. For the most part this has given way to containerization in the foreign commerce of the United States but is still very common in many developing countries. (Dividing a large shipment into several smaller ones is still known as breaking bulk.)

When several boxes are put together to make one unit, perhaps with steel straps or plastic shrink-wrap, you are dealing with *unitized cargo*. Because units can easily become too large and heavy to handle easily, they are often put on wooden or plastic platforms made so that small forklift trucks can pick them up and place them in a trailer. These platforms are *pallets*, and the cargo is said to be *palletized*. All the methods just described are known as less than containerload, or LCL, cargo.

The real revolution in export packing came with containerization. In shipping language, a container is a large metal box that can be loaded with cargo. There are various sizes, ranging from 20 to 53 feet long. A typical 40-foot container is 8 feet wide, $8^1/2$ feet high, and 40 feet long. It can hold about 2,347 cubic feet or 42,000 pounds of cargo.

The size of container used is determined largely by the weight/cubic measurement of the cargo; the availability of equipment, over-the-road maximum weight limitations at the origin and destination points; and the ship's configuration. Containers are taken off the truck's chassis by cranes at the port of origin and fitted like Legos below and on the deck of the containership. At the port of disembarkation, trucks pull up alongside the ship and the containers are lifted by crane and fitted directly onto the chassis. This process is called lift-on, lift-off or LOLO. With a roll-on, roll-off or RORO vessel, the trailers are rolled on-board the ship together with the chassis and both units are transported from origin to destination. Barges, a less common form of transport, carry breakbulk cargo, trailers, and some containers.

Export shippers can own or rent containers or can use "boxes" (as they are often called) that belong to steamship companies. Typically, a container is cleaned and checked for soundness (no water leaks, etc.), packed, locked and sealed, and sent to its destination. It may move by road or rail and then by ocean and is usually not opened until it reaches the importing country or sometimes even the importer's warehouse. When sealed by the exporter, the cargo is said to move under "shipper-load-and-count," meaning the shipper (not the carrier) takes all responsibility for declaring the true cargo (products), and the respective weights and piece counts. Any misrepresentation of this information is considered to be fraudulent. The numbers of the seals are recorded, so that it is nearly impossible for a thief to break into a container without leaving evidence of having done so.

There are specialized types of containers, the most common of which is the *reefer*, or refrigerated container. It is used especially for carrying fresh produce, which has become very important in the U.S. import/export trade. Systems have been developed, known as controlled atmosphere (CA) and modified atmosphere (MA), for containers to retard ripening of produce. There are usually temperature recorders placed in reefers so that, if produce arrives in poor condition, it will be easy to tell whether a mistake or equipment failure let it become too warm. Other types of containers have been designed to transport export commodities including tanks for frozen orange juice or other liquids, flatbeds for large pieces of equipment, hanging-garment vans to carry clothing on hangers, and ventilated vans for cocoa and similar products.

Containers are used also for airfreight. There are several standard sizes because of the large variation in the inside dimensions of aircraft. Exporters should check with their carrier about available container sizes and whether palletized cargo can be accepted. For fast turnaround, airlines will try to have a string of containers waiting when a plane arrives. Essentially, they will push out one string of metal boxes and push in another.

Many carriers have joint agreements to carry each other's freight, which lets them issue "through" airwaybills when cargo must be transshipped. The two most pressing air cargo issues for new and experienced exporters are availability of cargo space and frequency of service. There may not be enough regularly scheduled flights to meet an exporter's needs, or the connecting flights to the cargo's final destination may not be ideal, for example, leaving cargo sitting on the tarmac in the heat or missing a connection because of a delayed flight.

Break Bulk Packing

If your shipments are small, they will probably be sent break bulk, or LCL, which gives you a higher unit cost than that of larger volume shippers. Also, your packages will be subject to the potential risks of being dropped by handlers or handling equipment, crushed by heavy cargo, or soaked in seawater. Even cargo inside waterproof boxes can get wet if the ship sails through cold areas and moisture in the air inside the box condenses. That's why, in the old war movies, we used to see shipments of firearms coated with grease and wrapped in waxed paper. Now shippers can shrink-wrap cargo and/or add materials to the packages that absorb moisture.

Logic tells us that heavier boxes should be loaded on the bottom and lighter ones on the top, but most steamships call at several ports. What goes in first, or what will come out last, usually ends up on the bottom. That means there may be a bulldozer resting on your Ping-Pong balls.

Finally, some kinds of packing materials may get you in trouble with regulatory authorities. One importer wanted to bring wooden bowls packed in straw to the United States from Grenada but was prohibited from doing so because straw can harbor insect pests that might harm U.S. agriculture. Even wooden pallets can harbor insects and snails. I once heard of a South American exporter who was packing fresh garlic in mahogany boxes and was fined by his country's authorities for illegally exporting precious wood.

There is a noticeable trend toward the development and use of packaging materials that are friendlier to the environment. Many countries are adopting practices pioneered by Germany, which has strict regulations with respect to use of recyclable and reusable materials from pallets to corrugated cartons, packaging foams, and plastic crates. Shippers may even have to re-export certain materials, which of course adds to the cost of a transaction. Thus, it is important to know the regulations before you finalize a price.

All this means that you should pay attention to how your cargo is packed, even if you don't personally do the packing. Find out how the first few shipments from a principal or supplier are protected from hazards and, if you don't like what you see, try to get it corrected. Your Christmas ornaments packed in thin cardboard boxes may arrive intact the first time, but what might happen to them next time? There are several helpful sources of information on new and existing packaging, including the Institute of Packaging Professionals (IOPP), phone: (540) 428-0921, and fax: (703) 814-4961. Their web site is at www.IOPP.org, and you may click on "bookstore." Also, the World Packaging Organization is on the web at www.worldpackaging.com.

After You Pack It, Mark It

Companies that frequently pack goods for export should know how to mark them, but new exporters may have to be taught. There are several kinds of marks, which are usually printed or stenciled on boxes. In some trades, such as fresh produce, shipping boxes are being printed with colorful pictures of the products they contain.

Shipping boxes are usually marked "Made in [country of origin of merchandise]." They also give the gross weight, net weight, and outside dimensions, often in both metric and English systems. A few countries have special regulations—Libya, for example, frowns on the use of any language other than Arabic and any measuring system other than metric.

If there is more than one box in a shipment, each one is numbered. Often a box bears the exporter's name and the importer's (or his agent's) name, address, and order number. For cargo that is especially subject to pilferage (cameras, watches, etc.), however, there is a system of blind marks that supposedly prevents thieves from knowing the contents of boxes. Blind marks should be changed often because thieves have ways of learning which shippers they belong to. Fortunately, much of the cargo that thieves especially like is now shipped in sealed containers.

There are also cautionary markings on shipping boxes, sometimes in more than one language. Perhaps the most common ones are "Handle with Care," "Glass," "Use No Hooks," "This Side Up," "Fragile," "Keep in Cool Place," "Keep Dry," and "Open Here."

Because cargo handlers in many ports cannot read, however, the same instructions are communicated with symbols. A champagne glass means "Fragile," a hook with an X across it means "Use No Hooks," and so on (see Figure 8.1 for selected examples). Specialized books on export traffic show pictures of all these symbols.

Finally, there is an even more extensive set of symbols for marking boxes that contain hazardous materials. If you plan to deal in any product that is (1) explosive, (2) flammable, (3) spontaneously combustible, (4) water-reactive, (5) oxidizing, (6) poisonous, (7) radioactive, or (8) corrosive, you need to be sure your packing and marking are as required by the U.S. Department of Transportation, the Coast Guard, and/or the Civil Aeronautics Board. The captain of a vessel is the final authority with regard to carrying hazardous materials. If he thinks a shipment is unsafe, he can reject it, even though it may be in compliance with all regulations. Port authorities are also concerned about hazardous materials, and some ports prohibit loading or unloading the most dangerous kinds.

The risk of carrying hazardous materials may translate into higher rates for shippers. An exporter once told me that one drop of mercury in a container can cause that whole 40-foot box to be considered hazardous and thus increase the shipping rate.

Shippers may wish to consult with carriers regarding the carriage of hazardous materials, often referred to as "hazmats." Maersk/Sea-Land has developed information that is considered to have

Figure 8.1 Symbols Used in Handling of Goods

set much of the standard in the industry and is often a point of reference for government officials. Check with your local representative or their web site at www.MaerskSeaLand.com for key contacts in loss, prevention, and claims.

INTERNATIONAL TRANSPORTATION

Airmail

The business of international mail order, both to and from the United States, has grown tremendously, and one reason for this is the vast improvement made in many countries' post office departments. The U.S. Postal Service deserves several prizes for the way it has improved both its domestic and international services. In general, you can export and import packages as large as 42 inches in length and 79 inches in combined length and girth. The maximum weight varies, from 22 to 66 pounds, because of foreign countries' limits, although there are exceptions, depending on the country.

In May 2001, a 15-pound package shipped to London from the United States, using Airmail Parcel Post with the United States Postal Service (USPS), would have cost $62. The same package shipped via their Economy Mail service (surface) would have cost $41.25, but of course would have taken much longer to arrive. Insurance and registry are available, but indemnity limits vary by country. There is a special service known as International Surface Air Lift (ISAL) that was designed especially for mailing catalogs, books, and other merchandise. Please don't confuse this with the International Priority Air Mail (IPA), for business mailings of catalogs. Finally, there are other special services including Global Express Mail (EMS), Global Priority Mail (GPM), and Global Express Guaranteed (GXG). GXG resulted from an agreement between the USPS and DBL, a courier service. As the USPS seeks to lower its operating costs, you can expect to see more services contracted to courier companies. Check the web site at www.usps. com for more information.

You can import goods by mail, to a maximum value of $1,250 per day (except most textiles and apparel and leather goods), without having to complete a formal customs declaration. You will have to pay customs duty, if any is due, but not a penny for customs clearance.

An excellent example of international shipping by post is the company Isla, in San Juan, Puerto Rico. They sell Puerto Rican handicrafts with a beautifully illustrated catalog to customers in the United States, in U.S. territories and on military bases, and in foreign countries.

Courier Services

In mid-2001, the $62 USPS Airmail Parcel Post shipment mentioned in the previous section would cost you about $118.92 with Federal Express International Priority mail two-day service and $109.30 with the FedEx International Economy one-week delivery service. What would you get for the extra $50? FedEx is currently the largest express transport courier service in the world, with service to more than 211 countries. Customers receive free packaging materials, free shipping software, customs clearance (duties are usually paid and charged to the consignee), on-time delivery or your money back, and proof of delivery. If you can't go to any of the 39,000 drop-off locations, FedEx will pick up the package for a slight extra charge.

The size limitations are much more generous, also. International Priority Freight accepts packages with a maximum of 108 inches on any side and up to 68 kilograms. Other services include FedEx 10- and 25-kilogram boxes, International Extra Hours, and Improved Next-Day Service Within Europe. Major courier services now have sites on the World Wide Web where you can get just about whatever information you want except prices. The FedEx site, for example, is at www.fedex.com.

set much of the standard in the industry and is often a point of reference for government officials. Check with your local representative or their web site at www.MaerskSeaLand.com for key contacts in loss, prevention, and claims.

INTERNATIONAL TRANSPORTATION

Airmail

The business of international mail order, both to and from the United States, has grown tremendously, and one reason for this is the vast improvement made in many countries' post office departments. The U.S. Postal Service deserves several prizes for the way it has improved both its domestic and international services. In general, you can export and import packages as large as 42 inches in length and 79 inches in combined length and girth. The maximum weight varies, from 22 to 66 pounds, because of foreign countries' limits, although there are exceptions, depending on the country.

In May 2001, a 15-pound package shipped to London from the United States, using Airmail Parcel Post with the United States Postal Service (USPS), would have cost $62. The same package shipped via their Economy Mail service (surface) would have cost $41.25, but of course would have taken much longer to arrive. Insurance and registry are available, but indemnity limits vary by country. There is a special service known as International Surface Air Lift (ISAL) that was designed especially for mailing catalogs, books, and other merchandise. Please don't confuse this with the International Priority Air Mail (IPA), for business mailings of catalogs. Finally, there are other special services including Global Express Mail (EMS), Global Priority Mail (GPM), and Global Express Guaranteed (GXG). GXG resulted from an agreement between the USPS and DBL, a courier service. As the USPS seeks to lower its operating costs, you can expect to see more services contracted to courier companies. Check the web site at www.usps. com for more information.

You can import goods by mail, to a maximum value of $1,250 per day (except most textiles and apparel and leather goods), without having to complete a formal customs declaration. You will have to pay customs duty, if any is due, but not a penny for customs clearance.

An excellent example of international shipping by post is the company Isla, in San Juan, Puerto Rico. They sell Puerto Rican handicrafts with a beautifully illustrated catalog to customers in the United States, in U.S. territories and on military bases, and in foreign countries.

Courier Services

In mid-2001, the $62 USPS Airmail Parcel Post shipment mentioned in the previous section would cost you about $118.92 with Federal Express International Priority mail two-day service and $109.30 with the FedEx International Economy one-week delivery service. What would you get for the extra $50? FedEx is currently the largest express transport courier service in the world, with service to more than 211 countries. Customers receive free packaging materials, free shipping software, customs clearance (duties are usually paid and charged to the consignee), on-time delivery or your money back, and proof of delivery. If you can't go to any of the 39,000 drop-off locations, FedEx will pick up the package for a slight extra charge.

The size limitations are much more generous, also. International Priority Freight accepts packages with a maximum of 108 inches on any side and up to 68 kilograms. Other services include FedEx 10- and 25-kilogram boxes, International Extra Hours, and Improved Next-Day Service Within Europe. Major courier services now have sites on the World Wide Web where you can get just about whatever information you want except prices. The FedEx site, for example, is at www.fedex.com.

Airfreight

The way couriers have developed, you probably wouldn't want to use airfreight for that 15-pound box. If you have a 1,500-pound box, you might want to contact an airfreight company. You can contact them directly or through freight forwarders. In general, you will want to use a forwarder unless you are located near an international airport and don't mind taking your cargo there and completing an airwaybill. Foreign freight forwarders and customs brokers are discussed later in this chapter.

Many airlines have 800 numbers for international cargo reservations. You can get these numbers from advertisements in international trade magazines or by calling the main number listed for your airline in a telephone directory.

UPS Latin America advertises express overnight services for documents, freight, and small packages along with computerized reservation and package systems. UPS Air Cargo Latin America (formerly Challenge Air Cargo) handles flowers, other perishables, and some small animals such as chicks and tropical fish. It has a 6,000 square-foot refrigerated warehouse to handle cargo that needs to be kept cool. As international commerce grows, there is an increasing demand for warehouse space adjacent to airports, and some airlines are investing to meet this need.

Airfreight rates are nearly always higher than ocean rates, but other costs are often so much lower that air becomes the cheaper way to ship. Figure 8.2 gives you a format for comparing air and sea to see which is less expensive overall. Note the last item, "interest on value of goods in transit." If your $100,000 export shipment arrives ten days earlier because it was sent by air, you may get paid ten days earlier. The value of that to you, at twelve percent interest, is $100,000 × 10/360 × 0.12, or $333.

Shippers are encouraged to continue to check the rates. In one case, Guatemalan companies began exporting snowpeas and shipping them by air. Ocean carriers saw this as a revenue opportunity and worked with the exporters on trial ocean shipments.

Cost Item	Air	Sea
Export packing	$ 300	$ 800
Inland freight, country of origin	100	500
Freight forwarding	100	150
Shipping	3,800	2,000
Insurance	100	300
Customs clearance	80	150
Inland freight, country of destination	50	200
Interest on value of goods in transit	50	300
TOTAL	$4,580	$4,400
(Note: Assumes merchandise value approximately $50,000.)		

Figure 8.2   Air–Sea Freight Cost Comparison

The results were very favorable, and ocean rates for snowpeas were established below those for airfreight. This was beneficial to nearly everyone. Because of demand for cargo space, the airlines couldn't meet all of the needs, particularly as exports of refrigerated agricultural products increased. Once ocean rates were in place, exporters had both options and felt confident enough to increase their volume of shipments. Ocean rates are discussed in greater detail later in this chapter.

Shipping by Surface

A large part of the shipping between the United States and its partners in NAFTA, Canada and Mexico, is done by rail and road. The rapid increase in trade with Mexico and the terrorist attacks of September 11, 2001, have strained these methods of transportation, but they are gradually improving.

In trade with Mexico, railcars cross the border and are subject to customs inspection, but of course complete inspection of every package is impossible. They are then interchanged with rail services of the other country.

NAFTA allows each country's trucks to operate, with limits, in the other countries. This has, however, been the subject of

severe protests in California, where truckers and environmental-
ists say that trucks from Mexico are often poorly maintained and
operated by drivers with too little experience. This surely sounds
like protectionism; however, U.S. over-the-road truckers are proud
of their overall accident rate, which is something like one accident per *2 million* miles driven. It seems logical that, ultimately,
the intent of the signers of NAFTA will prevail, but there is at
least a temporary setback with regard to access by trucks.

With most international shipments, cargo moves by road and
perhaps by rail during at least part of its journey. Sometimes charges
are built into a "through rate," and sometimes they are separate.
Many shipments between the U.S. east coast and Asia, which
formerly would have gone through the Panama Canal, now travel
by double-stack train across the United States. Even though rail
connections to many of our ports are antiquated and inadequate,
rail is often the cheaper way to move cargo long distances on land.
Deregulation of the trucking industry, however, has made road
transport more competitive.

Ocean Freight

The largest volume of international cargo, by far, is moved by
ocean freight. The ability to handle huge weights and volumes
provides a huge cost advantage. One cannot even imagine all the
U.S. imports of oil and automobiles, or all the U.S. exports of
wheat and gas turbines, going by air.

Steamship services (the word "steamship" is still used even
though ships are no longer powered by steam) are either scheduled, nonscheduled, or charter. Nonscheduled lines are usually
cheaper but less reliable. You can get sailing schedules from steamship lines, freight forwarders, or specialized magazines such as
Shipper and Forwarder and *Steamship Digest*, but the handiest and
most current source is our old friend, the *Journal of Commerce*.
Five days a week, it publishes several pages of sailing schedules in
a supplement known as "Shipcards."

Figure 8.3 is a reprint of part of the inbound (to North America) schedule for Maersk Sealand, for September and October 2000. Note that the *American Feeder* arrives in Puerto Cortes, Honduras on September 7 and gets to Florida just three days later. Other ships bring cargo to it in Honduras and take cargo from it to other North American destinations.

Steamship lines are also classified as conference lines and independents. Lines sailing on many routes, as from the U.S. Atlantic and Gulf ports to West Africa, have banded together to form conferences. The lines in a conference compete with each other but maintain similar standards and charge the same rates. They have lower prices, known as *contract rates*, for shippers that agree to use conference carriers for most of their shipments on a given route, but even these rates can be higher than those charged by independent steamship lines.

Importers and exporters often complain about conferences and accuse them of being legalized cartels set up to keep prices high. The U.S. maritime industry is among the few that is not subject to antitrust legislation. The conference carriers reply that too much price competition would be ruinous to the industry and that they cannot provide safe, rapid, and dependable services unless their rates are high enough to cover the costs involved.

U.S. law also provides for nonvessel-owning common carriers (NVOCCs) and for shippers' associations. An NVOCC is a freight forwarder who reserves fixed amounts of space on certain vessels and then resells it to individual shippers, at lower rates than they would pay directly to the steamship line. A shippers' association is a group of shippers who pool their cargoes to make larger quantities and therefore obtain lower rates. Freight forwarders can tell you whether either of these kinds of service is feasible for you to use.

Using charter vessels is practical only for very large quantities, although sometimes a ship charterer or broker will know of a chartered vessel that has extra space and can carry your cargo for a low rate. The downside to the lower rate may be irregular service. You should explore various avenues to find a reasonably priced service that is acceptable. Using more than one carrier gives you a ready option in case your preferred carrier has a strike or other serious problem.

Two trends affecting international shipping today are *intermodalism* and *rationalization*. Intermodalism means combining more than one mode of transport. For example, a container may be transported from the factory to the port on a truck, which is then lifted onto a vessel and taken to the destination port and finally trucked to the consignee. Some shipments add rail to this scenarios so that your cargo might travel on three kinds of conveyances under one bill of lading.

Rationalization is occurring in the ocean shipping business much like in the air passenger business. Strategic alliances are formed between one or more carriers whereby space is allocated on each other's ships. While the carriers are still competitors and selling against one another, each of their schedules may be reduced in order to control costs. The end result is that exporters (like passengers) may find that their bill of lading indicates one carrier's name, but the cargo was actually moving on another carrier's vessel!

Shipping Rates

Shipping rates are a controversial and often misunderstood subject. The kind of service, kind of cargo, distance, and routing all enter into rate calculations. This is why it can cost less to bring a container of shirts to Boston from Hong Kong than from a Caribbean island. The factors that determine rates are operational costs (ships, crew, fuel, cranes, equipment, maintenance, port charges), the characteristics of the cargo (its value, perishability, risk, volume versus weight), and competition (number of carriers servicing a particular route and whether they are independent or belong to shipping conferences).

Both airlines and steamship lines have rate books, known as

Import Sailings

Central America to U.S.A. and Canada

Country	Port/City	Week 36 FEX 1 America Feeder 0024	Week 36 FEX 2 Maersk Santo Tomas 0074	Week 36 Gulf Goast Exp TBA 0038	Week 36 NCA Arktis Sun 0036	Week 36 WCCA Caravelle 0040	Week 37 FEX 1 America Feeder 0026	Week 37 FEX 2 Maersk Santo Tomas 0076	Week 37 Gulf Goast Exp TBA 0040	Week 37 NCA Arktis Sun 0038	Week 37 WCCA Jork 0044	Week 38 FEX 1 America Feeder 0028	Week 38 FEX 2 Maersk Santo Tomas 0078	Week 38 Gulf Goast Exp Angela Jurgens 0024	Week 38 NCA Arktis Sun 0040	Week 38 WCCA Caravelle 0042
El Salvador	San Salvador	9/4	9/8		9/7		9/11	9/15		9/15		9/18	9/22		9/22	
Guatemala	Guatemala City	9/3	9/7		9/7		9/10	9/14		9/14		9/17	9/21		9/21	
	Puerto Quetzal					9/7*					9/14*					9/21*
Honduras	Santo Tomas	9/6*	9/10*		9/10*		9/13*	9/17*		9/17*		9/13*	9/24*		9/24*	
	Puerto Cortes	9/7*	9/9*		9/9*		9/14*	9/16*		9/16*		9/14*	9/23*		9/23*	
	San Pedro Sula	9/6	9/8		9/8		9/13	9/15		9/15		9/20	9/22		9/22	
	Tegucigalpa	9/6	9/8		9/8		9/13	9/15		9/15		9/20	9/22		9/22	
Nicaragua	Managua	9/6	9/8		9/8		9/13	9/15		9/15		9/20	9/22		9/22	

Country	Port/City	Week 36 Arrives FEX 1	FEX 2	Gulf Goast Exp	NCA	WCCA	Week 37 Arrives FEX 1	FEX 2	Gulf Goast Exp	NCA	WCCA	Week 38 Arrives FEX 1	FEX 2	Gulf Goast Exp	NCA	WCCA
Canada	Halifax NS	9/20	9/23	9/22	9/21	9/24	9/27	9/30	9/29	9/28	10/1	10/4	10/7	10/6	10/5	10/8
	Montreal QC	9/19	9/22	9/21	9/19	9/22	9/26	9/29	9/28	9/26	9/29	10/3	10/6	10/5	10/3	10/6
	Toronto ON	9/19	9/22	9/21	9/19	9/22	9/26	9/29	9/28	9/26	9/29	10/3	10/6	10/5	10/3	10/6

	Port	9/7				9/14				9/21			
Mexico	Altamira												
	Ensenada				9/13*				9/20*				9/27*
	Manzanillo			9/10*				9/17*				9/24*	
	Mazatlan				9/11*				9/18*				9/25*
	Mexico City	9/7				9/14				9/21			
	Monterrey	9/6				9/13				9/20			
	Veracruz			9/9*				9/16*				9/23*	
United States	Atlanta GA	9/13	9/16	9/15	9/15	9/20	9/23	9/22	9/22	9/27	9/30	9/29	10/4
	Baltimore MD	9/14	9/16	9/15	9/16	9/20	9/23	9/23	9/23	9/28	9/30	9/30	10/4
	Boston MA	9/16	9/19	9/18	9/19	9/21	9/26	9/25	9/26	9/30	10/3	10/3	10/5
	Charleston SC	9/13	9/16	9/15	9/17	9/20	9/23	9/22	9/22	9/27	9/30	9/29	10/6
	Chicago IL	9/14	9/17	9/16	9/17	9/21	9/24	9/23	9/24	9/28	10/1	10/1	10/6
	Houston TX	9/15	9/18	9/17	9/15	9/22	9/25	9/24	9/22	9/29	10/2	10/1	9/29
	Jacksonville FL	9/12	9/15	9/14	9/15	9/19	9/22	9/21	9/22	9/26	9/29	9/28	9/29
	Long Beach CA	9/18	9/21	9/20	9/14*	9/25	9/28	9/27	9/21*	10/2	10/5	10/4	9/28*
	Miami FL	9/11	9/13*	9/16	9/22	9/18	9/20*	9/19*	9/23	9/25	9/27*	9/26*	9/30
	New Orleans LA	9/14	9/17	9/16	9/19	9/21	9/24	9/23	9/21	9/28	10/1	9/30	10/3
	New York NY	9/13	9/16	9/15	9/17	9/20	9/23	9/22	9/20	9/27	9/30	9/29	10/4
	Norfolk VA	9/14	9/17	9/16	9/16	9/21	9/24	9/23	9/21	9/28	10/1	9/30	10/5
	Oakland CA	9/19	9/22	9/21	9/18	9/26	9/29	9/28	9/25	10/3	10/6	10/5	10/2
	Philadelphia PA	9/14	9/16	9/17	9/16	9/21	9/23	9/24	9/23	9/28	9/30	10/1	10/1
	Port Everglades FL	9/10*	9/14	9/13	9/22	9/17*	9/21	9/20	9/29	9/24	9/28	9/27*	10/6
	Savannah GA	9/14	9/16	9/15	9/21	9/21	9/23	9/22	9/21	9/28	9/30	9/29	10/5
	Seattle WA	9/19	9/22	9/21	9/23	9/26	9/29	9/28	9/26	10/3	10/6	10/5	10/7
	Freeport	9/13*	9/13		9/20*	9/20			9/27*	9/27			

*Bold Dates—Direct Port of Call

Figure 8.3   Maersk Line "Shipcard" (Reprinted with permission of Maersk, Inc.)

tariffs, that show the rates for different kinds of cargo between specific areas of the world. They must be made available in the public domain (e.g., on the carrier's web site). You can obtain tariffs by calling the lines themselves, from your freight forwarder, or electronically. One electronic service, for example, is Freight Quote, phone (888) 595-6298, or on the web at www.freightquote.com.

There are general cargo rates, specific commodity rates, and container rates. The general rates are usually quite high, but fortunately there are specific commodity rates for most kinds of cargo. If there isn't a specific rate for your goods, you can apply for one to the airline, steamship line, or shipping conference. For example, a firm in Haiti wanted to ship bars of medicinal soap to New York. Because no one had made commercial shipments of soap from Haiti to New York before, there was no rate established. The exporter completed a form for the steamship line and obtained a new special rate. This rate was then available for all companies that shipped the same product on the same route with the same steamship line.

Rates are usually quoted on a weight/measure, or W/M, basis. Boxes that are large in relation to their weight are charged according to the amount of space they occupy, whereas boxes that are heavy in relation to their size are charged according to their weight. By air, the formula is 162 cubic inches = 1 pound. If the rate is $2.00 per pound, but it takes 243 cubic inches of your product to weigh a pound, you will be charged $3.00 for each pound you ship ($243/162 \times 2$). By sea, the formula is 40 cubic feet = 1 short ton.

Weight rates may reflect different units of measure (e.g., pounds, kilograms, or tons). Be careful to check which of the three kinds of tons apply in your case. A short ton is 2,000 pounds; a long ton is 2,240 pounds; and a metric ton is 2, 204 pounds (or 1,000 kilograms). Measurement cargo, which is usually bulkier or lighter weight, can be shown in the rates by cubic foot, hundred cubic feet (cwt), or cubic meter.

Air container rates show a minimum price for sending each kind of container, the maximum weight that can go for that price, and the charge for each kilogram above that maximum weight. By sea, you simply pay for the container, but there are sometimes weight limits.

Each air and steamship line has a *minimum bill of lading*, which means that a minimum charge is levied on very small shipments. The minimum weight may be as low as 1 kilogram in air tariffs but is much higher by sea. About the only place you have flexibility in using shipping tariffs is with weight categories. For example, if your air shipment weighs 290 pounds, you may be able to save money by calling it 300 pounds and paying less per pound to send it.

There are also miscellaneous charges, especially by sea. This becomes frighteningly clear with a real example—a quotation for shipping a 40-foot, refrigerated container of chicken parts from Pompano Beach, Florida, to Santa Domingo in the Dominican Republic in the spring of 2001:

Ocean freight	$2,750
Trucking, Pompano Beach-Port Everglades	$175
Dominican Republic ITBIS (tax)	$35
Shipper's Export Declaration	$100
Chassis recovery/wheel usage	$10
Consular fee (optional)	$150
Bunker surcharge	$180
Security surchage	$20
Consular administration	$25

Total shipping cost is $31,445 (note: $2,750 is the base ocean rate; $695 are *assessorial* [miscellaneous] charges). These charges do not include the other services of customs brokerage, freight forwarding, packing, and so forth, which are separate from the ocean freight quotation.

Exporters and importers are encouraged to obtain blank forms of typical transport documents (described more fully in the next chapter) to familiarize themselves with the terminology. Sometimes "shipper" is mistaken for "carrier," for example, and the "notify party" indication is extremely important. Take time to understand these details.

SHIPPING TERMS

In the early days of international trade, exporters and importers grew tired of having to negotiate all the individual conditions of every transaction. To solve this problem, they developed and defined standard packages (or sets) of conditions. Once trading partners agreed on the definition of a term, such as CIF, they could sell and buy CIF without discussing so many details.

Gradually, two similar sets of terms and their definitions were developed—the American Standard Foreign Trade Definitions and the International Commercial Terms, better known as INCOTERMS. Most international transactions now use INCOTERMS, which have been revised periodically to keep up with changes in trade procedures. Still, if you want to be sure there's no confusion, you should be very specific. Tell your foreign buyer that your quotation is CIF his port, "according to INCOTERMS, 2000 revision."

The 2000 revision includes thirteen terms, whose definitions specify essentially which party makes arrangements for shipping the goods, which party has title to them at each point in their journey, and which party is responsible for loss or damage at any point. The terms are in four groups, as shown in Figure 8.4.

As you move down the list, responsibilities and title to goods change hands progressively nearer the buyer. In an EX Works sale, the seller need only shove the goods out the door of his factory. In a Delivered Duty Paid sale, on the other extreme, the seller must actually enter the goods in the foreign country and deliver them to the buyer. Complete definitions of each term are in the

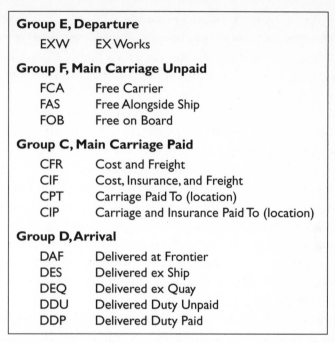

Group E, Departure

    EXW   EX Works

Group F, Main Carriage Unpaid

    FCA   Free Carrier
    FAS   Free Alongside Ship
    FOB   Free on Board

Group C, Main Carriage Paid

    CFR   Cost and Freight
    CIF   Cost, Insurance, and Freight
    CPT   Carriage Paid To (location)
    CIP   Carriage and Insurance Paid To (location)

Group D, Arrival

    DAF   Delivered at Frontier
    DES   Delivered ex Ship
    DEQ   Delivered ex Quay
    DDU   Delivered Duty Unpaid
    DDP   Delivered Duty Paid

Figure 8.4   INCOTERMS, 2000 Revision

publication *Incoterms 2000*, available from International Chamber of Commerce Publishing in New York City (see chapter 12 for more information)

The terms most often used when goods move by ocean are FAS, FOB, CFR, and CIF. They are sometimes written in capital letters and sometimes in lowercase letters with periods. In an FAS shipment, the seller must place the goods by the side of a ship, ready to be loaded, and pay all the costs to that point. Thus, they are free of encumbrances. With FOB, the seller must take care of any paperwork or expenses necessary to remove goods from his country and place them on an international carrier. Be careful of this term, though, because it is often used with other forms of transportation. If you buy FOB from a handcrafts exporter in the Sahara desert, and you expect the goods to be placed on board a ship while he only expects to place them on board a camel outside his workshop, there will be quite a problem. With regard to airfreight, the term FOB means the goods must be placed in the custody of an air carrier at an airport. It does not mean they must actually be loaded on a plane.

The abbreviation CFR has replaced the old C&F. It means the exporter is responsible for paying the freight bill. Ultimately, he will be repaid by the buyer. Once the goods are on the ship, however, the exporter is free of responsibility for subsequent loss or damage. With a CIF shipment, the exporter must also buy insurance. Technically, however, he sells the insurance policy to the importer along with the goods. Thus, if you import beer CIF and most of the bottles are broken, you will have to file a claim against insurance that was bought by the exporter. There may also be claims against that insurance by others whose cargo was damaged by the beer.

In U.S. trade by land, especially with Mexico, DAF is used widely. For example, a shipment of bathroom fixtures from Guadalajara will be placed on the U.S. side of the international bridge in Laredo, Texas. The importer will take charge of them at that point, before they are cleared through customs.

It takes some experience to learn how to decide which shipping term to use. In the beginning, try to make it easy for yourself. Export with a Group F term and import with a Group C term. Later, when you are more sophisticated, you can choose terms that minimize your cost and risk and are acceptable to both parties. You may be dealing with a big shipper who can get lower freight rates, so let her arrange transportation. You may want to use a term that lets you select the insurance company to make sure it's a good one, in case you have to file a claim. Some countries, however, require that import (and sometimes export) shipments be insured with their national companies.

One former client of mine was buying lovely wool sweaters from a small firm in Ireland that had no experience exporting. The solution was to buy FAS. My client arranged, through her

U.S. customs broker, for a shipping agent to take charge of the goods at the Irish port.

If you have a small export shipment to a major company in Europe, the sale may well be FCA. The buyer will be having several small shipments sent to a specialized firm that can consolidate them into one container for ocean shipment. Many other examples could be given.

Even experienced exporters, though, hesitate to get involved in shipping beyond CIF to developing countries. I was once asked to quote on an export shipment to be sent DDP to an importer in David, Panama. Besides being responsible for Panamanian customs clearance and duty, I would have had to arrange and pay for inland freight in the buyer's country. Although a multinational company might have agreed to that, I was willing to ship CIF and not an inch beyond. I once worked in Bolivia for an organization that had a new fax machine tied up in customs for six months. If the exporter had shipped this machine DDP, and did not receive payment in advance, he would have waited a long time for his money.

MARINE INSURANCE

In the early days of international trade, it was common for cargo to be lost when vessels ran into trouble with sand bars, storms at sea, or pirates. Shippers would demand compensation from the steamship companies, who often lacked the resources to make restitution in full.

Thus it was that ships' captains began sitting in Lloyds' coffee house in London, asking wealthy patrons to accept (for a small fee) the responsibility of repaying shippers when losses occurred. Finally a patron, whom others respected, would write at the bottom of a manifest the percentage of the risk he would accept and the fee he would charge. He was the *lead underwriter*. Other patrons, or *underwriters*, would add their percentages of risk and their signatures until finally the entire value of the cargo had been underwritten. From this small beginning, Lloyds of London and the gigantic industry of marine insurance were developed.

Nearly all international shipments are insured against loss and damage. A general cost guideline is 1 percent of the insured value, but this varies enormously with the type of goods, the mode of transportation, and other factors.

There are several types of limited coverage that major shippers use to save money on premiums, but most small-scale importers and exporters purchase "all risk" coverage. This covers nearly all risks. It does not cover loss or damage caused by war, strikes, riots, civil disobedience, or "inherent vice in the cargo." This means something in the cargo that destroys it, such as moth larvae in wool sweaters or deadly bacteria in shrimp. One can pay extra for *riders* or clauses that protect against these risks.

No standard cargo insurance covers late arrival or rejection of goods by buyers or government agencies. These are insurable risks, but the rates are high and many insurance companies refuse to insure.

It is vital that your marine insurance policy contain a *general average* clause. This means that, for example, if the ship is in a bad storm and some heavy cargo is jettisoned to save the rest, every shipper who was using that vessel is responsible for a portion of the value of the jettisoned cargo. Even though your cargo may be safe and sound, you cannot get it until the steamship line has been assured of payment for your share of the loss.

Also, insurance can be port to port, warehouse to warehouse, or some combination of the two forms. Warehouse-to-warehouse policies cover the goods from the time they leave the exporter's premises until they are in the importer's premises. They are becoming increasingly common.

What determines who must buy the insurance? The answer is the shipping term that is agreed upon. The definition of each INCOTERM says who is responsible for insuring the cargo.

Many problems can arise. Suppose, for example, that you are

exporting, CFR, on open account, and the cargo is lost. The foreign importer is obligated to pay you but may not do so until he collects from his insurance company. To speed up payment, you may get involved in helping your importer settle the claim. Or suppose you are importing CIF on a letter of credit and the cargo is lost. You will have to file a claim on the insurance company from which the *exporter* purchased coverage. This will be much easier if the exporter has used a sound, reliable company that has offices in the United States.

Whenever the other party to a transaction buys insurance to protect you, and you have doubts about the adequacy of coverage, you should consider purchasing contingent insurance. This costs about half as much as regular insurance and pays only if there is covered loss or damage and for some reason the primary insurer does not pay.

Small-scale importers and exporters usually buy insurance supplied by freight forwarders under their blanket policies, or directly from airlines, whereas medium-sized shippers buy through insurance brokers. Large importers and exporters have "open" policies that automatically cover all shipments of their normal merchandise in their normal trading areas. The importer or exporter simply reports each shipment to his insurance company.

It is customary to insure for the CIF value of a shipment, plus 10 percent of CIF. This means, for example, that if your goods are worth $9,000, the shipping cost is $900, and the insurance cost is $100, you should insure for $1,100 ($9,000 + $900 + 100 × 1.1). The extra 10 percent is to repay you for time and trouble, lost profit, and perhaps lost customers because you did not fulfill your obligations.

A few years ago, a friend of mine, a successful businessman, traveled to China and bought $5,000 worth of hand-carved wooden furniture to begin an import business. He had it shipped to the United States but did not tell the Chinese to insure it for CIF plus 10 percent. It was poorly packed and arrived with heavy damage, and only part of the loss was recovered.

You may trade for a lifetime and never have an insured loss. If you do have to file a claim, however, you will have to present the bill of lading, the insurance certificate, and a survey report with an invoice showing the amount of damage or loss. When a marine insurance company agrees that it has an obligation to pay, it usually makes payment from one to six months after a claim is filed.

BROKERS AND FORWARDERS

If you import a small shipment by air that has a value of $2,000 or less and doesn't include textiles, apparel, or leather goods, you can probably clear it through customs yourself. First call your carrier to verify this and ask what is needed. Then go to their cargo office at the airport, fill out a simple form (an informal entry), pay the duty if any is charged, and take the merchandise. Some possible complications to this scenario will be discussed in chapter 10.

If the shipment arrives by sea, is worth more than $2,000, or contains restricted products such as textiles, apparel, or leather goods, you should probably use the services of a licensed U.S. customhouse broker. Their functions are to locate your goods, fill out an entry form (a formal entry), and arrange for a customs inspector to clear your goods. Normally, brokers will send you one bill for services and for duty if any is paid. Brokers usually have two weeks to pay duty to customs, so they bill importers immediately and hope to be paid before they have to lay out cash of their own. Many now pay duties electronically.

A brokerage fee for a routine clearance is about $100, but these fees are unregulated and vary considerably. If your product needs approval by other agencies, such as the U.S. Food and Drug Administration (FDA), the broker will make the necessary arrangements. The cost of routine FDA clearance includes cartage to the FDA's office at the port or airport, the FDA fee, cartage back to customs, and a small extra broker's fee—usually $30 to $60 all together. If there are problems with documents, such as a missing or incomplete commercial invoice, the broker can usually resolve them. This, again, will cost you extra.

When your broker fills out customs forms (see chapter 10 for details), he will classify each product in your shipment by its Harmonized System number and report its value. (The Harmonized System of classifying and coding merchandise in international trade is explained in chapter 10.) Because the broker is your agent, you can be fined for any error that he might commit.

Also, in the process of clearing goods through customs, the duty that is paid is only an estimated duty. The inspectors at ports are very knowledgeable but are not product specialists. Customs has one year from the date of an entry for a product specialist to examine the paperwork and determine whether the correct duty was paid. If you paid too much, customs will send you a refund (it happened once in the year 1493). If you paid too little, customs will send you a notice and then a bill. If the product specialist wants to see a sample of the merchandise so as to determine its proper classification, customs will send you a Redelivery Notice. Customs can also ask for redelivery of a sample to check the labeling on your product and can do this as long as a year after your shipment has been entered.

Because importers usually receive their shipments before paying duty, customs needs a way to be sure it can collect. Also, there is a logical fear that an importer will bring in goods and pay too little duty, that within a year customs will try to collect the remainder, and that the importer will have passed away, gone broke, or gone into hiding in some faraway country. To reduce this risk, rules stipulate that, with few exceptions, each shipment that requires a formal entry must be covered by a bond. Provided that no approvals are required from other government agencies such as the Food and Drug Administration, the usual bond is equal to the value of the cargo plus duties and taxes. If other approvals are required, the bond must be equal to triple the estimated value of the merchandise.

You can go to a bonding company yourself and purchase either a *single-entry bond,* to cover just one shipment, or a *term bond,* to cover all your shipments for a year. Look for one near your port of entry. A bail bond firm in Topeka, Kansas, won't know much about customs bonds. The charge will be a percentage of the value of your shipment(s), with a minimum charge of about $60. Bonding companies will protect themselves by checking your income and financial position. If you use a broker to clear your shipment, however, he will get the bond for you. This may cost you as much or more but will be easier for you because bonding companies usually accept the word of a broker that an importer is honest and financially sound.

If there is a small problem with your entry, such as a missing document, the same bond will guarantee customs that the document will be submitted within sixty days.

In most ports, there are many licensed customs brokers. You should select one who will tell you clearly and honestly what the fees are and which services they cover. I once spoke with an importer who had been using the same broker for several years and had never received an itemized bill; as you might have guessed, the broker was overcharging but was a good friend of the company's president.

If you have special requirements, such as rush shipments or highly perishable cargo, look for a well-established brokerage firm that can guarantee the kind of service you need. I once had an urgent shipment of product samples land at Kennedy Airport on a Saturday with everything mixed up. The shipment was consigned to the wrong party, it contained quota goods and even a prohibited item, and *there were no documents at all.* My brokerage firm sent its number-one broker, a middle-aged lady about five feet tall with a voice like a Bengal tiger, and believe it or not the goods were out of customs and in Philadelphia by 6:00 P.M. on Sunday.

Once your goods are cleared through customs, you can pick them up, but an easier choice is to have the broker get them on a truck and delivered to your door. He or she will then be performing the function of a domestic freight forwarder. Some broker/forwarders have their own trucks for delivery, but more often they use the services of private trucking companies. In either case, you will be billed for forwarding, trucking, and perhaps insurance if the policy in force does not cover through to your warehouse.

I once met an importer who was having small shipments sent to him from Kennedy Airport by UPS. He said the charge was about $5, compared to $140 by truck. The moral is: Examine *all* your options.

On the export side, air and ocean forwarders can help you by:

- Supplying costs needed to prepare CIF quotations
- Booking space on vessels or aircraft
- Taking charge of cargo at the port or airport
- Arranging for packing if this is needed
- Preparing export documents
- Making sure the cargo is loaded on the vessel
- Collecting or assembling the documents and sending them to you or to your bank
- Tracking shipments that do not arrive as scheduled.

These are very valuable services. For example, if you receive a letter of credit that says you must ship by July 1, and your cargo reaches the port on time but cannot be loaded because you didn't book space on the only vessel available, your payment may no longer be assured.

Freight forwarders are paid by fees from their clients (usually exporters), plus commissions from the carriers they use. Fees are not regulated and vary considerably but are usually close to $100 for an air shipment and close to $200 for an ocean shipment. Commissions are around 2 to 5 percent but vary greatly, especially for ocean freight. It is illegal for forwarders to kick back any of their commissions to the shippers, but this is certainly done at times.

It *is* legal, however, for air forwarders to charge you, the shipper, whatever rate they care to set. For example, an airline could quote a price of $2,000 for a shipment and pay the forwarders 10 percent of that as a commission. The forwarder could charge you, the shipper, only $1,900, thus effectively giving you half the commission. You may come out better than if you dealt directly with the airline.

You will want to pick a forwarder who has offices near the ports or airports you use, who has experience with the kinds of cargo you will be shipping and with the destinations you will be shipping to, and who has friendly, competent personnel and good financial standing. This last criterion is especially important. If a forwarder should handle a shipment for you and you pay him for it, only to have the forwarder go out of business before paying the carrier, you will still be liable. This happened to me once, when I used a not-so-stable forwarder to air freight a friend's dog from Boston to Jakarta.

Also, it is worth checking directly with carriers from time to time to make sure your forwarder is giving you the lowest rates to which your cargo is entitled. All it takes is a phone call or two.

Many forwarders pick up freight at inland points of origin, and several can save you money through their roles as freight consolidators or NVOCCs. The moral, again, is to look at all your options.

Foreign freight forwarders (and brokers as well) are listed in telephone directories, port handbooks, and some trade magazines.

You can now find several customs house brokers and foreign freight forwarders on the Internet and learn more about their services. In fact, the AOL Web Crawler says there are more than *10,000* documents that match the term *customs brokers*. Some don't tell you where they are located, but they *do* of course give information about how to contact them. The following is a sample of some of the home pages you can tap into:

- BDB International (brokers and forwarders), www.bepint. com
- C. H. Greene International (forwarders), www. chrobinson. com
- Danzas (brokers and forwarders), www.danzas.com
- Panalpina (forwarders, customs brokers, logistics and supply chain), www.panalpina.com
- Poulton (brokers and forwarders), www.poulton.com/cargo.htm
- Schenker International (forwarders), www. schenkerusa. com

With increased access to information by shippers around the world, the traditional roles of customs brokers and freight forwarders have been changing. Large companies have bought smaller ones and are expanding into freight forwarding, customs clearance, warehousing, logistics, tracking shipments, and so forth. Look for more vertical integration and expansion of service in the future.

The National Customs Brokers and Forwarders Association can provide you with more information on this topic. Their home page can be found at www.tradecompass.com/ncbfaal. Trade Compass, by the way, is a trade information provider and is found on the web at www.tradecompass.com (e-mail trade_compass @msn.com).

CHAPTER **9**

Oh, Those Lovely Documents

There is an old expression: "Trade moves on paper." In today's ever more connected electronic age, this may change to, "Trade moves electronically," but this conversion is only beginning to happen internationally. What we're seeing is electronic transfer of documents, through fax and the Internet, but they still must be created and studied pretty much like in the old days.

Fortunately many of the prerequisite documents, like those between airlines and the airports they fly into and out of, are never seen by the importer or the exporter. Also, most shipments are reasonably uncomplicated. If you send rubber bands from the United States to England, by airfreight on open-account terms, documents won't be much of a problem. On the other hand, if you want to ship repeating rifles to Venezuela, by seafreight on a letter of credit, you'd better be prepared for reams of paper.

Most international trade documents can be placed into the following categories:

- Commercial documents
- Banking documents

- Transportation and insurance documents
- Government formalities documents

In general, the purposes of all of them are to facilitate, control, and keep track of international cargo movements. We will discuss each of them in turn.

COMMERCIAL DOCUMENTS

Commercial documents are those that move between the buyer and the seller. The ones to be discussed here are the following:

- Request for quotation
- Quotation
- Pro forma invoice
- Terms and conditions of sale
- Purchase order
- Order acceptance and confirmation
- Sales contract
- Commercial invoice

Buyers and sellers can exchange any number of letters, telephone calls, and fax and e-mail messages as the initial steps of an international transaction. This will normally lead to a *request for quotation*. This can be a simple fax or other form of message that says something like the following:

Dear Sirs:
Please send me your quotation for 50 Farm Best lawn tractors, Model number 307H. Please quote C&F Mombasa, Kenya. Payment will be by 90-day letter of credit.

Sincerely,

Seth Anjul, Monrobi Trading Company

You as the exporter would logically follow with a *quotation,* which is basically the price for which you can supply the goods for the specified shipping and payment terms (although you are free to propose alternate terms). All your costs, and your profit or commission, must be included. Your quotation should reference the number on the request, if there was one, and include a date until which it is valid. Figure 9.1 shows a simple example.

You will want the quotation to be as specific as possible, to

---

AGMARTRADE INTERNATIONAL
7823 Mistic View Court
Rockville, MD 20855-2275, USA

QUOTATION No. _____

This quotation is valid for 30 days from the date hereon: March 8, 2001.

Shipper: Agmartrade International, 7823 Mistic View Court, Rockville, MD 20855-2275, USA

Consignee: Monrobi Trading Company, 724 Serengetti Street, Mombasa, Kenya

50 lawn tractors, Farm Best Model 307 H as shown in their catalog dated January 2, 2001, packed for export by the manufacturer	US$42,100
Inland freight to the Port of Baltimore	1,000
Forwarding and freight to Mombasa, Kenya, by sea	5,125
Total C&F Mombasa	US$48,225

Marine insurance to be purchased by the Consignee.

Payment by 90-day irrevocable letter of credit from a first-class international bank.

Shipment to be made within 60 days after receipt of the letter of credit

---

Figure 9.1　Quotation

avoid misunderstandings. It is normally signed, and it is now possible to send e-mail messages with your signature on them (although these signatures are not accepted on contractual documents).

Sometimes an importer will want a more formal document that will help him or her get an import permit or foreign exchange authorization and/or to open a letter of credit; he or she may go one step further and ask for a *pro forma invoice*. This looks like a regular commercial invoice (see Figure 9.4 on page 157), except that it says "PRO FORMA" at the top. These words mean that the document in hand isn't the actual commercial invoice but is almost exactly what the actual invoice will look like.

Sometimes quotations and pro forma invoices are accompanied by other documents known as *standard terms and conditions of sale*. These give important information—such as "All shipments are made FOB McAllen, Texas"—that is not shown on quotations or pro forma invoices. This information is somewhat analogous to the "fine print" when you open a bank account or receive a credit card.

If the importer is satisfied with the quotation and/or pro forma invoice, he or she may place an order. This can be a simple oral or written statement such as "We hereby order as per your pro forma invoice number 627." More often there are additional details—for example, "We hereby order 100 dozen Model R FILEMAST bicycle pumps, CIF New York, to be shipped by ocean no later than January 1, 2002, with payment by irrevocable letter of credit." An order can include other conditions such as documents that should be provided and even what should be said on the documents. Figure 9.2 is an example of an international purchase order. Note that it shows how to mark the boxes and specifies payment by sight draft, documents against payment, and is signed.

The exporter should reply with a simple statement such as, "We accept your Purchase Order No. 291/91, dated May 2, 2002." In international trade, an order and an unconditional acceptance make a contract that theoretically can be enforced by either of

TREICO
93 Broad Street
Syosset, NY 11791   BANK: Citibank N.A.
USA   Syosset, New York

TO: Exportadors Uribe   P.O. DATE: Jan. 8, 2001
     77 Calle Inventada
     Rogelio, Panama   P.O. NO.:   3/86

                             SHIP TO: TREICO
                                          93 Broad Street
                                          Syosset, NY, USA

NO.	MODEL	DESCRIPTION	UNIT	TOTAL PRICE
10	S33	Cartons each containing 4 dozen Panama hats	$146.00	US$1,460.00
5	S29	Cartons each containing 4 dozen Panama hats	120.00	600.00
		TOTAL F.O.B. COLON, PANAMA Ocean Freight		US$2,060.00 421.15
		TOTAL C&F NEW YORK		US$2,481.15

MARKS: TREICO | 3/86 |
          Syosset, NY

PAYMENT: SD/DP

SHIPMENT: By sea, C&F New York

INSURANCE: TREICO will cover

PURCHASING DEPT.

Figure 9.2 International Purchase Order

the contracting parties. The next chapter includes some information about enforcement of contracts of sale.

In some cases importers order informally, by telephone, although this system has been partly replaced by fax, e-mail, and on-line web sites. The exporter then sends a *sales confirmation* (see Figure 9.3), which the importer signs and returns. This procedure creates a contract of sale.

The Finishing Touches

With large shipments between nonaffiliated companies, there are usually more formal contracts of sale. These can run to 30 or 40 pages. If you decide to buy or sell a shipload of copper, for example, I'd strongly suggest the services of a good attorney, expensive though they may be.

As an exporter, once you ship you will need to supply a *commercial invoice* that says how much the importer owes you (even if he has already paid) and for what. Each country has its own requirements for commercial invoices, which you can obtain from customs brokers/freight forwarders, consulates of the countries you are shipping to, or publications such as the Dun & Bradstreet *Exporters' Encyclopedia* and *Shipper and Forwarder* magazine. For example, on CIF shipments to many countries you are required to provide invoices that break out the prices of the goods, sales commissions, transportation costs, and so on.

Some countries such as Brazil have special forms for commercial invoices, which you can buy from their consulates or from UNZ & Company in Jersey City, New Jersey.

For shipments to the United States, the commercial invoice must show the following information:

- Port of entry of the merchandise
- Names of the seller and buyer, or shipper and receiver (usually addresses are shown as well, and these are required for some kinds of products)

_____ Corporation

Original for Seller

P.O. Box xxx, Taipei, Taiwan
Telephone: _____
Telefax: _____
Email: _____

Date: Feb. 20, 2002

SALES CONFIRMATION

Ref. No. SC-861013

(Please inicate the above
number in the covering LC)

Referring to   (BUYER)   LTD., USA

We confirm the following sale to you on the terms and conditions set forth
hereunder and on the reverse hereof.

Item No.	Description	Quantity	Unit Price FOB Taiwan Net	Amount
	P.O. 239			
4505	5 LBS/PR WRIST/ANKLE 6 PCS/ CTN/0.56'/15KGS	576PCS	US$2.02	US$1,163.52
4502	2 LBS/PR WRIST/ANKLE 12PCS/CTN/P.F7'/12.5 KGS	456 PCS	US$1.47	US$670.32
5016	16 LBS DUMBELL WTS. 4 PCS/CTN/0.26'/24.5 KGS	24 PCS	US$7.10	US$170.40
	TOTAL	1,056PCS		US$2,004.24

TOTAL IN U.S. DOLLARS TWO THOUSAND FOUR AND CENTS TWENTY FOUR ONLY.

PAYMENT: By Irrevocable and confirmed Letter of
Credit available against drafts drawn at sight in
Favor of Seller or transferable

SHIPMENT: Mar. 17, 19xx
DESTINATION: New York
VALIDITY: 30 DAYS SUBJECT TO UPDATE
REMARKS: IND.CO.

SHIPPING MARK
(BUYER)
NEW YORK
C/NO.
MADE IN TAIWAN
R.O.C.

SIDE MARK
STYLE NO:
QUANTITY
ORDER NO
N.W.:
G.W.:
MEA'T:

Agreed and accepted by:
Buyer:

(SELLER) CORPORATION

_____
(Buyer's signature)

_____
(Seller's signature)

Figure 9.3   Sales Confirmation (Reprinted with permission of Jonquil
International, Ltd.)

- Invoice date
- Country from which the shipment is made
- A detailed description of the merchandise including the name and quality of each item, marks used in domestic trade in the country of origin, and marks and numbers on the export packing
- The quantity of each item (some products are quantified by the number of pieces, others by weight, and others by volume, as specified in the product classification known as the Harmonized System)
- The purchase price of each item, in the currency actually used for the transaction (if the shipment is on consignment and there is no purchase price, the value must be shown)
- Charges involved in moving the freight from FOB vessel to where the U.S. customs inspection takes place may be shown on an attachment to the invoice, which the customs broker can prepare
- Any rebates or similar incentives the exporter will receive from his government for having made the exportation

The invoice should be in English or accompanied by an accurate translation. It should show any significant "assists" the importer gave the foreign producer, such as dies or manufacturing equipment.

A more detailed description of invoicing requirements is in the book *Importing into the United States,* published by the U.S. Customs Service and available from the Superintendent of Documents. Figure 9.4 shows a computer-generated invoice for an actual export shipment from New York to Saudi Arabia, with some information removed for confidentiality. Note the statements made at the bottom.

CHEW INTERNATIONAL CORPORATION
EXPORT DEPARTMENT
71 MURRAY STREET, 9TH FLOOR
NEW YORK, NY 10007-2114, U.S.A.
TEL: (212) 619-4300, FAX: (212:619-4273
	INVOICE PAGE: 1
	ORDER NO: A039608 DATE: 9/26/02
	REFERENCE DATA:
	  INVOICE NO: A039608/01
	    DATE: 26 JUN 2002
	  YOUR REF.:
	  ORDER DATE: 08 MAY, 2002

BUYER:
_____
ATTN: MR. _____
P.O. Box _____
ALKHOBAR, SAUDI ARABIA
	TERMS:
	    SALES: NET C&F DAMMAM
	  DELIVERY: NET C&F DAMMAM
	  PAYMENT: WIRE TRANSFER

CONSIGN TO: _____
NOTIFY: _____
ULTIMATE CONSIGNEE: _____
	SHIPMENT DATA:
	  SHIP VIA: OCEAN FREIGHT
	  ARRIVES AT: DAMMAM

MARKS: _____/ DAMMAM SAUDI ARABIA 1039608	THIS IS A COMPLETE SHIPMENT

TI	DESCRIPTION	NO. OF UNITS	UNTP	UNIT PRICE	AMOUNT US DOLL
1	6/10 WHOLE KERNEL CORN	375	Ctn	11.75	4,406.25
2	24/16 Oz. Whole Kernel Corn	375	Ctn	8.25	3,093.75
3	24/16 Oz. Sliced Beets Above 3 items--Super Fresh Brand: English/Arabic labels with m/e date (shelf live--2 years)	350	Ctn	9.50	3,325.00

NET C&F DAMMAM $12,824.50

THESE COMMODITIES LICENSED BY U.S. FOR UNTIMATE DESTINTION SAUDI ARABIA. DIVERSION CONTRARY TO U.S. LAW PROHIBITED.

WE CERTIFY THAT THIS PRODUCT DOES NOT CONTAIN PORT, ALCOHOL, GELATINE, SACCHARINE OR CYCLAMATE

PER _____, TRAFFIC MANAGER

BUYER INSURES

1-20'CONT.NO.IEAU-20845. SEAL NO. 10382
TOTAL CARTONS: 1315 DTNS
TOTAL GR. WT.: 45,728 LBS/20.742 KILOS

CERTIFIED TRUE & CORRECT   _____

FOR CHEW INTERNATIONAL CORP.

Figure 9.4   Commercial Invoice (Reprinted with permission of Chew International Corporation)

BANKING DOCUMENTS

The processes of paying and getting paid require relatively few documents. Cash in advance may be as simple as the importer sending the exporter a check or depositing it in his or her bank account. It is rarely more complicated than filling out a simple form to buy a bank draft or to order an airmail or cable transfer. Consignment, open-account, and credit card transactions are equally uncomplicated.

With payment by bill of exchange (sight or time draft), the exporter must complete a form to instruct his bank to prepare the draft and send it to the importer's bank. The first time you do this, you should sit down with your banker and go over each of the options that are presented on the form (see Figure 9.5). There is a more complete example in chapter 7.

A letter of credit sale is somewhat more complex than other forms of international payment. There are at least four documents involved, as follows:

- Application for letter of credit
- Letter of credit
- Advice of letter of credit
- Drafts (drawn on a bank for payment)

The application for a letter of credit must be completed by the importer and given to the opening bank. It is fairly complicated and should definitely be completed with the help of your banker the first few times. Major international banks now accept applications from established customers by computer. The importer simply fills in details on a form that is in his data-processing system and transmits it to his bank by modem.

The actual letter of credit is transmitted by the opening bank to its branch or correspondent in the exporter's country. It tells the exporter exactly which functions to perform and which docu-

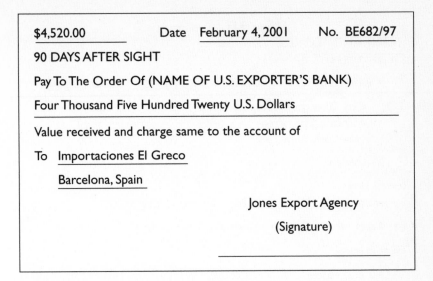

| $4,520.00 | Date | February 4, 2001 | No. BE682/97 |

90 DAYS AFTER SIGHT

Pay To The Order Of (NAME OF U.S. EXPORTER'S BANK)

Four Thousand Five Hundred Twenty U.S. Dollars

Value received and charge same to the account of

To   Importaciones El Greco

Barcelona, Spain

Jones Export Agency

(Signature)

Figure 9.5   Bill of Exchange

ments to provide, in order to get paid. There is a more complete example in chapter 7.

The advice of a letter of credit (see Figure 9.6) is a simple form that is sent to the exporter by a bank in his country. It says that a credit has been opened in his favor, and it is followed by the actual LC. It gives the exporting firm assurance that it can begin preparing the goods for shipment.

Finally, the exporter must present drafts for collection to the paying or negotiating bank. For example, if you receive a letter of credit that is payable upon presentation of documentary evidence that you have shipped as instructed, you can go directly from the port to the bank, armed with a draft for collection and the required documents. More likely, you will ask your freight forwarder to do this for you. To save time, the forwarder will probably send the draft and other documents to the bank by courier.

Still other documents will be involved in more complicated LC transactions—for example, when partial shipments are allowed

---

(Export LC, Confirmed)

(NAME AND ADDRESS
OF EXPORTER'S BANK)

Their Ref. No. <u>68392</u>   Our Advice <u>LC R23259</u>   Date <u>2/5/2001</u>

TO: City Directory Company
       650 East 11th Street
       New York, New York

<u>104-686943</u>

Instructions
Received from: Neopolitan Bank, Florence, Italy

For Account of: Cassata Importers, Florence, Italy

Gentlemen:

   Our correspondent, named above, has instructed us to advise you that they have opened their irrevocable credit in your favor, as designated above, for a sum or sums not to exceed the following:

FIFTEEN THOUSAND DOLLARS UNITED STATES CURRENCY ($15,000 USC)

Available by your draft(s):

For FULL invoice value of merchandise, to be described in your invoice as follows:

GUIDEBOOKS TO MAJOR NORTH AMERICAN CITIES

Your draft(s) must be accompanied by the following:
1.   Your commercial invoice, original and 3 copies
2.   Your ocean bill of lading issued to order, endorsed in blank evidencing shipment of the goods from New York to Florence.

Partial shipments are not permitted. Insurance is to be obtained by the buyers. We confirm this credit and affirm all drafts presented against it at (bank's address) by (date) will be honored.

This credit is subject to the Uniform   Yours truly,
Customs and Practice for Documentary
Credits as described in International
Chamber of Commerce Publication No. 500   Authorized Signature

Figure 9.6   Advice of Letter of Credit

or a credit is transferred or assigned from one beneficiary to another. There are also special documents for the seller to request, and the buyer to grant, amendments to LCs.

TRANSPORTATION AND INSURANCE DOCUMENTS

The old expression, "Goods move on paper," is becoming less true, but paper is still important. Goods don't move on paper, but neither do they move without some legal form of documentation. The transportation documents that will be mentioned in this section include:

- Packing list
- Delivery instructions to domestic carrier
- Inland bill of lading
- Dock receipt
- Insurance request, insurance certificate
- Shipper's letter of instructions
- Ocean bill of lading or airwaybill
- Booking request
- Arrival notice
- Carrier's certificate and release order
- Delivery order and freight release

The purpose of most of these documents is to keep track of merchandise as it passes from one hand to another and to make sure it isn't delivered to someone who is not supposed to receive it. If a shipper delivers goods to a trucking company, the shipper gets a receipt to show they have been delivered (the inland bill of lading). The truck driver needs proof of delivery when the goods are delivered to the dock (a dock receipt) or any other location.

If a shipment disappears, there should be a trail of documents that will tell investigators who had custody of it at the time it was lost.

There is another important aspect to this paper trail. No one wants to be held accountable for damage to merchandise that was caused by someone else. Therefore, each party who receives goods is supposed to make a visual inspection of the boxes. If a steamship company receives a box with no apparent loss or damage, it will simply accept it and issue a bill of lading (or sign the bill of lading previously prepared by the freight forwarder). If the box is wet or badly dented, however, the steamship company will note this as an exception on the bill of lading. The document will then be known as a *foul* bill of lading. Letters of credit often stipulate that an exporter must present to the bank a *clean* bill of lading in order to be paid for a shipment. If a box is damaged before being loaded on the ship, and a foul bill of lading is issued, the exporter's payment will be held up until the situation is resolved.

The *packing list* is a simple document that shows how many boxes there are in a shipment, how to identify each, and what is in each. If a box is missing, one can determine from the packing list which one it is and what it contains. Or, if you should need to find something specific in a shipment, the packing list should tell you which box it is in. The simple packing list in Figure 9.7 is from the book *A Basic Guide to Exporting*, prepared by the U.S. Department of Commerce and available from the Superintendent of Documents. Note that there are five cases of the same goods, numbered from one to five.

As an exporter, you are likely to be shipping goods by truck to ports and airports. You must provide delivery instructions to the domestic carrier. The carrier, in turn, will provide you with a signed inland bill of lading. This document shows that the carrier has received the goods and to whom they are to be delivered. The fine print on the back makes this bill of lading also a contract of carriage.

When your trucking company delivers goods to an ocean terminal, it will obtain a *dock receipt*. This is the domestic carrier's

PACKING LIST								
DEC. 15, 2002								
To: XYZ COMPANY								
LONDON ENGLAND								
Gentlemen:								
Under your order No. 123, the material listed below was shipped 12/5/02 via TRUCK AND VESSEL to LONDON								
PACK AGE	WEIGHT IN POUNDS OR KILOS			DIMENSIONS			QUAN TITY	CONTENTS OF EACH PACKAGE
NUM BER	GROSS WT. EACH	LEGAL WT. EACH	NET WT. EACH	HEIGHT	WIDTH	LENGTH		
1/5	300		250	25	25	25		SPARK PLUGS (AUTO PARTS)

Figure 9.7   Packing List (Reprinted with permission of U.S. Foreign Commercial Service, U.S. Department of Commerce)

proof of when and where it has made delivery. If the exporter is responsible for insuring the shipment, he or she will fill out an insurance request and obtain an insurance certificate. If you export CIF under a letter of credit, the insurance certificate will have to be included in the package of documents you present to the bank for payment.

Assuming the exporter uses the services of an international freight forwarder, he must tell the forwarder which goods she should receive for forwarding, where and when she should find them, and what she should do with the goods and with the documents. This information is communicated by means of a *shipper's letter of instructions*. Figure 9.8, from an export information manual published in Texas, is such a letter of instructions. It tells the forwarder to ship to La Paz, Bolivia, to prepay the freight, to insure the shipment, and to present the documents to the bank. Note that the shipment is consigned to a bank in Bolivia and is probably being sent with a to order bill of lading.

The ocean bill of lading, or airwaybill, serves as a receipt for the goods, a contract of carriage, and a temporary title document.

EXPORT SHIPPING INSTRUCTIONS   DATE: Feb. 9, 2002
                                    Shipper's ref. no. 78-456

Ship in name of: ABC MANUFACTURING COMPANY, ANY STREET, DALLAS, TEXAS
Consign to: BANCO DE AMERICA, APTDO. 666, LA PAZ, BOLIVIA
Notify: XYZ DISTRIBUTING COMPANY, APTDO 792, LA PAZ, BOLIVIA
Port of Discharge: LA PAZ   Final Destination: LA PAZ

MARKS AND NUMBERS	NO. OF PKGS.	DESCRIPTION OF COMMODITIES	VALUE	GROSS WT.(LBS.)	MEASUREMENT
XYX COMPANY LA PAZ P.O. 78-456 MADE IN USA CTN. #1	1 CTN.	CONTAINING OIL WELL DRILLING PARTS Partes para uso en la industria petrolera 6 #2489 O rings @ 2.89 10 #6723 gaskets @ 1.59 4 #8932 seals @ 8.79 18 #8056 bushings @ 9.30 1 #5742 shim TOTAL F.O.B. DALLAS	 $17.34 15.90 35.16 167.40 12.68 $250.04	83	

Letter of Credit Expires: _____   Bank Documents Through: **BANCO DE AMERICA**

Value for Customs Clearance: _____   License No.: _____

Inland Fright to be Charged to: _____   Export Carrier: _____

Port Charges to be Charged to: _____   Port of Origin: **DALLAS, TEXAS**

Air/Ocean Freight Prepaid or Collect: **PREPAID**   Name of Supplier: _____

Insurance Requirements: **INSURE SHIPMENT**   Inland Routing: _____

Send Documents to: ___ **BANK** ___   Car No./ Truck Line: _____

OTHER INSTRUCTIONS

Consular Declaration or Other: _____
_____
_____

Figure 9.8 Shipper's Letter of Instructions

You may run into various types of bills of lading including "short form" and "long form," "received for shipment" and "on board," and "straight" and "to order." For example, if you ship goods by sea, FOB vessel with payment by sight draft, you will probably use a long-form, on board, to order, ocean bill of lading. Complicated sounding—it can be, but only until you have made your first few shipments.

Figure 9.9 is an example of a short-form, intermodal bill of lading. The goods are being sent by two modes of transportation,

A. FREIGHT FORWARDER, INC. DALLAS, TEXAS	SHORT FORM INTERMODAL BILL OF LADING Not Negotiable Unless Consigned "To Order"			

Shipper/Exporter
  ABC MANUFACTURING COMPANY
  ANY STREET
  DALLAS, TEXAS
	Document No.			

	Exporter References:
	  D-74896
	  P.O. NO. 78-456			

Consignee
  BANCO DE AMERICA
  APARTADO 666
  LA PAZ, BOLIVIA
	Forwarding agent name and address -
	references
	  A. FREIGHT FORWARDER, INC.
	  DALLAS, TEXAS			

	Goods accepted for carriage at DALLAS/FORT WORTH, TEXAS			

Notify Party
  XYZ DISTRIBUT8ING COMPANY
  APARTADO 792
  LA PAZ, BOLIVIA
	Domestic routing export instructions
	  ALSO NOTIFY:
	    HERMANOS SOLARES
	    APARTADO 456
	    La Paz, Bolivia			

Pier				

Export Carrier
  A.N.Y. AIRLINES
	Port of Lading
	  MIAMI
		Goods engaged for delivery at		

Port of Discharge LA PAZ, BOLIVIA	For transhipment to			

PARTICULARS FURNISHED BY SHIPPER

MARKS AND NUMBERS	NO. OF PKGS.	DESCRIPTION OF PACKAGES AND GOODS	GROSS WEIGHT	MEASURE MENT

XYZ COMPANY
LA PAZ
P.O. 78-456
MADE IN USA
CTN. #1
	1 CTN.	CONTAINING:
		
		OIL WELL DRILLING PARTS
		
		Partes para uso en la industria
		petrolera
		
		  6 #2489 O RINGS -Anillos @ 2.89
		10 #6723 GASKETS -Empaques @ 1.59
		  4 #8932 SEALS -Sellos @8.79
		18 #8056 BUSHINGS-Bujes @9.30
		  1 #5741 SHIM -Planchas
		
		     TOTAL F.O.B. DALLAS, TEXAS
			83 LBS.
			
			$ 17.34
			15.90
			35.16
			167.40
			12.68
			
			$250.04	

FREIGHT CHARGES		PREPAID COLLECT	Received by _____ for shipment by ocean vessel, from port of loading to port of discharge, and from place of acceptance and/or oncarriage to place of delivery as indicated above, the goods as specified above in apparent good order and condition unless otherwise stated. The goods to be delivered at the above mentioned port of discharge or place of delivery, whichever applies, subject to terms contained on the reverse side hereof, to which the shipper agrees by accepting this bill of lading. In witness thereof three (3) Original Bills of Lading have been signed, if not otherwise stated above, one of which to be accomplished, the other9s) to be void.
INLAND FREIGHT DALLAS/MIAMI	XXX.XX		
OCEAN FREIGHT (MIAMI/LA PAZ)	XXX.XX		A. FREIGHT FORWARDER, INC.
TOTAL	XXX.XX		MO. DAY YEAR B/L NO.

Figure 9.9 Intermodal Bill of Lading

air from Dallas to Miami and sea from Miami to La Paz, Bolivia. The bill of lading, issued by a freight forwarder, is called a forwarder's bill of lading. It would not be accepted for payment if the importer's letter of credit specified an on board ocean bill of lading.

If both you and your freight forwarder are doing your jobs, the forwarder will send a *booking request* to the chosen carrier as soon as you give him the information he needs to do so. Then, when the goods reach their country of destination, the air or steamship line will send an *arrival notice* to the importer or his customs broker. Airlines usually phone in addition to mailing the notice. Then the carrier will provide customs with a carrier's certificate and release order, the consignee will give his broker or the carrier a release order, and the carrier will provide the consignee with a freight release. More and more, this transaction is being conducted electronically between the carrier, the broker, and U.S. customs. It is known as Electronic Data Interchange, or EDI.

GOVERNMENT FORMALITIES DOCUMENTS

The U.S. and foreign governments all want to know which goods enter and leave their countries. They need information, which is provided by documents, both for statistical purposes and to facilitate control. A country can't limit imports of certain goods, or restrict exports to certain countries, unless it knows what is moving in and out. In many developing countries, import and export documents serve to maintain employment in the bureaucracy and preserve the power of bureaucrats, including in many cases the power to extract bribes from importers and exporters.

The government control documents we will mention in this section include:

- Import license, foreign exchange authorization
- Export license application, validated license

- Certificate of origin
- Inspection report
- Commercial, special, and consular invoices
- Shipper's export declaration
- Customs entries

The United States does not use import licenses (except for a few commodities) or foreign exchange authorizations. In many countries, however, importers have to present pro forma invoices to their government authorities to get permission to import goods and/or to pay for them in hard currency. This is becoming less prominent as economies are liberalized. Many developing countries play tricks with exporters' foreign exchange earnings such as giving them only a small percentage in hard currency and giving them the rest in local currency, at artificially set exchange rates.

U.S. exporters have to be sure they don't ship to importers who need licenses or authorizations before these are actually in hand, unless payment is assured whether or not the importer gets his authorizations. Sometimes importers will instruct their vendors to ship, before the licenses are in hand, assuming they can obtain the required documents the correct way (or another way). If you get paid up front, and have no moral qualms about this kind of arrangement, it's probably all right to go ahead and make the shipment.

Some foreign countries require all their exporters to be licensed and/or to apply for a license to make each shipment. That way they can control what leaves the country and make sure that at least most of the foreign exchange comes into the country.

In Ecuador, a large quantity of eucalyptus logs was stopped just before being loaded on a ship. Although it was clearly illegal to export this product from Ecuador, the exporter claimed he had permits from the country's central bank. I never learned whether there were repercussions from that incident, but I did hear that the logs stayed in the country and were sold cheaply to local sawmills.

Like many foreign countries, the United States requires that all significant outgoing shipments be accompanied by export licenses. Unlike many countries, however, U.S. exporters can give themselves licenses to ship most goods to most destinations. This is explained in the next chapter in the section on regulations for exporters.

In the instances when a validated license is required, the U.S. exporter must complete an export license application. This is obtained from and sent to the U.S. Department of Commerce. If your shipment requires a validated license, *do not try to send it* until and unless this requirement is met (see chapter 10 for more information about export licensing in the United States).

Every national government wants to know the country of origin of imported goods, and often an exporter must provide this information by means of a formal document called a *certificate of origin*. Its purpose is to make it harder for importers to falsify the country of origin in order to pay lower duties, avoid quotas, or bring merchandise from prohibited countries. Because there are U.S. import quotas on textiles and apparel items from many countries, but not from all countries, importers are sometimes tempted to transship in third countries and use false labeling and certificates of origin. This is especially true with regard to wearing apparel made in China. Customs inspectors are pretty sharp, however, and those who try to deceive them often get caught.

A U.S. exporter who needs a certificate of origin can usually obtain it from the nearest large chamber of commerce by sending three copies of his commercial invoice, a letter stating that the goods are of U.S. origin, and a check (usually around $10–$30) for the chamber's fee. The chamber will certify on the invoice that the goods are of U.S. origin, and the certified invoice then becomes a certificate of origin. In some locations, such as New Orleans, the customs brokers' association has been certified to conduct the same service. This saves the exporter both time and money. A few countries (Japan, South Africa, Israel, and Nigeria) require special forms of the certificate; these are available from their consulates or from UNZ & Company.

Chambers of commerce vary in their policies toward giving certificates of origin, but most accept the declarations of exporters that their products are of U.S. origin, at least until something happens to show that a particular exporter is dishonest. Chambers usually provide better service and lower fees to companies who are members, but most will issue certificates of origin to nonmembers, as well.

U.S. import shipments must be accompanied by certificates of origin if they are intended to be duty-free under the preferential arrangements that are in force with Israel, Canada, Mexico, most developing countries in general, and most Caribbean and Andean countries in particular. For imports from developing and from Caribbean and Andean nations, the form used is Form A, Certificate of Origin. This is an international form that is theoretically not available in the United States. Your foreign exporter must provide it.

Figure 9.10 is a sample Form A. The important part is at the bottom right, where the exporter declares in which country the merchandise was produced.

Country of origin declarations are complicated by the fact that relatively few goods are produced entirely in one country. A shirt can be made with Egyptian cotton, spun and woven in England, cut in the United States, and sewn and finished in the Dominican Republic. What is the country of origin? For Generalized System of Preferences (GSP), Caribbean Basin Initiative (CBI), and Andean Trade Preference Act (ATPA) shipments, the country of origin is generally the country from which the product is shipped to the United States, provided that at least 35 percent of the value of the product was added in that country (or sometimes in a combination of eligible countries). Under CBI and ATPA rules, up to 15 percent of the 35 percent can be U.S.-made materials or components.

Suppose, for example, that the Egyptian cotton that goes into a shirt is valued at $0.40. When the finished cloth reaches the United States for cutting, the value has increased to $1.60. After the cloth is cut into parts of a shirt and delivered to the Domini-

1. Goods consigned from (exporter's business name, address, country) (DELETED)	Book No. 154260
	Reference No. **EI** 7712984
	GENERALIZED SYSTEM OF PREFERENCES CERTIFICATE OF ORIGIN (Combined declaration and certificate)

2. Goods consigned to (consignee's name, address, country) (DELETED)	**FORM A**
	Issued in ....**INDIA**.. (country)
	See notes overleaf

3. Means of transport and route (as far as known) **BY SEA VIA JNPT (INDIA) TO NEW ORLEANS (U.S.A.)**	4 For official use

5. Item number	6. Marks and numbers of packages	7. Number and kind of packages & description of goods	8. Origin criteria (see notes overleaf)	9. Gross weight or other quantity	10. Number and date of invoices
1	1 TO 95 PKGS	**EXPORT WORTHY 95 PACKAGES PACKED IN RAFFIA Garfil 3 STR COMBO REPE (MADE FROM 67% NON-FIBRILATED ROPE) IN WHITE COLOUR ONE RED TY-PPMF OF 600 FEET**		6021.820 LBS 16378.100 KGS	

11. Certification It is hereby certified on the basis of control carried out That the declaration by the exporter is correct.	12. Declaration by the exporter The undersigned hereby declares that the above details and statements are correct and that all the goods were produced in ....**INDIA**................................ and that they comply with the origin requirements specified for those goods in the generalizes system of preferences for goods exported to ....**USA**.. (importing country)

Figure 9.10 Form A Certificate of Origin (reprinted by permission of The Irwin Brown Company)

can Republic, the value has reached $2.40. The FOB country of origin value of the finished shirt is $3.60. That makes the value added in the Dominican Republic $3.60 minus $2.40/3.60, or about 33 percent. By including the value of the processing in the United States, the 35 percent rule is satisfied, and the shirt can be considered a product of the Dominican Republic.

There are many cases in which governments or importers (and sometimes exporters, as well) demand *inspection reports*. Some developing countries insist on inspection of outgoing shipments to make sure their exporters are not sending illegal or low-quality merchandise. Also, some developing countries want inspection of imported goods to make sure the importers are declaring the goods they actually bring in and are not falsifying the prices paid or other costs. Finally, some importers want goods to be inspected by independent organizations as a condition for payment to be made to the exporter.

The three major inspection companies in the world are SGS, from Switzerland; SSI, from Great Britain; and Bureau Veritas, from France. All have offices in major U.S. cities. In some cases, inspections are performed by small independent firms or by government agencies, such as the U.S. Department of Agriculture and the FDA.

Your commercial invoice, discussed previously, is a government control as well as a commercial document. Importing country authorities use it to see types and quantities of goods, countries of origin, and values.

As discussed previously, some countries have special forms for commercial invoices or special requirements as to the information that must be provided on these documents. Both exporters and importers should take steps to ensure that their invoices contain all the required data.

There are a few countries that still require documents known as *consular invoices*. This is a special form that must be "legalized" by a consulate of the country you are shipping to. It is theoretically a device to prevent prohibited or overpriced (or underpriced) goods from being shipped to a country, but its main function is probably to give some countries' consulates a bit of extra income.

Each export shipment from the United States worth over $2,500 ($500 for mail shipments, but this should be increased soon), whether or not it requires a validated export license, must be accompanied by a shipper's export declaration. An exception was made early in 1991 for shipments to Canada that are to *remain* in that country. A shipper's export declaration is a document on which exporters report their shipments to the U.S. Department of Commerce, both for statistical purposes and to help in enforcement of export control regulations. There are three versions of this form—a 7525-V for most shipments, a 7525-V-Alternate for intermodal shipments, and a 7513 for in-transit goods. They can be purchased from the Superintendent of Documents, from UNZ & Company, or from a good commercial stationer. Because carriers charge $100 for the paper version of this transaction, there is a real incentive to move to electronic filing. Most freight forwarders now do this.

Figure 9.11 is a blank form 7525-V. Note, at the bottom of this document, the statement to the effect that both civil and criminal penalties can be imposed for making fraudulent statements, omitting requested information, or violating U.S. laws upon exportation.

Finally, there is a customs entry, which you or your broker must file with customs authorities when you import. There are many types of customs forms; however, the most important for you will probably be the Immediate Delivery Entry and the Entry Summary. These will be discussed in chapter 10.

A FEW MORE THOUGHTS ON DOCUMENTS

Some of the things in this chapter do not apply entirely to trade with Canada and Mexico because of provisions of NAFTA. Chapter 11 presents selected information on provisions of NAFTA.

Sometimes documents have to be translated from English to

Form **7525-V** (7-25-2000)   **SHIPPER'S EXPORT DECLARATION**   OMB NO. 0607-0152

1.a. U.S. PRINCIPAL PARTY IN INTEREST (USSPI) (Complete name and address)			
ZIP CODE		2. DATE OF EXPORTATION	3. TRANSPORTATION REFERENCE NO.
4a. ULTIMATE CONSIGNEE (Complete name and address) ··· INTERMEDIATE CONSIGNEE (Complete name and address)			
5. FORWARDING AGENT (Complete name and address)		6. POINT (STATE) OF ORIGIN OR FTZ NO.	7. COUNTRY OF ULTIMATE DESTINATION
8. LOADING PIER (Vessel only)	9. METHOD OF TRANSPORTATION (Specify)	14. CARRIER IDENTIFICATION CODE	15. SHIPMENT REFERENCE NO.
10. EXPORTING CARRIER	11. PORT OF EXPORT	16. ENTRY NUMBER	17. HAZARDOUS MATERIALS ___Yes ___No
12. PORT OF UNLADING (Vessel and air only)	13. CONTAINERIZED (Vessel only) ___Yes ___No	18. IN BOND CODE	19. ROUTED EXPORT TRANSACTION ___ Yes ___ No

20. SCHEDULE B DESCRIPTION OF COMMODITIES (Use columns 22-24)					
D/F or M (21)	SCHEDULE B NUMBER (22)	QUANTITY - SCHEDULE B UNIT(s) (23)	SHIPPING Wt. (Kilograms) (24)	VIN/PRODUCT NUMBER/VEHICLE TITLE NO. (25)	VALUE (U.S. dollars, omit cents) (Selling price or cost if not sold) (26)

27. LICENSE NO./LICENSE EXCEPTION SYMBOL/ AUTHORIZATION	28. ECCN (When required)
29. Duly authorized officer or employee	The USPPI authorizes the forwarder named above to act as forwarding agent for export control and customs purposes.
30. I certify that all statements made and all information contained herein are true and correct and that I have read and understand the instructions for preparation of this document, set forth in **the "Correct Way to Fill Out the Shipper's Export Declaration."** I understand that civil and criminal penalties, including forfeiture and sale, may be imposed for making false or fraudulent statements herein, failing to provide the requested information or for violation of U.S. laws on exportation (13 U.S.C. Sec. 305; 22 & S.C. Sec. 401; 18 U.S.C. Sec. 1001; 50 U.S.C. App. 2410).	
Signature	Confidential - For use solely for official purposes authorized by the Secretary of Commerce
Title	Export shipments are subject to inspection by U.S. Customs Service and/or Office of Export Enforcement
Date	31. AUTHENTICATION (When required)
Telephone No. (include Area Code)	E-mail address

Figure 9.11   Shipper's Export Declaration (reprinted by permission of The Irwin Brown Company)

a foreign language, or vice versa. There are services that let you send your documents to them electronically and receive translations the same way, with very fast turnaround, but you should still have their work checked by a native speaker.

Most important, the computer revolution is in the process of changing radically the way documents are written and moved. The Irwin Brown Company in New Orleans, for example, is a customs broker and foreign freight forwarder that has established electronic data interchange (EDI) with its agents, customers, and import/ export service firms. An exporter can flash information to Irwin Brown, with which it can create documents to transmit electronically to steamship lines and other parties to the transaction. On the import side, Irwin Brown can receive electronic arrival notices from the steamship lines and then communicate by computer with import customers and with U.S. customs. In general, steamship lines have moved further with electronic data interchange than airlines have, but the gap is narrowing. U.S. Customs is strongly encouraging Electronic Data transaction of documents through its Electronic Data Interchange (EDI) and the Automated Broker Interface (ABI). The latter is used with a release form to allow for delivery of cargo, with an entry permit. The Automated Clearing House (ACH) is a new system whereby customs duties are simply deducted from the importer's bank account. The disadvantage is that, if for any reason too much duty is deducted, it may take quite a while for the importer to get a reimbursement.

Import/export service firms that do not keep up with the computer revolution are in danger of losing out completely to those that do. There are several firms that sell software, especially for importers and exporters, including Exits, Inc., in Easton, Connecticut, phone (203) 396-0022, fax (203) 374-8733. Their products include Quick Assistant for Export Documentation and Quick Advisor for the Exporter. Some others are Shipping Solutions at (888) 890-SHIP or www.shipsolutions.com, and Integrated Trade Systems at (888) 439-7676, or www. tradesolutions.com.

CHAPTER 10

Regulation of Foreign Trade

Like it or not, we live with a lot of regulations, and foreign trad-ers live with more than most other people do. On the import side, this is mainly because countries want to protect their industries from foreign competition, keep harmful products from entering the country, and earn revenue from customs duties. On the ex-port side, regulations are made to increase exports, keep some prod-ucts in the country for use there, and sometimes to keep strategic materials out of the hands of foreign competitors or enemies. Note that export regulation seems contradictory because it includes both incentives and restrictions.

This chapter looks in some detail at regulations on interna-tional trade, why they exist, and how to deal with them. Notice that I didn't say, "How to get around them." In most cases, that can't be done legally. We'll start with the U.S. Customs Service.

U.S. CUSTOMS SERVICE

The U.S. Customs Service is in the Department of the Treasury, which also includes, for example, the Federal Mint and the Internal Revenue Service. It is a potent government department, headquartered in Washington, D.C., and with offices throughout the United States and abroad. The main task of the customs service is to enforce the laws of the country at its borders, with respect to nearly everything except living human beings. The Immigration and Naturalization Service takes care of them.

Customs is responsible for enforcing laws with regard to both incoming and outgoing cargo. It can inspect part or all of any shipment and is normally not held liable for damage to products that might occur in the inspection process. It works closely with other U.S government agencies and with the customs departments in foreign countries.

After September 11, 2001, customs increased the percentage of cargo inspected as well as the intensity of its inspection procedures. This caused delays at ports and led to new efforts to use technology to make inspections faster and more effective. It also instituted the Customs Trade Partnership Against Terrorism. The partnership is between customs and participating importers. In addition, there are now some inspections of U.S.-bound shipments, performed in the countries of origin.

Your First Contact

To get a feel for customs and what it's all about, you should log on to the Customs web site at www.customs.gov. There is an incredible amount of information, so it can take a while to find what you want.

The following are some addresses on the site that will take you to specific kinds of information:

- Headquarters main telephone numbers: www.customs.gov/top/office.htm
- Ports of entry, with addresses and telephone numbers: www.customs.gov/top/office.htm

- Publication on U.S. import requirements, text and ordering instructions: www.customs.gov/top/contact.htm
- Harmonized Tariff Schedule of the United States, Annotated: www.dataweb.usitc.gov/scripts/tariff/toc.html
- Marketing country of origin: www.customs.gov/top/contact.htm
- NAFTA, A Guide to Customs Procedures: www.nafta-customs.org/docs/us/guideproc.html

Your concerns will probably relate to specific products that you are considering importing. For each such product, you will want to know its rate of duty and other regulations including how it should be marked. The rate of duty on a product depends on its country of origin and its tariff classification or Harmonized System (HS) number. This system is discussed in the next section.

To ask about duties and other information about specific products, you should have the HS numbers. This can be obtained from the book *The Harmonized System* in libraries, or on the U.S. Customs web site at www.customs.gov. Your computer will need Adobe Acrobat software. Also, you can call customs in your local port. With the HS number, the best way to get accurate information is by calling the national import specialists at New York Seaport Customs at phone (646) 733-3000 and fax (646) 733-3250. You can also buy an HS book, but get it from a U.S. government bookstore. The ones sold by private companies are expensive.

You can even get a binding ruling as to the classification and therefore the rate of duty on your product, which your customs broker can present to customs at whichever port your goods come in to. To get this, send a request in writing to the National Commodity Specialist Division, U.S. Customs, Attn. Classification Ruling Requests, New York, NY 10048. Please include all the information that will be needed to make a classification including specifications and perhaps a photograph. You can send a sample if you wish; however, it will not be returned.

The Harmonized System

On January 1, 1989, the United States adopted a new system of classifying and coding products in international trade—the Harmonized System. This system is very logical and has been adopted by most of the world's nations; it replaced several separate coding and classification systems that made statistical comparisons nearly impossible.

Figure 10.1 is a page from the *Harmonized Tariff Schedule of the United States* (2001). This particular page, from chapter 42 of the schedule, covers trunks, suitcases, and so forth. There are 99 chapters in all. If you follow the classification down, you will see that the classification "Handbags . . . of wood" is HS number 4202.29.20. Customs declarations should give the actual number (No.) of bags rather than some other unit of measure such as kilograms (kg) or dozens (dz). The rate of duty is 33 1/3 percent,

Harmonized Tariff Schedule of the United States (2001) (Rev. 1)
Annotated for Statistical Reporting Purposes

Heading /Subheading	Stat. Suf- fix	Article Description	Units of Quantity	Rates of Duty		
					1	2
				General	Special	
3302		Mixtures of odoriferous substances and mixtures (including alcoholic solutions) with a basis of one or more of these substances, of a kind used as raw materials in industry; other preparations based on odoriferous substances, of a kind used for the manufacture of beverages:				
3302.10		Of kind used in the food or drink Industries:				
3302.10 .10	00	Not containing Alcohol	Kg	Free		25%
		Containing Alcohol				
3302.10 .20	00	Containing not over 20% of alcohol by weight	Kg	Free 1/		$0.44/kg +25% 1/
		etc.				

1/ Imports under this provision are subject to Federal Excise Tax (26 U.S.C. 5001) if they contain one-half of 1 percent or more of alcohol by volume and if they are determined to be fit for beverage use.

Figure 10.1 Part of a page from the Harmonized Tariff Schedule of the United States. This figure has been retyped and reformatted to fit into this book.

3.3 percent, 1.0 percent, or free, depending on the country of origin.

The 33 1/3 percent duty is charged on wooden handbags from "Column 2" countries, which are not members of the World Trade Organization (WTO, formerly the GATT) and are not friendly with the United States. In 2001 these rates applied only to products of Afghanistan, Cuba, Laos, North Korea, and Vietnam, and trade relations with Vietnam should be normalized in 2002. There were a few other countries, such as Libya and Iraq, with which trade was almost entirely prohibited.

The rate of 3.3 percent is charged on handbags from "General" countries, that is, those that are WTO members but do not qualify for any of the various special privileges. These privileges are indicated in the "Special" column, which uses the following designations:

- A for countries that qualify for the Generalized System of Preferences, or GSP, which gives nearly all developing countries duty-free treatment on a wide variety of products. A* means that there are GSP products on which one or more countries lost the GSP privilege because they shipped too much to the United States.

- B is for products and countries that qualify under the Automotive Products Trade Act, C for those that qualify under the Agreement on Trade in Civil Aircraft, K for those that qualify under the Agreement on Trade in Pharmaceutical Products, and L for those that qualify under Uruguay Round Concessions on Intermediate Chemicals for Dyes.

- CA and MX indicate Canada and Mexico, our partners in NAFTA. Separate categories are still needed because Canada already receives duty-free treatment on nearly all products, but free trade with Mexico is being phased in over several years. See chapter 11 for more information about this.

- *D* indicates duty concessions under the relatively new African Growth and Opportunity Act.

- *E* and *E** indicate duty preferences under the Caribbean Basin Economic Recovery Act, under which most countries in the Caribbean and Central America receive duty-free treatment on all products except textiles, apparel, leather goods, and petroleum and its products, watches and watch parts, and canned tuna. The asterisk means the same as it does for GSP countries. There is now a "Caribbean Trade Partnership" which gives Caribbean countries approximately the same preference that NAFTA countries enjoy.

- *J* and *J** give almost the same preferences to the beneficiaries of the Andean Trade Preference Act, Colombia, Bolivia, Ecuador, and Peru. This provision of law expired on December 4, 2001, but was expected to be renewed.

- *IL* is for the United States–Israel Free Trade Act, which created a nearly complete free trade area of these two countries.

Note that our wooden handbags can enter free of duty from A, E, and J countries and from Israel and Canada. Mexico is charged a usurious 1 percent.

More about Customs Duties

U.S. Customs duties range from 0 to about 120 percent, with the average around 4 percent. This is one of the lowest average rates in the world. Duties raise money for the federal government and also give domestic producers some protection against products from abroad. Duties are negotiated in international "rounds" under the auspices of what is now the WTO and must be ratified by Congress.

Nearly all duty rates are ad valorem, which means a percentage of value, but they can also be "specific" (so much per item or per kilo) or "mixed" (ad valorem plus specific). Specific duties encourage importation of better grades or qualities of an item because the incidence (percentage of the value of the item) goes down as the value increases.

The United States charges duty on the first cost of an item, which normally is what you pay in the country of origin. That can be anywhere from ex factory to f.o.b. vessel, depending on the terms of sale. The United States does not charge duties on international transportation and insurance, although there are some countries that do. If you buy from an agent abroad, it may be better to use one who works for you rather than for your supplier. This is because buying commissions are not dutiable, while selling commissions are.

If there is a high duty on your product, you may want to consult a customs attorney or at least a good broker to see whether there is any way it can be reduced. The most common way is to make some change in the product that changes the HS number to one that has lower rates of duty.

Marking and Labeling

U.S. law requires that nearly all products be marked with the country of origin, in such a way that the final buyer can see and read the mark. The country name in English should be used, but the type and location of the marks vary. It should be on a sticker glued to the bottom of a crystal ash tray, die-stamped in most metal parts, sewn in the back of the neck of shirts, and so on. Be sure to ask customs about the country-of-origin mark for your product, and see "Marking Country of Origin" on the web site at www.customs.gov.

There are some products, such as clocks, for which separate marking of each major part is required. There are also cases of "transformation" which is not considered "substantial." For example, crude pistachio nuts from Iran that are roasted and bagged in the United States must still be identified as Iranian produce.

In a few instances, containers for products must be marked separately, in case they are emptied in the United States and then sold.

Proper marking is no laughing matter. If you import 100,000 candy bars, and the Swiss exporter doesn't put his country's name on them, you won't be able to sell them until they are marked properly. You might be able to get them released from customs by posting a bond, but you cannot deliver them to a customer until you have marked them, redelivered a sample to customs, and received approval. Sometimes customs will even clear and release goods that are improperly marked and then (within 30 days) request redelivery. If you can't take the shipment back to customs, you will be assessed a marking duty plus a penalty.

You should also ask a classification specialist what other information should be on the product or its package, or ask importers and study labels in a store. Some possibilities are instructions for laundering (apparel), ingredients and nutritional content (processed foods), and safety warnings (cigarettes). It is illegal to sell an imported product that lacks any of the required information.

In addition, you might ask which other federal agencies regulate the importation or sale of your product. There are several possibilities including the Food and Drug Administration, the Consumer Products Safety Commission, and the Department of Transportation. These will be discussed later in this chapter.

GETTING DEEPER INTO CUSTOMS

In some cases, especially with apparel products, the customs officer won't be able to tell you with certainty over the phone the classification of your product. If this occurs, make an appointment to visit customs with your product. A customs specialist can nearly always look at your product and tell you the exact classification and the correct rate of duty, although in some cases even they can disagree. Try it yourself: Are chocolate-covered cherries fruit or candy? Is a pointed piece of wire, with threads but no slot in the head, a screw or a nail? There are many other examples.

In some cases, a customs specialist can help you by suggesting ways of modifying the product to reduce the rate of duty. For example, dry onion powder from developing countries is charged a higher rate of duty than dry onion *flakes*. Maybe your buyer will take small flakes instead of powder. There was an extreme case a few years ago, before the Harmonized System was adopted: The trademark on a shipment of blue jeans was held to be ornamental because the *e* in the mark was slanted rather than straight, and that increased the rate of duty.

Customs Procedures

When your goods arrive at a port of entry, the air or steamship line should notify the party named on the documents. Of course, you should know, long before that, which ship or plane your goods will be on. You will want to act fast; you have only five working days to pick up the merchandise before it is taken to a customs warehouse. If that happens, you will have to pay cartage to the warehouse, storage charges, cartage out, and an extra broker's fee.

As stated before, you can clear shipments worth less than $2,000 (less than $250 for most textile, leather, and a few other products from most countries of origin) with an informal entry form. If the value is over $2,000 or if the shipment contains textile or leather products and you try to clear it yourself, you will be asked to complete an Immediate Delivery Entry Form and pay duty. Figure 10.2 lists the kinds of information you will need for this form.

You must also sign the following statement: "I hereby make application for entry/immediate delivery. I certify that the above information is accurate, the bond is sufficient, valid, and current, and that all requirements of 19 CFR Part 142 have been met." The CFR is the huge, huge *Code of Federal Regulations* of the United States.

Contents of an Immediate Delivery Entry

Arrival date of the goods and entry date through customs

Type of entry (usually "Consumption" and entry number)

Single transaction bond information (if you need a bond)

File numbers of the broker, consignee, and importer (which could all be the same)

Name of the ultimate consignee and the importer (which could be the same)

The carrier code and number and location of the goods

The vessel code or name and the port of unlading

The manifest number, the "G.O." number, and the total value

The bill of lading or airway bill code and number

The quantity, HS number, country of origin, and manufacturer's number for each kind of merchandise in the shipment

---

Figure 10.2 Contents of an Immediate Delivery Entry

As you can see, this entry form is not one that you can easily fill out yourself the first time you try it. It is usually wise to use a customs broker the first time so you will have an example to follow.

After filing the Immediate Delivery Entry Form, the broker has 10 working days to file an entry summary with the commercial invoice and other documents and a check for the duty. Customs then has 30 days in which to accept or reject it. UNZ & Company sells both of the preceding forms and, of course, customs offices have them, as well. The Entry Summary asks for forty numbered kinds of information, which can be summarized as shown in Figure 10.3. The entry summary for goods that are under quota, such as textile and dairy products, must be filed when the goods arrive.

Contents of an Entr y Summar y

Entry number, type, and date

Port code, bond number, type of bond

Manufacturer's identification number and reference number

Foreigh port, mode of transportation, bill of lading, or air waybill number

Country of origin, exporting country, export date

Broker or importer number, importer name and address

Ultimate consignee name, address and number

Importing carrier, U.S. port, import date

Merchandise commodity numbers, weights, quantities, values, duty rates, duty amounts, taxes, other charges

Location of goods in the USA

Figure 10.3   Contents of an Entry Summary

In other words, you will normally have your merchandise before the duty is paid. How does customs know you will pay the duty? That is one function of the bond that was discussed in chapter 9.

In some cases, especially when goods are highly perishable, your broker may be able to get them precleared so they will be released from customs as soon as they arrive in the United States. This is becoming increasingly common, especially as more shipping lines, customs brokers, and ports begin using the Automated Manifest System and the Automated Broker Interface (with customs). You should, however, ask if there will be preclearance fees.

The final step in the entry process is called *liquidation*. This is when a commodity specialist reviews the entry, within one year, and decides whether the proper duty was paid. When this happens, you will receive a notice that liquidation has taken place. If you feel that customs has charged too much for duty, you have 90 days from the date of liquidation to file a protest. If this protest is denied, you have 180 days from the date of the denial in which to file a summons with the U.S. Court of International Trade. This gets you into the big time, and you will need a big-time customs attorney.

There is also a customs user fee charged on entries of goods other than from Canada, Mexico, Israel, and the Caribbean and Andean countries. This fee is 0.21 percent of "customs value," with a minimum of $25 and a maximum of $485 per entry. In some cases, there are small fees (no more than $9) charged on informal entries as well.

Quotas on Imports

Most textiles and apparel, cheese, chocolate, and other products are subject to U.S. import quotas. They serve to protect domestic industry, by limiting the supply and therefore raising the prices of foreign products to U.S. consumers, and to allocate production among supplying countries. For example, quotas on ladies' blouses from Korea, China, and Hong Kong limit their sales to the United States and so permit several other countries to take part of the market.

Most of the quotas are fixed ceilings on the quantities of an item that can be imported each calendar year from each country. For example, the 2001 quota on men's cotton shirts from Malaysia is a certain number of dozens. There are also *tariff rate quotas*, which means that the rate of duty increases each year when a certain quantity of an item has cleared U.S. Customs.

Foreign governments need systems for deciding which of their companies will be able to use their quotas in the U.S. market, and, of course, they want to get the highest possible value of exports from the allowable quantities. They use different systems to allocate quotas, including auctioning them in blocks. Holders of quotas are often permitted to sell them to other suppliers who can get higher prices from their U.S. buyers.

U.S. Customs helps many countries enforce their quota arrangements by requiring that import shipments of quota goods be accompanied by visas, issued by the competent authorities in the exporting countries. This means that, if your shipment of men's cotton shirts from Malaysia reaches U.S. Customs and there is no visa among the documents, they cannot be entered. You can apply to the Malaysian Consulate for a visa, but it will not be granted unless the responsible agency in Kuala Lumpur gives its consent.

Classification specialists in customs' district offices should know the details of quotas on the items they handle, but even they cannot always tell you the annual quota on a specific item from a specific country or how much of the year's quota is still available. They can, however, translate the HS number of your product into a quota category number. Then you can check the web at www.customs.gov/impoexpo/impoexpo.htm to find out the quota and the status of its fulfillment. It will take you a while to learn to interpret this data. Also, you can look for the "Quota Watch" column in the *Journal of Commerce*.

Occasionally, a product will be in a special *watched* status. In such a case, you will need a visa to import it, even if it is not actually under quota.

Extra Duties

There are occasionally circumstances in which importers are charged extra duties. For example, if the U.S. government determines that a foreign country is subsidizing its exports and that, for members of the GATT (General Agreement on Traffic and Trade), imports of the subsidized goods are hurting American producers, a *countervailing duty* can be applied to counteract the subsidies. Also, if the government finds that a country is "dumping" goods on the U.S. market (selling in the United States at less than the fair market value in the country of origin), an antidumping duty may be charged.

In addition, there are sometimes extra duties or import prohibitions to try to pressure foreign countries into opening their markets to U.S. goods or protecting intellectual property (patents, copyrights, and so forth) of U.S. firms. In 1990, for example, very high duties levied on several Brazilian products had a lot to do with opening Brazil's market to U.S. computer products.

Temporary Entries

If you want to ship goods through the United States without paying duty on them, such as from Mexico to Canada, you can do so with a bond and a special kind of customs entry. The same applies to goods that are in the country temporarily for repair or to be exhibited in a trade show. Your customs broker can help you with this kind of temporary importation under bond, or TIB.

You can also use a special customs entry to bring goods into the United States and warehouse them, without paying duty, until you either reexport them or enter them into the commerce of the United States. Only minor processing, such as repackaging, can be done in a bonded warehouse.

If you care to bring the goods into a *foreign trade zone*—an area under customs control that you can find in major ports and some inland cities—you can do almost any kind of processing. You can, for example, import foreign parts for small engines and combine them with U.S. parts in a foreign trade zone. If you export the engines, you never pay customs duty on the imported parts. If you sell them in the United States, you can pay duty on the imported parts or on the finished engines, whichever is lower. The raison d'être of these zones diminishes as import duties decrease.

Finally, you can bring goods such as components into the United States under a *drawback* entry. Then, if you later reexport them, even if they have been combined with U.S. components to make finished goods, you can "draw back" most of the duty that was paid. You can even draw back duty if the components you export are not the same as the ones you brought in with a drawback entry, as long as they are identical.

There are still other types of customs entries that you can find out about in the book *A Basic Guide to Importing*, prepared by the U.S. Customs Service. Every importer should buy a copy in a U.S. government bookstore or order one from the Superintendent of Documents, U.S. Government Printing Office, Washington, DC 20402, or read it on the web.

OTHER FEDERAL REGULATIONS

There are numerous federal laws that affect both domestic and imported goods. The detailed text of each is printed in the *Code of Federal Regulations*, but importers usually get information about them from the concerned government agencies. The following is a summary of some (though not all) of these laws. Much of the information is from the book just mentioned, *A Basic Guide to Importing*.

Food Products

The Federal Food, Drug and Cosmetic Act is the basic legislation governing imports of products that go in or on the body, including both human and animal bodies; the responsible agency is the Department of Health and Human Services of the Food and Drug Administration (FDA), Rockville, Maryland 20857. The telephone number of the Division of Import Operations and Policy is (301) 443-6553. Each FDA district is the final authority for products entering through ports in its area. You can't get a ruling in Florida that says your canned strawberries can be imported in Oregon.

Moreover, the FDA will not analyze your product before you import it to tell you whether it will pass inspection. You should probably have it analyzed yourself by a private company that is familiar with FDA regulations. Otherwise, you will risk bringing in a shipment that cannot enter into the United States. One such company is Food Products Laboratory in Portland, Oregon (phone (503) 253-9136).

Neither will the FDA tell you, anymore, whether the label on your can, bottle, or package is satisfactory. This is important because there are numerous requirements about information on labels on food products, and they were changed as recently as May 2001. A significant example is the special nutrition label, which must be on most processed foods whether produced in the United States or abroad. Very small manufacturers are exempt from this requirement, but even medium-sized firms overseas may not have enough information on the nutritional content of their products to produce a correct label.

If you are considering importing processed foods, you may want to use the services of a specialized consultant such as Phoenix Regulatory Associates in Virginia, phone (703) 406-0906, fax (703) 406-9513. You could copy the label of a similar product and try it on a small shipment, but try to ask customs when that shipment comes in if the label is all right. Otherwise, the inspector might overlook a technicality but stop your next (larger) shipment. Also, copying a nutrition label would be very risky because the composition of products can vary greatly.

A food product must meet certain criteria to be given a *statement of identity* such as "catsup." Requirements for "catsup," "dill pickles," and so on are spelled out in the *Code of Federal Regulations*, Title 21, Parts 100–169. The label should also give the net weight of the product in ounces (in the lower 30 percent of the label), the ingredients in descending order of predominance by weight, and the name and place of business of the manufacturer, packer, or distributor.

Food products processed at high temperatures are more likely to meet FDA standards than other food products, provided they are properly handled and packed. There is a category of so-called "low acid" canned foods for which the producer must obtain a special Food Canning Establishment, or FCE, number in order to export to the United States. The process of obtaining this can be long and complex.

The FDA is keeping up with the times and has begun using an Electronic Entry Processing System (EEPS). This system requires the use of an FDA code for each commodity. Contact your nearest FDA office for the easiest way to get an EEPS number in your area.

Meat and Poultry

Fresh and frozen meat, poultry, and related products are allowed only from foreign factories that have been approved to export to the United States. The fear is that meat from diseased animals will be processed and shipped or that conditions in the slaughterhouse will be unsanitary. Even some industrialized Western countries do not sell raw meat to the United States because none of their factories have the necessary certification. The recent problems with "mad cow" disease and hoof-and-mouth disease have shown the importance of regulating imports of animals, meat, and hides.

The principal agencies involved with these products are the Food Safety and Quality Service and the Animal and Plant Health Inspection Service, both of the U.S. Department of Agriculture (USDA). For some kinds of poultry, such as quail, you should also consult the Fish and Wildlife Service or the Department of the Interior.

Fresh Fruits and Vegetables

Because of increased health consciousness and other factors, U.S. imports of fruits and vegetables have skyrocketed in recent years.

When fresh produce comes in counterseasonal to production in this country, consumers and middlepersons are very pleased and U.S. producers do not get hurt. In fact, some U.S. farming organizations have stabilized their incomes throughout the year by becoming importers as well as producing in the United States.

Fresh produce imports are limited to specific items from specific countries, upon approval by the Animal and Plant Health Inspection Service of the USDA (which has also recently begun checking some export shipments). This is to control the entry of insect pests that might damage U.S. agriculture. There are also strict limitations on pesticide residues, established by the Environmental Protection Agency and enforced by the FDA. Finally, several kinds of produce are subject to "Marketing Orders," related to quality. These are established by the Agricultural Marketing Service, USDA, Washington, DC 20250. Look on the web at www.ams.usda.gov.

Dairy Products

Many types of cheese are under quota and require import licenses. Contact the Foreign Agricultural Service, USDA, Washington, DC 20250, or search the customs or USDA web site. Milk and cream are regulated by both the FDA and the USDA. Milk is under a tariff rate quota, which, as you saw earlier in this chapter, means that the duty goes up after a specific quantity is imported each year. Condensed and evaporated milk, cream, and ice cream are under absolute quotas.

Other Food Products

There are quotas on various food products including several species of fish, potatoes, chocolate, sugar, and peanuts. Candy containing more than 0.5 percent alcohol is prohibited entirely.

Unexpected things can happen. A few years ago, U.S. companies found that it was profitable to import food products containing large amounts of sugar, extract the sugar, and sell it. This was possible because the price of sugar in the United States is maintained at more than twice the world price in order to protect the beet growers in the south and midwest and the cane growers in Hawaii. The government responded to this sugar extraction business by temporarily banning imports of a category of miscellaneous foods items, some of which did not contain any sugar at all. The measure was put into effect so suddenly that quite a bit of merchandise that had been bought and shipped was illegal by the time it reached the United States.

Textiles and Apparel

Textile and apparel imports are subject to numerous requirements. They must be labeled with the country of origin, fiber content, laundering instructions, and the name or trademark of the producer, importer, or marketing organization. A registration number, or RN, obtained from the Federal Trade Commission, can be substituted for some of this information. The Federal Trade Commission, Washington, DC 20580, can give you information about requirements of the Textile Fiber Identification Act and the Wool Products Labeling Act. Also, there is extensive information on the customs web site.

When the Harmonized System took effect in the United States on January 1, 1990, the soft-goods importing community expected massive confusion because of changes in the codes, classifications, and duty rates of so many items. In-depth information was presented in numerous publications and seminars, and the transition was made with very little trouble. One problem is that many fabrics are blends of different materials, such as polyester and cotton. For proper classification, you need to know the relative content, by weight, of each kind of fiber.

You should check also on regulations enforced by the Consumer Products Safety Commission, especially with regard to flammability of fabrics. Their address is 4330 East-West Highway,

Bethesda, MD 20814, and they are on the web at www.cpsc.gov. In the United States and several other countries, some products cannot be imported if they are flammable. Be very careful about ordering items such as children's pajamas, especially from developing countries.

Regulations on importing textiles and apparel from Caribbean Basin and many African countries were liberalized early in 2001, but they are still onerous. For example, if you say your product is made in Jamaica, but Customs finds that it was not made entirely in Jamaica and does not satisfy the "country of origin" requirements in the Caribbean Basin Trade Preference Act, you can be subject to a severe penalty.

Alcoholic Beverages

Imports to the United States of beer, wine, and liquor are so highly regulated that you will probably want to avoid dealing with these products. First, you'll need an Importer's Basic Permit from the Bureau of Alcohol, Tobacco and Firearms, Department of the Treasury, Washington, DC 20226, phone (202) 927-8110. You will have to fill out forms and pay a fee (technically a tax) of around $500, and you are unlikely to be approved if you have a criminal record or have ever declared bankruptcy. You will also need a wholesaler's permit from the state to which you plan to import. This usually costs more than the Importer's Basic Permit but is easier to obtain. Unfortunately, you need a different permit for each state in which you plan to sell. This regulation is being challenged by Internet merchants, and the outcome is uncertain.

For wine and liquor, the bottles must be in metric sizes and the labels must be approved in advance by the Bureau of Alcohol, Tobacco and Firearms. There are several label requirements, one of which is the government health warning. Another, in several states, is that the alcohol content be printed on the label. In some states, beer labels also need prior approval.

For liquor, you will need to buy federal red strip stamps to place on the bottles. These are evidence that the excise tax has been paid. If you import liquor without the strips, you will have to buy them and paste them on before making deliveries. Alcoholic beverages are also subject to inspection by the FDA.

Motor Vehicles

Two kinds of laws apply to cars, trucks, and motorcycles—safety and environmental cleanliness. Imported vehicles manufactured after December 31, 1967, must conform to safety regulations. For information, contact the Office of Enforcement, Motor Vehicle Program, National Highway Traffic Safety Administration, U.S. Department of Transportation, Washington, DC 20590. *All* imported vehicles must meet the requirements of the Clean Air Act. Information about this is available from the Public Information Center, Environmental Protection Agency, Washington, DC 20460. Finally, used vehicles must be fumigated by the Department of Agriculture.

It used to be fairly easy for an individual to go overseas, buy a new or used car, and import it to the United States. It could be brought up to U.S. standards in the foreign country or in the United States. Now, however, usually only authorized importers can bring in automobiles. The stated reason for this is to make sure that all imported vehicles meet the safety and clean air standards. Of course, there may be another reason—to help automobile dealers by reducing the number of people who import their own cars.

Contact the customs district office in your area to find out which firms have been approved to import motor vehicles. For general information, call customs at (202) 354-1000.

Other Products

Household appliances are subject to consumer products safety, energy efficiency, and energy labeling laws. For information, contact the Public and Consumer Affairs Office, U.S. Department of Energy, Washington, DC 20585, and the Division of Energy and Product Information, Federal Trade Commission, Washington, DC 20580.

Electronic products that emit radiation must meet standards enforced by the Center for Devices and Radiological Health, FDA, 1390 Picard Drive, Rockville, MD 20850. For electronic products that broadcast on the airwaves, contact the Federal Communications Commission, Washington, DC 20554.

Plants and plant products must always be inspected at the border, by the Animal and Plant Health Inspection Service of the USDA, for potentially destructive insect pests.

Drugs and cosmetics must be safe for human use and are subject to inspection and approval by the FDA. The testing period is long and the standards are strict. One result is that many remedies are much cheaper abroad than in the United States or are simply not available in this country. The FDA receives a lot of pressure to reduce its standards, but its main concern is the health and safety of the public.

Pesticides and toxic substances are regulated by the Office of Pesticides and Toxic Substances, Environmental Protection Agency, Washington, DC 20460. The telephone number of the Toxic Substances Control Act Assistance Information Service is (202) 554-1404.

Hazardous substances, such as dangerous chemicals, must meet regulations enforced by the FDA and the Consumer Products Safety Commission. Their transportation is closely regulated by the Hazardous Materials Safety Bureau, U.S. Department of Transportation, Washington, DC 20590.

STATE AND LOCAL REGULATIONS

Government authority in the United States is fragmented among various jurisdictions. Individual states regulate some products. Toys for children, for example, can't be sold in many areas without being approved by the consumer protection offices of the state governments. With imported toys, it is usually the importer who has to apply for (and pay for) state approval.

I once assisted a Chilean company that was making light switches and other simple electrical goods and was planning to export them to the United States. Federal regulations presented no difficulties, but no city or county would buy the products unless they met local standards. We had to begin by contacting Underwriters Laboratories (UL) in Northbrook, Illinois, and having both the products and the factory in Chile inspected by UL personnel. Then, even with UL approval, we had to establish that the products met building standards in some of the cities where they were to be sold.

Counties and towns often regulate the thickness of insulation in houses, the color of trash cans, the size of mail boxes, and so on. If you import 1-inch-high street numbers for houses, and a new county law specifies 2-inch numbers, you'll have to find a new supplier or get your existing supplier to retool in a hurry.

How do you find out about these kinds of regulations? First, look carefully at products like yours in stores to see whether there is any mark or label on them that you don't understand. If there is, find out what it is and why it is there. Second, ask people in the trade as well as local government authorities. Look especially for new environmental regulations.

At the same time, keep your eyes open for new ordinances that are about to be enacted. If your town is debating a dog litter law, there may be a market for leashes and pooper scoopers. If it is about to start a complete trash recycling program, every house will need containers for glass and tin, newspaper, wet garbage, and miscellaneous trash.

REGULATION OF EXPORTS

A lawyer specializing in international trade could probably list a hundred laws that affect small-scale export operations. I will mention just a few—those that are most likely to be encountered by small-scale exporters. They are the Trading with the Enemy Act, the Business Practices and Records Act, the Anti-Boycott Law, and those involving tax incentives.

Trading with the Enemy Act

The Trading with the Enemy Act authorizes most of the U.S. export control regulations. These regulations are to prevent harming the U.S. national interest by exporting products that are in scarce supply at home (very few) or that should be kept in the United States in order to maintain this country's military and industrial positions. In general, the less friendly a country is with the United States, the fewer products can be exported under open general license (OGL). An OGL is for nonrestricted product–destination combinations. An exporter can give such a license to him- or herself, by simply writing "G-DEST" (general license for this destination) in the box reserved for the license symbol (box 27) on the Shipper's Export Declaration. Also, the less friendly a country is with the United States, the harder it is to get "validated" licenses for products that require them.

The first step in complying with export control legislation is to find your product on the Commodity Control List (CCL). You can look on a Commerce Department web site (www.bxa.doc.gov), or in 15 CFR, Section 399. Also you can find the list in the book *U.S. Export Administration Regulations,* available from the Superintendent of Documents, U.S. Government Printing Office, Washington, DC 20402, phone (202) 512-1800. When you find your product on this list, you will see a four-digit Export Commodity Control Number (ECCN). You will also see a letter, from A to M (not all letters from A to M are used). This letter indicates the country groups for which your product requires a validated license.

Next, you must look at the Country List, which is available

on the web site, at Department of Commerce field offices, and is in 15 CFR, Part 370. For example, the letter G after your ECCN on the commodity control list means that your product needs a validated license for S and Z countries. From the Country List you can tell whether your destination is an S or Z country. If it is, you need to get a rather complicated form and submit it to the Department of Commerce for approval of your export shipment. You can now do this on the Internet through the "BXA" site given agove. The same web site gives names, telephone numbers, and e-mail addresses of persons who can help with this process.

Applications for export licenses are supposed to be approved within two weeks, unless they have to be reviewed also by the Department of Defense. Then it can take much longer. Sometimes requests even go to Congress, as when Saudi Arabia places a major order for military equipment with a U.S. firm.

There are some special types of export licenses, and there are often requirements that applications be accompanied by special statements or certificates. You may have to state on your bill of lading or airway bill that the product cannot be diverted to a third country without authorization from the U.S. government, and your buyer may have to provide a written statement that the product will not be diverted. Every shipment that requires a validated license, no matter what its value or destination, also requires a shippers' export declaration.

If you want to find out what is happening to your application for a license, call Stela. Her complete name is System for Tracking Export License Applications, and her telephone number is (202) 482-2752. There is also an Automated License and Information Network, or ALAIN.

With the changes in Eastern Europe, the export license categories are under nearly constant review. Many of us hope that, in the near future, the licensing process will be simplified and licensing itself will become less important.

Business Practices and Records Act

The Business Practices and Records Act replaced the Anti-Foreign Corrupt Practices Act, which was commonly known as the "anti-bribery law." The intent is to enhance the United States' image by reducing bribery by U.S. firms abroad. The primary means of enforcement is by the recordkeeping requirements that are built into the act.

Essentially, this law makes it illegal for U.S. exporters to bribe foreign officials to do something that is not one of their normal functions. Of course, the definitions of *bribe, foreign official,* and other terms are critical. It is legal to give a small payment to a foreign customs inspector to get your shipment cleared expeditiously. The small payment would not be considered a bribe, the customs inspector would not be considered a foreign official, and clearing your shipment expeditiously is one of his normal functions. It is *not* legal to give the brother of the Minister of Health several thousand dollars to bring about the purchase of your line of antibiotics. If your foreign sales agent pays a bribe and you didn't know about it, you can still be held accountable if the Justice Department believes that you *should* have known about it.

Most recent U.S. government administrations, however, have realized that not being able to offer bribes puts U.S. firms at a competitive disadvantage with regard to firms of other countries. Therefore, the law has not been enforced very diligently. Still, there have been major convictions with regard to selling aircraft to The Netherlands, petroleum equipment to Mexico, and so on. Also, other countries are slowly joining the United States in trying to reduce corruption.

Anti-Boycott Law

Talk about a law that has teeth in it! The fines imposed on one who violates the Anti-Boycott Law can be high enough to really hurt! This legislation was designed to counter the Arab boycott of Israel, but it applies to any boycott that the U.S. government does not support.

You may, for example, be asked by a buyer in Syria to certify that your goods are not of Israeli origin, were not made by an Israeli-owned company, and will not be shipped on Israeli vessels. If you make such a statement, you will be in violation of U.S. law. You can usually make a positive statement, such as certifying that the goods *are* a product of the United States.

If you receive a boycott request, it should be reported to the USDC in Washington, D.C. Your USDC field office or a specialized attorney can advise you as to what you can and cannot do to avoid getting into trouble. If you receive a letter of credit that contains boycott provisions, your bank will probably refuse to handle it.

DISCs and FISCs

You may have heard of tax incentives known as DISCs and FISCs, perhaps because U.S. exporters would like to make them more useful while foreign exporters would like to see them abolished. The former is a domestic international sales corporation, and the latter is a foreign sales corporation. Both are legal devices to reduce the tax burden on U.S. exporters.

The DISC law allowed U.S. exporters to channel their exports through shell corporations, on their own premises if they wished, and to postpone payment of income tax on part of the export profits. When the GATT ruled that this was a subsidy, the rules of DISCs were changed, effective January 1, 1985, to make them less attractive and FISCs were created.

A FISC must be a separate corporation, which is set up offshore in an approved country and which has personnel to handle export paperwork. Export transactions (not actual merchandise) are routed through the FISC, and income taxes on a portion of the profits are waived. Your company alone may be too small to own its own FISC, but the law allows trade groups and associa-tions to set up FISCs that serve all their members. If you become a substantial exporter, these tax incentives will definitely be worth looking into.

An easy way to get more information is on the web site of Export FSC International Ltd., www.exportfsc.com.

Foreign Import Regulations

Remember that, in addition to U.S. regulations on exports, you will have to consider foreign countries' import regulations. These vary considerably and can be quite stringent. However, help is available from several sources including your foreign buyers, the U.S. Department of Commerce, and consulates of the countries to which you are selling.

For example, exporters of foods, food additives, dietary supple-ments, cosmetics, and animal feeds must sometimes provide what is known as a "Certificate of Free Sale." This says, essentially, that the product complies with all U.S. laws and standards. This cer-tificate is available from some trade associations and state gov-ernment export promotion offices. It is also available from the U.S. Food and Drug Administration, for just $10, but there may be a delay of several weeks in receiving it.

CHAPTER 11

NAFTA, GATT, and Other Trade Pacts

If you're planning on becoming a globe-trotting (at least by telephone and e-mail) international businessperson, it is vital that you have at least a rudimentary understanding of how international trade is being affected by recent and upcoming trade agreements between nations. NAFTA, the GATT, and other pacts may seem like abstractions, but they will have serious impact on your business. Here is a brief rundown of those agreements, how they will affect your business, and what the future might hold.

WHAT ARE THESE THINGS, ANYWAY?

Historically, countries have restricted imports for reasons already mentioned in this book. For the law of international comparative advantage to work, by increasing specialization according to the different countries' endowments, barriers to trade must be low. In most cases, however, countries have not seen fit to lower their import barriers *unilaterally*. They have negotiated with one or more other countries to lower barriers simultaneously for their mutual benefit. The resulting agreements are normally categorized as follows:

- *Free trade areas*, in which member countries eliminate most or all of their tariff and quota barriers to trade with each other, but each keeps its own barriers to the rest of the world. The countries must then agree on *rules of origin* to prevent foreign products from coming into the country that has the lowest duty and then moving freely to the other member countries

- *Customs unions*, in which member countries eliminate most or all of their tariff and quota barriers to trade with each other and agree on a *common external tariff* to the rest of the world

- *Common markets*, which are customs unions that also reduce or eliminate barriers on movement of labor and capital

These simple concepts get very complicated in practice because traded goods (and services) affect and are affected by many elements of a country's economy and society. Regulations to preserve and protect the environment, for example, vary greatly from one country to another. If Country X establishes free trade with Country Y, must it accept merchandise whose *production* hurts the environment in Country Y? Must it accept merchandise that is legal in Country Y but whose *use* might hurt the local environment? Should it try to impose its environmental standards and regulations on Country Y, which may be at a lower stage of development and unable to afford them? Alternatively, should it accept Country Y's lower standards to make the trade agreement work smoothly? There are thousands of these kinds of questions that must be faced in the implementation of a trade agreement.

For example, you may have heard that in June of 2001 a part of the United Nations known as the Convention on International Trade in Endangered Species (CITES) determined that the Caspian states of Russia and Turkmenistan should not be allowed to export more caviar unless they presented a feasible plan for protecting stocks of sturgeon. This small statement by a little-known organization affected carriers, importers, distributors, restaurants, and consumers in a variety of countries.

The more countries that are involved in a trade agreement, the harder it is to negotiate and implement. That is why the European Union, formerly the European Community, and before that various other names, has developed slowly over many years and has such a large and costly bureaucracy. Yet application of the theory of comparative advantage is much more useful when applied to several countries with diverse economies. Joining two countries that produce apples in autumn is not nearly as beneficial as joining two that produce apples in different seasons or one that grows apples (South Korea) and another that grows bananas (Taiwan).

By the way, the Theory of *Comparative* Advantage is in large part giving way to the newer Theory of *Competitive* Advantage. "Comparative" advantage says that a country will export things it can produce the cheapest, relative to its trading partners, based on natural endowments such as land, minerals, and labor. "Competitive" advantage recognizes the importance of policies, skills, and so forth. For example, a country will be less competitive if it has a tax on exports and more competitive if its government helps with market research or promotion.

Opposition to Free Trade

While freer trade nearly always has net benefits to a society, not everyone is a winner. The industries that are high-cost producers because they do not have comparative advantages are often injured. Industries that do have comparative advantages but are inefficient because they have enjoyed high protective tariffs are also injured. One could argue that they deserve to be, but this does not stop them from trying to embarrass and influence the government that, as they see it, is signing away their livelihoods.

The United States is no exception with regard to opposition to trade agreements. The first attempt to form a world trade organization, after the Second World War, failed because the U.S. Congress would not ratify it. In its place, 23 nations signed a simpler document, a "General Agreement on Tariffs and Trade," which became known as the GATT and was expanded through the years. Almost 40 years later, the Secretariat of the GATT was effectively turned into the World Trade Organization, or WTO.

In recent years we have seen or at least become more aware of ultranationalists who dislike trade agreements because they fear that the United States will lose its autonomy. While it is true that any agreement imposes restrictions on the parties to it, trade agreements are carefully negotiated and have escape clauses so that countries do not give up many of their prerogatives. Also, in many cases complete autonomy is not for the common good. If one country keeps out the products of another because of, for example, claims that they are unhealthful, it should have to substantiate the claims, admit the product, or at least tell the truth about why it will not admit the product.

Other very nationalistic persons, such as Ross Perot and Pat Choate, say they are against trade agreements because they will cost U.S. jobs. Several studies have shown that, when the United States enters into a trade agreement, there is usually a net job *gain*. Unfortunately, the word *net* means only that there are more winners than losers. If new exports create 100 new and high-paying jobs, while new imports cause a smaller number of lower paying jobs to be lost, the country as a whole will be better off. It is, however, quite logical that the people whose jobs are lost will be bitter and will complain. It is also logical that the political process will produce candidates who reflect the feelings of these people.

THE GATT AND THE WTO

The GATT and the WTO are the world's most far-reaching global trade arrangements.

About the GATT

After its formation in 1947, the GATT developed into an international forum and organization devoted to increasing international trade. It did this mainly by bringing trading nations together in meetings called *rounds* to negotiate reductions in their import duties. Each round lasted several years. Members were to give equal treatment (*nondiscrimination*) to all member countries, except that they could discriminate *in favor of* less developed countries by giving them special privileges such as the Generalized System of Preferences. Also, member countries could enter into trade agreements, such as free trade areas, and give preferential treatment to their partners in these agreements.

The GATT also provided a forum for discussion and settlement of trade disputes. After much discussion and negotiation, it could even *authorize* a country to retaliate by raising trade barriers against a nation that is violating GATT rules by keeping its products out.

The coverage of GATT agreements has extended to most manufactured goods traded by well over 100 countries. Trade in agricultural products was not included until only recently, at least in part because European countries did not want an agreement by which they would have to reduce their subsidies to farmers. Trade in services was also a difficult issue because developing countries are weak as service providers. They feared that an agreement in this area would lead to dominance in their markets by banks, insurance companies, and the like from the United States, Western Europe, and Japan.

The Uruguay Round

The Uruguay Round of the GATT lasted several years and culminated in a series of agreements, which were signed by 113 countries in Morocco on May 3, 1994. Six other countries withheld their signatures until their governments could ratify the agreements.

The governments signed the GATT 1994 as well as agreements in the following areas:

- Agriculture
- Application of Sanitary and Phytosanitary Measures
- Textiles and Clothing
- Technical Barriers to Trade
- Trade-Related Investment Measures
- Implementation of Article VI of the GATT 1994 (on dumping)
- Implementation of Article VII of the GATT 1994 (on valuation of goods)
- Preshipment Inspection
- Rules of Origin
- Import Licensing Procedures
- Subsidies and Countervailing Measures (to counteract exporting countries' subsidies)
- Safeguards (against harm to a country's industries)
- Trade in Services
- Trade-Related Aspects of Intellectual Property Rights
- Rules and Procedures Governing Settlement of Disputes
- Trade Policy Review Mechanism
- Plurilateral Agreements on Trade in Civil Aircraft, Government Procurement, Dairy Products, and Bovine Meat Products

There were also 24 Ministerial Commitments and Declarations and an Understanding on Commitments in Financial Services. One wonders how this round could *ever* be completed, but finally it was.

The bulk of the negotiations, of course, related to the *tariff concessions* that each country would make. Essentially, each country began with a list of what it would give and what it wanted in return. With 20,000 or so products in the Harmonized System, you can imagine how long some lists were and how hard it was *in each country* to reach decisions about what to offer and what to negotiate for. Many countries do not have the organization or the resources to do this well. One result is that some of these countries later submitted *rectification* proposals, which essentially means that they wanted to change what they agreed to and keep barriers to imports of selected products higher or keep them longer.

All in all, the Uruguay Round of the GATT can be considered highly successful. It will contribute to an expansion in world trade and therefore to higher standards of living.

The WTO

The GATT may have looked like an organization, but technically it wasn't one. It was an agreement with a secretariat to help implement it. Proponents of freer trade had long believed that an entity with more legal standing was needed to advance the process of trade liberalization and help keep nations from sliding backward into protectionism. On April 15, 1995, in Marrakech, Morocco, this was achieved. Article I of the Agreement Establishing the World Trade Organization says simply, "The World Trade Organization (hereinafter referred to as 'the WTO') is hereby established."

The scope of the WTO is, among other things, to "provide the common institutional framework for the conduct of trade relations among its Members." In general, its functions are to facilitate the implementation of trade agreements, to provide a forum for future trade negotiations, to administer the Understanding on Rules and Procedures Governing the Settlement of Disputes and the Trade Policy Review Mechanism, and to further greater coherence in global economic policy-making.

The WTO is to hold a meeting of its trade ministers every two years. According to the organization's director-general, the top priority of the meeting held in Singapore in December 1996 was "to advance enactment of trade liberalization commitments already undertaken and of negotiations already scheduled." He also called attention to important trading nations that were not yet WTO members but were pursuing membership, including China and Russia, and to the need for more concessions to help the least developed countries. Together, the 48 least developed countries had a population of 550 million people but accounted for less than 0.4 percent of total world trade. Their average per capita income was less than $500 per year.

The general meeting in 1998 was more or less peaceful and progressive, but you probably remember the troubles in Seattle in the year 2000. There were large numbers of protestors, some of whom were violent. They represented various beliefs and organizations, but in general felt that expanding world trade was giving large corporations too much power and was harming the environment, workers, less developed countries, and some sectors in the developed countries. The police in Seattle had not expected such opposition to the WTO, and so were not well prepared for it.

Still, the number of member countries has grown to 141 with the accession of Lithuania in May 2001. China joined on January 1, 2002, and Taiwan was admitted as a unique customs territory.

The WTO also has a General Council that meets more frequently and acts as a dispute settlement body, a Council for Trade in Goods, a Council for Trade in Services, and a Council for Trade-Related Aspects of Intellectual Property Rights. These councils can establish subsidiary bodies as they are needed. Finally, there are committees on Trade and Development, Balance-of-Payments Restrictions, and Budget, Finance and Administration. The secretariat of the GATT simply became the secretariat of the WTO. Selecting a director for an international organization is always very complex; after much debate, Renato Ruggiero of Italy was selected in 1995 to be the first leader of the WTO. Developing countries in general favored Carlos Salinas de Gotari, the outgoing president of Mexico, but political and economic problems in that country doomed his candidacy.

The bottom line of all this is that the WTO was established as a legal entity, to which each member state should accord "such privileges and immunities as are necessary for the exercise of its functions." It is the champion of all of us who are involved in importing and exporting.

NAFTA AND THE FTAA

The North American Free Trade Agreement (NAFTA) is real and is important. This section attempts to describe it in a few pages. The Free Trade Area of the Americas (FTAA) is scheduled to come into being on January 1, 2005. Will it, or won't it? The USDC says we are achieving "concrete progress." My heart says "right on" but, if I had to place a bet, it would be on the negative side.

NAFTA

International economists said for years that free trade in North America would be a boon to all the countries, but few people actually believed it could happen. In the early 1990s, Mexico was progressing and there were pro-trade governments in all three countries. Miraculously, an agreement was negotiated and signed in December 1992. Despite political battles in all three countries, the agreement was ratified in all three and went into effect on January 1, 1994. To a large extent, it was an expansion of the U.S.–Canada Free Trade Agreement, which had taken effect five years earlier.

NAFTA is intended to enhance prosperity in its member countries by increasing trilateral trade and investment, through elimination of both tariff and nontariff barriers. It eliminated some tariffs at the outset, and others are being reduced to zero over a period of years (a maximum of 15 years for the most sensitive products). There are complex Rules of Origin to determine whether an item is indeed a product of one or a combination of the three member countries. These rules are especially complex in the case of textile and apparel products. The basic rule is called *yarn-forward*. This means essentially that, for an item to be considered a NAFTA product, all processes, beginning with weaving of the yarn, should be done in the region.

There is a special Certificate of Origin form that must be used for shipments for which NAFTA duty rates are requested. This must be completed and signed by the exporter. On the form there are several "preference criteria," or ways that a good can qualify as a NAFTA product. There are also special rules on marking the country of origin.

The agreement also covers trade in services, investment, protection of intellectual property rights, and settlement of disputes. There are supplemental agreements relating to labor standards and environmental issues, although the effectiveness of these is still a subject of debate.

In the first year of NAFTA, two-way trade between the United States and Mexico increased by a phenomenal 23 percent. The early winners were U.S. exporters, but soon the Mexican peso was "cut loose" and allowed to find its value in the marketplace. This resulted in a sharp devaluation, which benefited Mexican importers. Since about 1996, growth in trade has been more balanced among the member countries.

All three countries have contact points to help their international traders take advantage of NAFTA. The U.S. section of the NAFTA secretariat is at the U.S. Department of Commerce, phone (613) 992-9388. The Mexican section is in Mexico City at phone 011-525-629-9630. Of course, there are numerous sites on the Internet that have information (and opinions) about NAFTA. The official site, that of the secretariat itself, is at www.nafta-sec-alena.org.

The FTAA

In June 1994, when the heads of state of nearly every country in the Western Hemisphere agreed to create a free trade area of the Americas in 10 years, it seemed that the obstacles could all be overcome. NAFTA already included three of the principal countries. Chile was expected to be the next to join, Trinidad was lobbying to be one of the first, and other countries were defining their positions.

But that was in June 1994. Shortly thereafter, the problems in Mexico and the U.S. congressional elections disrupted the process. Early accession for Chile was forgotten, and the Latin American and Caribbean nations began expanding their own trade areas. There are more than 20 of them, including the Southern Cone Common Market (MERCOSUR), the Andean Community, the Central American Common Market, and the Caribbean Community and Common Market (CARICOM). These various groups of countries could later merge into a larger trade area, especially if they had similar rules in such areas as valuation of goods, country of origin labeling, and sanitary and phytosanitary procedures. Some efforts are being made to harmonize decisions in these areas, but it has been very difficult for any country grouping to adopt the procedures followed by another grouping.

The trade ministers of participating countries are to meet once a year and to invite ideas and information from the business community. At the meeting in Colombia in March 1996, there was an Americas Business Forum immediately preceding the meeting of ministers. Incredible as it sounds, the Colombian hosts succeeded in publishing a report of the forum, in two languages, just hours after it ended. The Toronto Ministerial meeting in 2001 produced a number of declarations that were designed to keep the process moving. For more information, see the FTAA web site at www.alca.ftaa.org.

The bottom line of all this is, of course, that trade agreements create opportunities for traders. The closer we come to forming a

Free Trade Area of the Americas, the easier it will be for importers and exporters to buy, sell, transport, enter, and pay for merchandise. Also, lower (or zero) import duties will free up money that will somehow be shared by producers, merchants, and consumers. Two-way trade between the United States and its Latin American and Caribbean neighbors, which was valued at more than $190 billion in 1995, should expand considerably.

OTHER TRADE AGREEMENTS

Aside from these primary agreements, there are myriad other trade agreements with potential implications for your business.

Western Hemisphere

We have already seen that there are more than 20 trade agreements just in the Western Hemisphere. For the record, the most recent list reads as follows:

- Andean Community
- Association of Caribbean States
- Bolivia–MERCOSUR Trade Agreement
- Bolivia–Mexico Trade Agreement
- Caribbean–Canadian Common Market
- CARICOM
- Central American Free Trade Agreement
- Chile–Colombia Free Trade Agreement
- Chile–Ecuador Free Trade Agreement
- Chile–Mexico Free Trade Agreement
- Chile–Venezuela Free Trade Agreement
- Colombia–CARICOM Trade Agreement
- Colombia–Venezuela–Central American Free Trade Agreement

- Group of 3 (Colombia, Mexico, and Venezuela)
- Latin American Integration Association
- MERCOSUR
- Mexico–Central American Free Trade Agreement
- NAFTA
- Organization of East Caribbean States
- Rio Group (Mexico and most South American countries)
- U.S.–Andean Trade Preference Act
- Venezuela–CARICOM Trade Agreement

These can all be seen as steps on the way to hemispheric free trade; or as obstacles to it. I personally believe they are essential. Unification cannot come all at once; it must take place little by little. I doubt that it will take place by the year 2005, but I would love to be proven wrong.

A new trade agreement between the United States and Vietnam took effect on December 10, 2001, and it appears that an agreement between the United States and Chile will be finalized in 2002.

Other World Areas

Outside the Western Hemisphere, the most important grouping by far is the European Union (EU). It has grown to 15 countries and may someday absorb others. It cooperates closely with the European Free Trade Association (EFTA), which includes seven additional countries. This means that many U.S. and Canadian exports to Europe are at a disadvantage because they face entry barriers that are not faced by their competitors in Europe. This has led many firms to begin producing in Europe when they would not otherwise have done so. Our southern NAFTA partner, Mexico, faces fewer barriers because it is a beneficiary of the European Union's Generalized System of Preferences. For more information about the EU, see the web site, www.s700.uminho.pt/

ec.html. The site for EFTA is much simpler; it is www.efta.int (but can take a long time to come up on your screen).

Exporters to Europe must now pay great attention to the "green" movement there, which affects both products and their packaging. There has been a dramatic increase in the need for exporters to be certified to one of the various environmental standards and to have their products appropriately labeled. For example, bed linens and T-shirts should be manufactured without using harmful substances such as azo coloring agents. The fabric used should not be made of fiber that was produced with the use of toxic substances. Also, packaging must be brought into conformity with the European Directive on Packaging & Packaging Waste. There are waste reduction targets and designated ways of identifying packaging materials, such as PVC, for polyvinyl-chloride, which *must* be complied with as of January 1, 2001.

In Asia, the major organization of importance to world traders is called Asia Pacific Economic Cooperation, or APEC. The name bothers people because it isn't followed by a noun such as "Association" or "Group." Made up of 21 members—15 Asian nations and the United States, Canada, Mexico, Chile, Peru, and Russia—it is essentially a high-level organization for discussion and study of economic cooperation, but odds are that it will develop into a full free trade area. On the web see www.apec.org and www.apecsec.org.sg. Also, the ten-member Association of Southeast Asian Nations has established a free trade area. See www.asean.or-id.

Other groups worth mentioning are the Gulf Cooperation Council in the Middle East and the Economic Community of West African States. Other attempts at free trade have been and will be made, but it has been difficult to make them work as they should. A few powerful individuals, who may be hurt by free trade, can keep an entire country from reaping its benefits.

There may be changes in trade agreements between the United States and other countries or regions as a result of the war against terrorism. Both importers and exporters should be alert to commerical policy actions that might affect them.

CHAPTER 12

Sources of Information and Help

So, now you're set up in the import/export business. You're going to need information and help as you go along. There is surely *no one* who knows all the sources, and if someone did know them all today there would be new ones tomorrow. This chapter bears little resemblance to its counterpart in earlier editions of *Building an Import/Export Business*.

This chapter lays out a variety of places to get information and help, some of which have been mentioned earlier in this book and some of which have not. It follows the sequence of the book, but some chapters have been grouped together to avoid repetition. There is emphasis on low-cost sources that will be useful to international microentrepreneurs. Prices are not given in most instances because they change too frequently. Also, mailing addresses are not given because readers of this book surely do not have time to write letters and wait for responses by mail.

Besides the sources listed here, you can often get help from import/export associations, world clubs, international trade service companies, and private consultants.

SETTING UP YOUR BUSINESS

- Airlines on the Internet: low-cost fares if there are seats at the last minute. USAIR, www.usair.com. Call (888) 359-3728 for reservations; Northwest, www.nwa.com. Call 1-800-692-6961 for reservations; American, www.amrcorp.com. Call 1-800-344-6702 for reservations; Continental, www.flycontinental.com. Call 1-800-523-3273 for reservations.

- Columbia Cascade: Export Expert, software to help new small businesses get started exporting. Phone (703) 620-9403.

- GMS Publications: *Guide to Importing.* Phone 1-800-206-5656.

- *Inc., Entrepreneur,* and other magazines for small business owners. Phone 1-800-274-6229, www.inc.com and www.entrepreneur.com.

- The *Journal of Commerce,* Phillipsburg, New Jersey: *Export ABCs, a Guide to Getting Started.* Phone (908) 859-1300, www.joc.com.

- Microsoft: Small Business Resource site. Web site www.bcentral.com; also try www.microsoft.com/industry.

- Money Hunter: business planning template. Web site www.moneyhunter.com.

- NEBS, Groton, Massachusetts: mail-order stationery house; also provides TRW credit information on individuals and businesses. Phone 1-800-225-6380.

- Small Business Exporters Association, Annandale, Virginia: a nonprofit organization of small-scale exporters. Phone (703) 761-4140, fax (703) 750-9655.

- Smart Business Supersite: a large amount of information on starting and running a small business. Web site www.smartbiz.com.

- Trademark Services. Phone 1-800-487-2336, web site www.4trademark.com.

- Internet sites for small business help: There are many that can be useful to you. Two, for example, are www.smallbiz help.net and www.bizmove.com.

- U.S. Small Business Administration, Washington, D.C., and field offices: many publications including *Breaking into the Trade Game: A Small Business Guide to Exporting*; also the video *Basics of Exporting*. Phone 1-827-5722 or (202) 205-6720, web site www.sbaonline.sba.gov.

BEGINNING WITH A BUYER, CHOOSING PRODUCTS AND SUPPLIERS, AND MARKETING IN THE UNITED STATES AND ABROAD

- Access Frontiers International: information on countries and cultures. Phone (212) 370-4915, www.acrossfrontiers. com.

- Africa Business: information on selling to Africa. www.africa-business.com.

- American Demographics: on-line information on the U.S. market. Web site www.marketingtools.com.

- BigEx.com. Web site www.bigex.com

- De Paula Publishing, New York, New York: sells directories for exporters and importers including guides to U.S. wholesale and retail buyers. Fax (212) 629-4542.

- Dun & Bradstreet: Exporters' Encyclopedia, credit information and so forth. Call any D&B office, or see www.dnb.com.

- Economic Intelligence Unit on-line bookstore: www.store. eiu.com.

- Economic Intelligence Unit Data Services: www.eiu.com/ data.

- European information on-line. Web site www.apollo. co.up:80/import-and-export-europe.html.

- Interdata, Poulsbo, Washington: *Export Leads*, a newspaper. Phone (360) 779-1511, fax (360) 697-4696.

- Globaltech International Ltd.: has links to a huge, repeat, *huge*, number of sources of information on international trade. Web site www.coolone.com or phone 1-800-478-8763.

- Global Information Network: Phone (630) 513-9304 or www.ginfo.net.

- Grey House Publishing, Lakeville, Connecticut: directories of catalogs and information resources for international trade. Phone 1-800-562-2139 or (860) 435-0868, fax (860) 435-0867.

- Hong Kong Trade Development Council: This site gives a large amount of information, principally about buying from suppliers in Hong Kong and China at www.tdctrade.com.

- International Press Publications, East Brunswick, New Jersey: sells directories of interest mainly to exporters. Phone 1-800-679-2514, fax (905) 946-9590.

- International Strategies, Boston, Massachusetts: *Export Hotline*, a service that offers more than 5,000 reports on markets. See www.exporthotline.com.

- Journal of Commerce Publishing Company, New York, New York: the *Journal of Commerce* newspaper with the "Global Commerce" supplement on Wednesdays.

- Latin American Trade Council of Oregon: information on trading with Latin America. www.latco.org.

- News of the Caribbean. Web site www.caribnet.net.

- Nihon Keizai Shimbun, Japan: on-line business news from Asia. Web site www.nni-nikkei.co.jp.

- NYNEX Information Technologies Company: yellow pages listings from throughout the United States. Web site www.bigyellow.com (and computer software that provides the same information).

- PIERS: Through this service you can buy very accurate records of U.S. import and export shipments by sea. PIERS also sells nationwide (U.S.) directories of importers and exporters. There are now on-line versions that are more up-to-date and complete than the printed versions at www.piers.com.

- Trade Compass: international trade information, leads, and matchmaking. Phone: 1-800-598-3220, www.tradecompass. com.

- U.S. Bureau of the Census, Washington, D.C.: National Trade Data Bank on CD-ROM. Call the Trade Information Center for information at 1-800-782-8872.

- U.S. Chamber of Commerce, Washington, D.C.: International Business Exchange Network (on-line). Phone 1-800-537-IBEX.

- U.S. Department of Agriculture, Washington, D.C.: huge amount of information and assistance for exporters of agricultural products. Contact the Office of Outreach and Exporter Assistance. Phone (202) 720-7420, fax (202) 690-4374.

- U.S. Department of Commerce, International Trade Administration, Washington, D.C.: Phone 1-800-USA-TRADE or (202) 482-0543, web site www.ita.doc.gov. For international trade statistics, go to www.stat-usa.gov; the help line for this is (202) 482-1986. For the Trade Information Center, phone 1-800-872-8723 or e-mail tic@ita.doc. gov. Ask for the *Internet Resource Guide*. Sometimes there are on-line counseling sessions. The USDC has numerous products and services for exporters.

- WorldAtOnce.com: www.worldatonce.com. gives information on companies, worldwide.

MONEY MATTERS; PACKING, SHIPPING, AND INSURANCE; OH, THOSE LOVELY DOCUMENTS; AND REGULATION OF FOREIGN TRADE

- Clear Cross: www.clearcross.com.
- Export-Import Bank of the United States. Phone 1-800-565-3946, web site www.exim.gov.
- From2: www.from2.com and Global Commerce Zone: www.gczone.com. Both are on-line sources of help with trade logistics.
- Global Sources: www.asia.globalsources.com. Includes list of Asian freight service providers and banks.
- International Chamber of Commerce, New York, New York: large number of publications on technical and legal aspects of international trade. Phone (212) 206-1150, fax (212) 633-6025, web site www.iccbooks.com.
- Sandler & Travis Trade Advisory Services, Miami, Florida: seminars nationwide on technical aspects of exporting. Phone 1-800-5TRADE5, web site www.strtrade.com.
- Serra International Freight Forwarders and Customs Brokers. On-line freight rate quotations, trade leads, etc.: www.serraintl.com.
- Tower Group International, Buffalo, New York: information on tariffs, customs, and NAFTA. Phone 1-800-889-8723.
- UNZ & Co., New Providence, New Jersey: has international trade forms, software, books, and seminars. Phone 1-800-631-3098, web site www.unzexport.com.
- U.S. Customs Service, Washington, D.C.: *International Mail Imports, Publication 514; Marking Country of Origin, Publication 539; How to Obtain Copyright, Trademark, and Patent Protection from the U.S. Customs Service, Publication 563; NAFTA, Publication 571.* Phone (202) 354-1000, or see www.customs.gov.

- U.S. International Trade Commission: *The Harmonized Tariff*. web site www.usitc.gov.
- U.S. Small Business Administration, Washington, D.C., and field offices: some export financing, counseling, and training. Contact your nearest SBA district office.
- World Trade Organization. Web site www.wto.com.

NAFTA, GATT, AND OTHER TRADE PACTS

- NAFTA Office of the Mexican Government: www.naftaworks.org.
- PricewaterhouseCoopers LLP: *Doing Business in Mexico*. Phone 1-800-579-1646.
- Software for traders using NAFTA. Phone 1-800-554-4883, fax (604) 986-0869, www.infertek.com.
- U.S. Small Business Administration: *Opportunity in Mexico: A Small Business Guide*. Call your local field office, or phone (202) 606-4000.

AND STILL MORE SOURCES

This small section hardly seems necessary anymore, now that Amazon.com and Barnesandnoble.com each has thousands of books on international trade. I will, however, list a few information sources that you might want to look at in your local library or buy from your bookstore or on the web.

- Adams Media Corporation: *Exporting, Importing, and Beyond: How to Go Global with Your Small Business*, by Lawrence W. Tulleer, 1997.
- AMACOM: *Export/Import Procedures and Documentation*, by Thomas E. Johnson, 1997.

- Business News Publishing: *World Trade* magazine, phone 1-800-640-7071.

- Dearborn Trade, Chicago, IL: *The Global Entrepreneur: Taking Your Business International*, by James Foley, 1999.

- Dryden Press: *International Marketing*, by Vern Terpstra and Rave Sarathy, 1997.

- Executive Excellence: *7 Secrets of Marketing in a Multicultural World*, by G. Clotaire Rapaille, 2001.

- Export Today: *Global Business Online*, www.globalbusiness mag.com.

- Global Training Center, *Inc.: Export/Import Letters of Credit and Payment Methods: A Guide for Payments in International Trade*, by John S. Gordon, 2000.

- McGraw-Hill, New York, NY: *Import/Export. How to Get Started in International Trade*, by Carl A. Nelson, 2000.

- McGraw-Hill Professional Book Group: *Selling to the World. Your Fast and Easy Guide to Exporting and Importing*, L. Fargo Wells, 1996.

- McGraw-Hill, New York, NY: *Riding the Waves of Culture: Understanding Diversity in Global Business*, by Alfons Trompenaars, 1997.

- NTC Publishing Group: *A Basic Guide to Importing*, by U.S. Customs Service, Department of the Treasury, 1995.

- West Information Publications Group: *International Business Transactions in a Nutshell*, by Ralph H. Folsom, 2000.

- World Trade Press: *A Basic Guide to Exporting*, by U.S. Department of Commerce, Alexandra Woznick, 2000.

There are hundreds of other sources that you can find by surfing the Internet. In the academic community, for example, Michigan State University's Center for International Business Education and Research, or CIBER, has an "Export Tutor," and its Small Business Development Center has an "Export Answer Book" and the "Target" series of publications about specific countries. At Ohio State University, the Center for Information Technologies has available an "Export Process Assistant."

Sample Market Study Outline

Most small businesses start with inadequate market studies or with none at all. Yet, a market study is almost the only way to support your income (sales) projections and your marketing plan.

The following is a topical outline for a report on the market, for any product being exported from one country to another. If you can produce or buy this kind of information before you begin, you might decide to try another product or another market. If the results are positive and you do go ahead, your chances of success will be increased considerably.

Also, a solid market study looks very good to potential investors and lenders.

Basic Information

- Product name and Harmonized System (HS) number
- Country of origin, exporting country, importing country

Regulations

- Exporting country controls and taxes
- Importing country controls and taxes:
  - Import restrictions, quotas, etc.
  - Import duties
  - Marketing and labeling laws
- Other regulations

Supply and Demand

- Availability of supply in the exporting country
- Domestic production less imports in the importing country (five years' statistics with trend calculation)
- Imports for consumption (five years' statistics with trend calculation)
- Percentage of product for consumption that is imported
- Industry experts' perception of current and future supply and demand in the importing country
- Selected buyers' perceptions of same

Competition

- Survey of producers in the importing country
- Description of selected producers
- Sources of imports (countries), with import market share of each
- Average f.a.s. and c.i.f. prices from each country

Target Markets

- The market and market segments
- Characteristics of important market segments
- Kinds of industrial users
- Main industrial users and a brief description of each

Product Description

- Main types/varieties of the product
- Required or desired product characteristics
- Required or desired packaging and labeling

Distribution

- Normal distribution system in the importing country
- Principal importers and wholesalers
- Principal industrial distributors

Pricing

- Representative prices and markups at each level in the channel
- Price trends
- Discounts used in the trade

Promotion

- Methods of promotion used in the trade
- Promotional assistance usually expected of exporters
- Approximate costs of this assistance

Logistics

- Steamship lines and airlines serving the route
- Usual method of shipping this product
- Availability of vessels (planes) and cost of shipping
- Shipping term normally used
- Payment term normally used

Other Considerations

- Local laws on the product, label, distribution, pricing, promotion
- Distributors' and consumers' openness to new suppliers
- Image of exporting country in the importing country

Sources of Industry Information

- Industry experts including consultants
- Associations and trade publications
- Trade exhibits
- "Off-the-shelf" market study reports
- Government organizations
- Other information sources

APPENDIX B

Guidelines for Business Planning

Appendix B is reprinted with permission of the Small Business Development Center of Howard University, Washington, D.C. These "Guidelines for Business Planning" are exceptionally thorough and provide a format for a complete business plan that would probably take you several weeks of full-time work to prepare. More streamlined versions are available in books, on the World Wide Web, and from business assistance organizations.

In place of Section V, "Production Processes," a nonmanufacturing importer or exporter could amend the outline, as follows:

V. Operations
    E. Product sourcing and ordering
    F. International transportation and insurance
    G. Payment for merchandise
    H. Customs clearance and duties
    I. Quotas
    J. Warehousing
    K. Legal considerations

Gratitude is expressed to the Small Business Development Center of Howard University for providing this excellent material. Some minor changes have been made for editorial consistency.

GUIDELINES FOR BUSINESS PLANNING

The business plan is your pathway to profit. It can mean the difference between success and failure. A business plan with goals and actions can

231

guide you through turbulent economic times with alternative channels that you can fall back on as changes dictate.

Through the development of a business plan, you will be able to identify your areas of strengths and weaknesses and spot opportunities and threats that may loom on the horizon. You will review the competitive conditions of the marketplace and isolate opportunities and situations that seem advantageous to your business.

The business plan will communicate your understanding of the industry in which you operate, the competitive situation you face, the capability of your management, the suitability of your location, and the capacity of your particular business. It will make reasonable assumptions and forecasts of your expectations concerning sales, expenses, cash flow, and attainment.

Letter of Transmittal

You should enclose a letter explaining why your business plan is being sent to the addressee and what he or she is expected to do with it. The contents of the letter of transmittal typically include:

- The identity and purpose of the business
- A very short history of the business
- The purpose of the plan (e.g., financing proposal)
- Identity of the person requesting money
- The amount and type of financing required
- The amount of equity already invested in the business
- The productive purpose for which the money will be used
- When the money will be needed
- The goals and market potential of the business with the new funds
- Collateral and other security offered

Title Page

You should start the plan with a title page that identifies the name of the business; a title of the plan; a date, copy, and revision number, if applicable; and instructions regarding confidentiality, reproduction, and dissemination of the plan.

Executive Summary

A one-page summary of the plan should be presented next. It is not necessary to cover the contents of the letter of transmittal or all of the sections of the plan in the executive summary. The summary must identify the purpose of the business, its short- and long-term goals, and the means by which they will be reached.

Table of Contents

The table of contents lists the major divisions and subdivisions of your plan. The page number where the section begins is also indicated. Sections are usually numbered and appendices are lettered. Typical contents, and the contents of this outline, include:

Outline of the Business Plan

I.   Description of the Business

The purpose of this section is to explain to the targeted reader what you are as a business, who the intended customer is, what you are trying to accomplish through your business, and where you wish to go in the future.

A.   *What is the current status of the business?*

   1.   What is the business, or what will it be?
   2.   What market do you intend to service, and what is the size of the market and your expected share?

3. Why can you service that market better than your competition?
4. Why have you chosen your particular location?
5. What management and other personnel are required and available for the operation?
6. Why will your investment or someone else's money (debt/equity) help make your business profitable?

B. *What is your business?*

1. What type of business is it: *primarily* merchandising retail, manufacturing, wholesale, or service?
2. What is the nature of the product(s) or service(s)?
3. What is the status of the business: new, expansion of a going concern, or takeover of an existing business?
4. What is the form of legal organization: sole proprietorship, partnership, or corporation?
5. Who are the customers or clients?
6. Why is your business going to be profitable?
7. When will (did) your business open?
8. What hours of the day and days of the week will you be (are you) in operation? If yours is a seasonal business, or if hours will be adjusted seasonally, make sure that the seasonality is reflected in your replies to the two previous questions.
9. What have you learned about your kind of business from outside sources (trade suppliers, banks, other business people, publications)?

C. *For a new business*

1. Why will *you* be successful in this business?
2. What is *your* experience in this business?
3. Have you spoken with other people in this type of business about their experience, challenges, and rewards? What were their responses?
4. What will be special about your business?
5. Have you spoken with prospective trade suppliers to find out what managerial and/or technical help they will provide?
6. Have you asked about trade credit?
7. If you will be doing any contract work, what are the terms? Reference any firm contract and include it as a supporting document in an appendix.
8. Do you have letters of intent from prospective suppliers or purchasers?

D. For an existing business

1. When and by whom was the business founded?
2. Why is the owner selling it?
3. How did you arrive at a purchase price for the business?
4. What is the trend of sales?
5. If the business is going downhill, why? How can you turn it around?
6. How will *your* management make the business more profitable?

E. What are the short- and long-term goals of the business?

1. Are these goals realistic, measurable, and attainable?
2. Do these goals offer adequate protection and return income to you, your investors, and debtors?
3. What issues must be addressed related to the chosen goals?
   a. New products/services/markets
   b. Capabilities and number of employees
   c. Financing amount and source
   d. Capacity of plant and equipment
4. What steps must be taken in order to meet your desired results?
   a. Time frame with necessary "controls"
   b. Critical check points to measure progress
   c. Reporting and monitoring?

Note: A personal financial statement must be included as a supporting document in your plan if it is a proposal for financing. Also, include your resume as a supporting document.

II.   Products or Services Offered

This section describes your products or services in sufficient detail so that the reader knows what you are offering, what utility the customer receives from your product or service, and how the customer prefers to buy and pay. Remember who is reading your plan. Generally, this section should be written such that it is easily understood by a layperson.

A. What are the specific products or services that you sell (or plan to sell)?

B. Do you possess any proprietary positions on your products or services such as patents, copyrights, trademarks, market position, or

legal or technical considerations? Place applicable diagrams and documents in an appendix.

C. What are some of the other factors that your customers perceive as a part of their purchase?

1. Savings
2. Convenience
3. Personal service
4. Status
5. Safety

D. How do your products or services compare to those of your competitors?

1. If they are not unique, why would people buy from you?
2. Are you able to differentiate your products or services from those of your competitors based on the above?
3. Do you plan to market future "new" products or services?

III. Market Analysis

Provide an analysis of the industry, customers, market, and competition in sufficient detail that the reader knows that you understand what it takes to succeed in your industry.

A. The industry

1. What industry are you in?
2. What are the major trends within the industry?
3. Is the industry in a growth phase?
4. What uncontrollable variables (government regulations, economy, technology, etc.) could affect the industry?

B. Customers

1. Who are your target markets (to whom do you sell)?
    a. Who are your main customers?
    b. What is their buying trend with you?
    c. Who are the people making the buying decisions, and what needs are they trying to fulfill?
    d. Why do your target markets buy your products or services?

2. When do they do their purchasing?
    a. Sporadically (car, travel)?
    b. Weekly (groceries, gas for the car)?
    c. Annually (insurance)?
    d. Seasonally (holiday items, sporting goods)?
3. How does the customer like to pay for the product or service?
    a. Cash or credit?
    b. How will you offset delinquent payment by your customer?
4. Do your customers purchase in small or large quantities?
5. How do your target markets find out about you? Describe your advertising and promotion plans.

C. *Market size and trends*

1. What are the characteristics of your target markets?
    a. Demographics (age, sex, income, profession)?
    b. How were these characteristics determined?
        1. Survey
        2. Literature review
        3. Manufacturer or trade association
        4. Discussions with customers, suppliers, distributors, etc.
2. What is the current size of the market(s) you serve?
3. Is the market competitive?
    a. Does your business retain a profitable share?
    b. Does the market have potential for added growth?
4. If the market does grow, do you have the resources that are needed to maintain your current share?
5. In what ways will you attract additional customers to your business?

D. *Location*

1. Where is the business located?
2. How would you describe the area? Is it compatible with the needs your customers are trying to fulfill?
3. For the area of your location, what are the expected population trends?
4. What are the advantages of your business location?
    a. Easily accessible?
    b. Close to your customers?
    c. Close to your suppliers?
5. Do you know the local zoning laws?

6. Are there any new area developments upcoming in the next five years that could affect your business?

E. Competition

1. Who are the key competitors in your market and market segment?
2. Are their businesses currently increasing, decreasing, or steady?
3. What are your competitors' strengths and weaknesses?
4. Do your business strengths and weaknesses match up favorably with theirs?
5. How will your operation be better than theirs?
6. Why will customers buy from you rather than them?

IV. Marketing Strategy

This is your opportunity to express your philosophy toward sales. All businesses must sell—be it to other businesses, the government, or the general public. Your philosophy toward service, returns, promotion, and price will markedly affect your sales and, ultimately, your success as a business. Factors typically considered in the selling process follow.

A. Overall strategy and approach

1. Major sales emphasis
   a. Service
   b. Price
   c. Convenience
   d. Philosophy concerning the customer

B. Selling tactics

1. Direct
2. Executive selling
3. Manufacturers' representatives
4. Distributors
5. Retailers
   a. National chains
   b. Regional chains
   c. Independents
   d. Mail order
   e. Telemarketing

C. *Pricing objectives*

1. Profit-oriented—Maximizes profit (practiced over a long time period). Look at total output rather than single items. Uses return on sales, percentage of return on sales to net sales, or sales to net investment.
2. Sales-oriented—Increases percentage over previous periods. Might use a lower price to increase market share or to gain a foothold in the market.
3. Status quo—Uses price leadership with the leader stabilizing the price or competitive pricing where the others follow the leader.
4. Market-oriented
    a. Skimming—Initially high price then lower price according to demand.
    b. Penetration—Lower initial price to gain a market share foothold and then, once established, raise prices to meet competition.
    c. Premium—Price above competitive price if firm is able to differentiate its product/service as having higher quality, superior features, etc.
5. Margin-oriented—Cost and profit margins on each item are the primary consideration.

D. *Sales terms and conditions*

1. Credit
2. Bad debt
3. Returned items
4. Complaints

E. *Merchandising—the attractive display of goods or services*

F. *Channels of distribution—transferring the goods or services from the production location to the location of the final consumer*

V.   Production Processes

Whether you are a service business, manufacturer, retailer, or whatever, you must produce. The production may be a product or something as intangible as a smile, but something must be produced. This section addresses how you plan to deliver the goods or services that form the basis of your business. Considerations include the following.

A. *Physical layout*

B. *Required furniture, fixtures and equipment*

C. *Review of operations flow and quality control*

D. *Inventory and inventory control*

E. *Vendors*

VI.   Management and Personnel

Your proposal is only as strong as the people you have available to assist you in executing the plan. Here you detail the key players who you have already identified or the qualifications of successful candidates if you must recruit. It is wise to have already selected your most important personnel.

A. Management structure

1. What is your business background?
2. How does your background/business experience help you in this business?
3. What management experience do you have?
4. Do you have managerial experience in *this type of business?*
5. Do you have managerial experience acquired elsewhere— whether in totally different kinds of business, or as an offshoot of club or team membership, civic or church work, etc.?
6. What weaknesses do you have and how will you compensate for them; that is, will you hire employees or pay consultants who have management abilities/expertise that you don't have?
7. What education do you have (including both formal and informal learning experience)? Does it have a bearing on your managerial abilities or knowledge of the industry?
8. What is your personal data: age, where you live and have lived, special abilities and interests, and reasons for going into business?
9. Why are *you* going to be successful at *this* venture?
10. Do you have direct operational experience in *this type of business?*
11. Who is on the management team?
12. What are the duties of each individual on the management team?

13. Are these duties clearly defined? How?
14. Who does what? Who reports to whom? Where do final decisions get made?
15. What and how will management be paid?
16. What additional resources have you arranged to have available to help you and your business (accountant, lawyer, etc.)?

B. Personnel structure

1. What are your personnel needs now? In the near future (three years)? In five years?
2. What skills must they have?
3. Are the people you need available?
4. Will your employees be full-time or part-time?
5. Will you pay salaries or hourly wages?
6. Certain employee benefits are mandatory. Do you know what they are?
7. Will you provide additional fringe benefits? If so, which ones? Have you calculated the cost of these additional fringe benefits?
8. Will you utilize overtime? If so, you may be required by law to pay time and a half, double time, and/or other extra costs.
9. Will you have to train people for both operations and management? If so, at what costs to the business?

VII.   Financial Data

The proof of the business plan is in its pro forma financial reports. Many readers read the cover letter first, the summary second, and skip back to the financial data before reading the rest of the plan. The discussions contained in the other sections of the plans should be reflected in the revenue and expense columns of the projections.

A. List the sources and uses of the proposed funding

B. List the productive purposes to which the money will be put

C. Develop pro forma balance sheets for three years

D. Prepare projective purposes to which the money will be put

1. Detail by month for the first year.
2. Detail by quarter for the second year.

    3.   Provide an outlook for the third year.

    4.   Explain how you were able to develop the projections. Provide a list of major assumptions.

E. Prepare projected cash flow statements

    1.   Detail by month for first year.

    2.   Provide notes of explanations and assumptions.

F. Prepare financial statements for businesses already in existence

    1.   Balance sheets for the past three years

    2.   Income statements for the past three years

    3.   Personal and business tax returns for the past three years

G. Develop a break-even analysis

H. Develop key financial ratios and a comparison with standards

I. Develop a cost/benefit analysis

J. Develop a calculation of the payback period

VIII. Summary and Conclusions

This section summarizes the major goals in your plan and reiterates how you will achieve them and what the company will become if you are successful. This section should be short and to the point and contain the most important aspects of your plan—the ones you want the reader to retain.

IX.   Appendices and Supporting Documents

Provide clear and legible copies of pertinent documents that will help you to prove your case. These documents typically include the following, which are presented as appendices.

A. Corporate or partnership documents (if applicable)

B. Personal resumes of owners and key management personnel

C. Letters of recommendation or support

D. Any other documents relevant to the business

FINANCIAL DATA

Sources and Applications of Funding

Sources

1. Mortgage Loan
   (Applications 1 and/or 3) $ _____

2. Term Loan
   (Applications 2 and/or 3) $ _____

3. Line of Credit
   (Applications 3 and/or 4) $ _____

4. Reserved Loan
   (Application 6) $ _____

5. Personal Equity Investments
   (Applications 1 through 5) $ _____

6. Outside Equity Investments
   (Applications 1 through 5) $ _____

7. Other _____
   (Application 7) $ _____

   TOTAL $ _____

Applications

1. Building (Purchase)
   (Sources 1, 5, and/or 6) $ _____

2. Equipment and Furniture (Purchases)
   (Sources 2, 5, and/or 6) $ _____

3. Renovations
   (Sources 1, 2, 5, and/or 6) $ _____

4. Inventory
   (Sources 3, 5, and/or 6) $ _____

5. Working Capital (Operating Expenses)
   (Sources 3, 5, and/or 6) $ _____

6. Reserve for Contingencies
   (Source 4) $ _____

7. Other _____
   (Source 7) $ _____

   TOTAL $ _____

Capital Equipment and Furniture Lists

Major Equipment & Accessories	Model	Cost or List Price
_____	_____	$_____
_____	_____	_____
_____	_____	_____
	Total:	$_____

Minor Equipment	Model	Cost or List Price
_____	_____	$_____
_____	_____	_____
_____	_____	_____
	Total:	$_____

Furniture	Model	Cost or List Price
_____	_____	$_____
_____	_____	_____
_____	_____	_____
	Total:	$_____

Grand Total $_____

Break-Even Analysis

Sales	$_____
Less Cost of Goods Sold	$_____
Gross Profit	$_____
Operating (Fixed) Expenses	$_____
Pretax Profit (Loss)	$_____

Step 1: Divide gross profit by sales to show the percentage relationship:

$$\frac{\text{Gross Profit}}{\text{Sales}} \quad = \quad \text{Gross profit as a percentage (\%) of sales}$$

Step 2: Divide fixed expenses by gross profit as a percentage of sales, expressed as a decimal (gross profit % divided by 100):

$$\frac{\text{Fixed Expenses}}{\text{Gross Profit \%}} \quad = \quad \text{Break-Even Sales}$$

Projected Balance Sheet

Assets

Current Assets

Cash $ _____

Accounts Receivable _____

Merchandise Inventory _____

Supplies _____

Prepaid Expenses _____

Total Current Assets $ _____

Fixed Assets

Furniture $ _____

Vehicles _____

Equipment _____

Leasehold Improvements _____

Building _____

Land _____

Total Fixed Assets $ _____

TOTAL ASSETS $ _____

Liabilities & Net Worth

Current Liabilities

Accounts Payable $ _____

Current Portion of Long-Term Debt _____

Other Current Liabilities _____

Total Current Liabilities $ _____

Long-Term Liabilities

Notes Payable $ _____

Long-Term Debt _____

Other Loans Payable _____

Total Long-Term Liabilities $ _____

Total Liabilities $ _____

Net Worth: Owner's Equity $ _____

TOTAL LIABILITIES & NET WORTH $ _____

1. Accounts Payable Display

Name of Account	Amount
a. _____	_____
b. _____	_____
c. _____	_____

2. Long-Term Liabilities

Name of Account	Amount
a. _____	_____
b. _____	_____
c. _____	_____

Projected Income Statements
First-Year Summary

	Quarter I 200____	Quarter II 200____
Sales	_____	_____
Less Cost of Goods Sold	_____	_____
Gross Profit	_____	_____
Operating Expenses		
Salaries	_____	_____
Commissions		
Outside Labor	_____	_____
Payroll Expenses (taxes, etc.)	_____	_____
Advertising & Promotion	_____	_____
Car & Delivery	_____	_____
Gen. Office Admin.	_____	_____
Legal & Accounting	_____	_____
Operating Supplies	_____	_____
Bad Debts	_____	_____
Rent	_____	_____
Repairs & Maintenance	_____	_____
Utilities	_____	_____
Insurance	_____	_____
Taxes & Licenses	_____	_____
Depreciation	_____	_____
Interest	_____	_____
Other Expenses	_____	_____
(specify each)	_____	_____
TOTAL OPERATING EXPENSES	_____	_____
PRETAX PROFIT (LOSS)	_____	_____
INCOME TAXES	_____	_____
NET PROFIT (LOSS)	_____	_____

Quarter III	Quarter IV	Total
200_____	200_____	
_____	_____	_____
_____	_____	_____
_____	_____	_____
_____	_____	_____
_____	_____	_____
_____	_____	_____
_____	_____	_____
_____	_____	_____
_____	_____	_____
_____	_____	_____
_____	_____	_____
_____	_____	_____
_____	_____	_____
_____	_____	_____
_____	_____	_____
_____	_____	_____
_____	_____	_____
_____	_____	_____
_____	_____	_____
_____	_____	_____
_____	_____	_____
_____	_____	_____

Projected Income Statement

	Month 1	Month 2	Month 3	Month 4	Month 5
Total Net Sales					
Cost of Sales					
Gross Profit					
Controllable Expenses Salaries					
Payroll Taxes					
Security					
Advertising					
Automobile					
Dues and Subscriptions					
Legal and Accounting					
Office Supplies					
Telephone					
Utilities					
Miscellaneous					
Total Controllable Expense					
Fixed Expenses Depreciation					
Insurance					
Rent					
Taxes and Licenses					
Loan Payments (interest)					
Total Fixed Expenses					
TOTAL EXPENSES					
NET PROFIT (LOSS) (before taxes)					

Month 6	Month 7	Month 8	Month 9	Month 10	Month 11	Month 12	Total

Cash Flow Projections

	Start-up or prior to loan	Month 1	Month 2	Month 3	Month 4
Cash (beginning of month)					
Cash on Hand					
Total Cash					
Income (during month) Cash Sales					
Collects from Customers					
Other Cash Income					
Total Income					
TOTAL CASH and INCOME					
Expenses (during month) Inventory or New Material					
Wages (including owner's)					
Taxes					
Equipment Expenses					
Overhead					
Selling Expense					
Transportation					
Loan Repayment					
Other Cash Expenses					
TOTAL EXPENSES					
CASH ON HAND (end of month)					

Month 5	Month 6	Month 7	Month 8	Month 9	Month 10	Month 11	Month 12	Total

Possible Sources of Financing for Your Business

The following are potential sources of financing for your new business. Some are equity (shares of the business), while others are debt (loans). Equity investors will look for potential profits and increases in value, while lenders will be concerned about "cash flow," which for them boils down to whether you can generate enough cash every month to make your principal and interest payments.

In general, one cannot get financing without putting some of his/her own money into the business. Also, both investors and lenders look at the ratio of debt to equity to make sure it is not dangerously high.

Your Own Resources

- Equity: Your personal savings
- Debt: Personal loans, especially home equity loans
- Note 1: It is usually quicker, easier and cheaper to use personal loans for a business startup than to try to get a loan to the business itself.
- Note 2: Try to avoid using credit cards. The interest rate is too high, and it is usually unwise to use short-term debt for a long-term purpose such as a business startup.

Friends, Fools, and Family

- Equity: Shares in the company (usually requires incorporating)
- Debt: Loans from friends, fools, and family
- Note: If the business fails, equity investors usually lose their money (and the entrepreneur may lose their friendship). Lenders usually expect to be repaid, sooner or later.

Small Business Financiers

- Equity: "Strategic" investors, such as suppliers, who will gain if your business succeeds. Also Small Business Investment Corporations (SBICs), which are scattered throughout the United States and usually have federal government assistance.
- Debt: Microcredit organizations, bank loans, loans and loan guarantees from the U.S. Small Business Administration (SBA):
  - 7(a) Loan Guaranty Program (apply through a bank)
  - Prequalification Loan Program (for veterans, women, and minorities)
  - Low Documentation Loan (up to $150,000)
  - SBA Express (up to $150,000, 50% guaranteed by SBA)
  - Caplines (75% guarantee for working capital loans)
  - Export Working Capital (guarantee for individual transactions)
  - International Trade Loan (for established businesses)
  - 504 Loan Program (mainly for job creation)
  - 7(M) Microloan Program (for nonprofit lending organizations)
  - Small Business Investment Company Program
  - Angel Capital Electronic Network
  - Community Adjustment & Investment Program
  - Preferred and Certified Lenders Program
- Note: Some states, counties and cities operate loan programs for new, small, and/or minority-owned businesses. Many of these have funding from the SBA.

Alternative Methods of Financing

- Leasing: Leasing equipment, such as computers, can save your money for use as working capital.

- Fixed Asset Financing: If you already own land or equipment, you may be able to use it as collateral for obtaining loans.

- Trade Credit: When you have even a small track record, suppliers will often give you 30 days or more in which to pay them.

- Export Credit: The U.S. Export Import Bank, and similar organizations in some states, can lend (or guarantee loans to) your foreign importers so they can buy from you and pay you immediately.

- Factoring Receivables: If you make large sales on credit, either in the United States or overseas, you may find a "factor" who will take over the collection process and lend you money before he or she collects. Sometimes you can even sell a receivable "without recourse," which means that, if the buyer does not pay, it is the factor who loses.

APPENDIX D

Sample Supply Agreements

The sample supply agreements were provided for an earlier edition of this book by the New York law firm of Kaplan Russin Vecchi & Kirkwood. The first is between a foreign exporter and a U.S. selling agent, and the second is between a foreign exporter and a U.S. importer/distributor. *These are given only as examples*; each commercial relationship is different and is likely to require special terms and conditions in the enabling agreement.

AGENCY AGREEMENT
(between foreign exporter and U.S. selling agent)

THIS AGREEMENT is made this _____ day of _____, 20__.

BETWEEN ___A CORP___ incorporated in _____ with its registered office at:

_____

_____

_____

(hereinafter called "A Corp") of the one part

AND: ___B CORP___ incorporated in _____ with its principal office at:

_____

_____

(hereinafter called "B Corp") on the other part

WHEREAS
(A)   A Corp designs, develops, manufactures and sells widgets and ancillary equipment for use in the widget industry.
(B)   In view of its previous experience in marketing widgets and ancillary equipment for the widget industry in the United States, its valuable contacts in that industry and its general marketing expertise and organization, B Corp wishes to undertake, and A Corp is willing to support, the marketing of widgets and ancillary equipment manufactured by A Corp in the United States under an agency from A Corp.
(C)   The parties now wish formally to record the terms and conditions which shall govern their association for the purposes outlined in Recital (b) above.

NOW, THEREFORE IT IS AGREED AND DECLARED AS FOLLOWS:

Clause 1.   SCOPE

The parties agree that the terms and conditions set forth in this Agreement represent the entire agreement between the parties relating to the Agency of B Corp for A Corp and shall supersede any and all prior representations, agreements, statements and understandings relating thereto. The parties further agree that neither party places any reliance whatsoever on any such prior representations, agreements, statements and understandings except to the extent expressly set forth in this Agreement.

Clause 2.   APPOINTMENT OF AGENT

A Corp hereby appoints B Corp to be its exclusive Agent in the United States during the currency of this Agreement for the sale of all widgets and ancillary equipment listed in Schedule 1. All such widgets and ancillary equipment are hereinafter collectively referred to as "The Products." A list of The Products which are standard as at the date of this Agreement is set forth in Schedule 1 to this Agreement and A Corp undertakes to give B Corp prompt written notice of any additions to or deletions from such list.

Clause 3.   DUTIES OF THE AGENT

3.1 B Corp shall during the currency of this Agreement:
   3.1.1   Use its best endeavors to promote the sale of The Products to customers and potential customers throughout the United States and solicit orders for The Products to be placed with

A Corp as per Clause 9 hereof. Without prejudice to the generality of the foregoing B Corp shall:

3.1.1.1 maintain close marketing relationships with customers and potential customers so that their relevant equipment needs and future plans are ascertained.

3.1.1.2 draw the attention of customers and potential customers to The Products suitable to their needs and ascertain the equipment and technical commercial proposals being offered by A Corp's competitors.

3.1.1.3 B Corp shall not, during the currency of this Agreement act as agent or distributor for any products directly competitive in price and specification to The Products.

3.1.2 Establish and maintain a product support service having the capacity of:

3.1.2.1 dealing with routine service enquiries from customers either by telephone or telex advice or in the field.

3.1.2.2 maintaining liaison with customers.

3.1.2.3 assisting customers in the implementation of the A Corp Warranty for The Products.

3.1.3 Promptly draw to the attention of A Corp any new or revised legislation, regulation or orders affecting the use or sale of The Products in the United States of America as and when such legislation, etc. come to its attention.

3.1.4 Employ such technically competent sales, commercial and service staff as may be reasonably necessary.

3.1.5 Receive within its B Corp's offices temporary visiting staff of A Corp and afford to such staff reasonable office, secretarial and communications services.

3.2 Recognizing its obligations to protect the reputation of A Corp, B Corp undertakes that it shall not undertake any obligations in respect of the performance of The Products in excess of the limits specified by A Corp in respect of The Products concerned and shall not offer any time for delivery earlier than that given by A Corp pursuant to the inquiry and order procedure provisions of this Agreement.

Clause 4. SUPPORT OBLIGATIONS OF A CORP

During the term of the Agreement, A Corp shall:

4.1 Continue to develop The Products to meet the requirements of the United States market.

4.2　Supply at its own cost B Corp with all reasonable requirements for technical data in reproducible form for use in catalogues, sales literature, instruction books, technical pamphlets and advertising material relating to The Products including developments of The Products as envisaged under Clause 4.1 above, and will pay the equivalent of ___% of the prior 12 months' gross billing, in every year, for the preparation of such material.

4.3　Make potential customers within the United States aware of the support available from B Corp as agent of A Corp and of A Corp's support of such agency.

Clause 5.　DELIVERIES BY A CORP

5.1　Throughout the term of this Agreement A Corp shall assist the sales efforts of B Corp by holding a stock of certain of The Products in an authorized warehouse within 50 miles of B Corp's headquarters at a level not lower than that set forth in Schedule 2 annexed hereto, which schedule may be changed from time to time by the signature of both parties on the revised version thereof.

5.2　A Corp shall provide adequate and suitable storage accommodations for such stock at its authorized warehouse and all deliveries will be dealt with through that warehouse. The costs and charges of the warehouse company shall be billed directly to and settled by A Corp.

5.3　All stock belonging to and warehoused by A Corp as set forth is and shall at all times remain the exclusive property of A Corp, and neither title nor possession thereof or in part thereof, shall pass to B Corp or to any third party customer of B Corp save or until the precise terms and conditions of Clause 5.4 herein below have been completely and exclusively complied with.

5.4　B Corp shall have the authority to instruct A Corp's warehouse to release not more than 5 widgets on any given day. As to widgets released and shipped in accordance with the above authority, B Corp must receive payment in one of the following alternative ways: (a) By cash payment for the widget within 48 hours of such shipment; or (b) by delivery to Barclays Bank, N.Y., Jericho branch, within 48 hours of such shipment, of an irrevocable 45 day Letter of Credit, in the amount of the payment due.

Clause 6.　PRICE

6.1　Customers solicited by B Corp shall pay the prices agreed or to be agreed from time to time and annexed as an Exhibit A hereto. Payment shall be made in accordance with paragraph 5.4 hereinabove. The parties hereto further agree that the said prices shall be reviewed every six months beginning on the date of this Agreement.

6.2   A Corp undertakes that it will give not less than three months' notice of any changes to its United States Dollar prices for the sale of The Products. A Corp further undertakes that any non-standard Products and agreed modifications to The Products shall be priced on a basis consistent with its normal pricing arrangements under this Agreement.

Clause 7.   COMMISSIONS EARNED

Upon delivery of, and payment for, each Product pursuant Clauses 5 and 6, B Corp shall be entitled to a commission in the amount of _____ percent (___%) of the list price of each of The Products as set forth in Exhibit _____ hereto less any discounts or other allowances made by B Corp in these prices to achieve the sale and any freight, packing, insurance, or other charges. Commissions shall be calculated at the end of each calendar month based upon deliveries during the preceding month. Payment shall be made within 10 days of the end of the calendar month to B Corp.

Clause 8.   DIRECT SALES AND FOREIGN ORDERS

A Corp agrees not to solicit sales for use within the United States during the currency of this Agreement. However, nothing in this Agreement is intended to operate nor shall it be construed as operating to prevent A Corp from selling, should it receive direct orders from and to any customer within the United States or to any customer outside the United States which customer whether within the knowledge of A Corp or not, intends to resell or actually resells to a customer within the United States. In the event of a direct sale by A Corp to a customer within the United States then A Corp shall grant B Corp a commission upon such sale in an amount of _____ percent (___%) of the sale price charged by A Corp to such customer provided always that thereafter The Product support obligations of B Corp pursuant to this Agreement shall apply in respect of the sale of The Product so made by A Corp to the said customer. A Corp shall notify B Corp of each and every such sale. Further and in addition, if B Corp obtains any order for A Corp's products for shipment outside the United States, A Corp shall grant B Corp the same said commission on such sale.

Clause 9. PROPRIETARY RIGHTS

9.1 The due and proper performance of its obligations and the exercise of its rights hereunder by B Corp shall not be deemed to be a breach of copyright or infringement of patent trademark or other proprietary right owned by A Corp.

9.2 B Corp shall not under any circumstances acquire any rights whatsoever in any copyright, patent, trademark or other proprietary right of A Corp nor shall B Corp acquire any rights whatsoever in relation to the design of The Products.

Clause 10. DELIVERY

10.1 A Corp reserves the right to specify and change delivery dates and shall not be responsible for any delay in delivery or failure to meet delivery schedules where such delay or failure arises due to any cause outside the reasonable control of A Corp.

10.2 The parties hereto agree that, in the event that delivery of Products is delayed by an act or omission of a customer, B Corp shall invoice such customers for the reasonable storage charges incurred by A Corp as a result thereof, and will use reasonable efforts to effect collection. Upon receipt of payment against such invoice, B Corp shall remit such payment to A Corp after deduction of B Corp's commission and costs of such collection.

Clause 11. WARRANTY

11.1 A Corp's warranty on all of The Products is limited to the following: A Corp will repair or replace at its option any Product at its own expense, save as to freight as to which it shall pay 50% of the round-trip cost for all validated warranty claims, as to which Product any defect in design, material or workmanship arises within a period of one year from commencement of operation of such Product or eighteen (18) months from the date of delivery of such Product, whichever shall first occur.

11.2 The warranty contained in Clause 11.1 above is subject to:

   11.2.1 The Product not being used for any purpose other than the normal purpose for its specifications.

   11.2.2 the observance by the user of all operating instructions and recommendations issued by A Corp in relation thereto.

   11.2.3 prompt written notice being given to A Corp within 30 days following discovery of such defect.

11.3 B Corp shall promptly issue a report to A Corp in respect of each warranty claim brought to its attention.

Clause 12. PATENT INDEMNITY

12.1 In the event that any claim should be brought against B Corp that The Products infringe letters patent or other protected proprietary right, valid at the date of acceptance by A Corp of B Corp's order for such Product, owned by any third party, not being an employee or officer or shareholder of B Corp and not being a subsidiary or associated company of B Corp, then A Corp shall indemnify B Corp against and hold B Corp harmless from any and all damages which may be awarded against B Corp by any Court of competent jurisdiction provided that:

    12.1.1 B Corp notifies A Corp in writing within 30 days of learning of any such claim as aforesaid.

    12.1.2 B Corp permits A Corp to conduct the defense to any such claim as aforesaid and the negotiation of any settlement thereof.

    12.1.3 B Corp provides at the expense of A Corp such assistance as A Corp may require in the defense or settlement of such claim as aforesaid.

    12.1.4 such indemnity and undertaking as aforesaid shall not apply if the infringement relates to any use other than a use authorized by A Corp.

    12.1.5 such indemnity and undertaking as aforesaid shall not apply where the infringement relates to the combination of The Products with equipment not designed, manufactured or sold by A Corp, unless A Corp specifically was aware of and approved such combination in advance thereof.

12.2 A Corp reserves the right to settle any such claim as aforesaid on the basis of substituting non-infringing Products for the alleged infringing Products providing that such substituted Products are capable of performing substantially the same functions as The Products so replaced.

12.3 Such indemnity and undertaking as aforesaid shall not apply in the event the designs, the subject of such claim as aforesaid, were supplied by B Corp's customers. In that event B Corp shall request such customers to indemnify A Corp against any claims made against A Corp alleging the infringement of letters patent or other protected proprietary rights arising out of the use of such designs or the manufacture or sale of Products utilizing such designs.

Clause 13. LIMITATION OF WARRANTY

13.1 The parties hereto agree that the express undertakings of A Corp pursuant to the provisions of the Warranty contained in Clause 11 constitute the only warranties of A Corp and the said undertakings of Clause 11 are in lieu of and in substitution for all other conditions and warranties express or implied INCLUDING WITHOUT LIMITATION ANY WARRANTIES AS TO MERCHANTABILITY OR FITNESS FOR PURPOSE and all other obligations and liabilities whatsoever of A Corp whether in contract or in tort or otherwise, and B Corp shall so inform customers and potential customers. B Corp shall not offer or assume nor authorize anyone to offer to assume for or on behalf of A Corp any other Warranty or similar obligation in connection with The Products other than as authorized by Clause 11 and this Clause 13.

Clause 14. CAPACITY OF THE PARTIES

14.1 B Corp undertakes that it will at all times material to this Agreement make clear to customers and potential customers that it acts in the capacity of agent of A Corp. Except as specifically authorized under the terms of this Agreement, B Corp is not authorized to bind or commit or make representations on behalf of A Corp for any purpose whatsoever, and B Corp shall make this clear to customers and potential customers.

14.2 This Agreement is not intended nor shall it be construed as establishing any form of partnership between the parties.

Clause 15. ASSIGNMENT

The obligations and duties of B Corp hereunder are personal to B Corp and shall not be subcontracted to any third party without the prior written consent of A Corp nor shall B Corp assign this Agreement or any part thereof to any third party without the prior written consent of A Corp.

Clause 16. CONFIDENTIALITY

Any information which may during the currency of this Agreement be divulged by either party to the other on the express written basis that such information is confidential shall be so regarded and be protected whether in storage or in use. Furthermore, any such information shall not be used by the party receiving same otherwise than for the express purpose for which it is divulged and shall not further be divulged except to such of the said party's own servants and agents as may have a "need to know" for the purposes of this Agreement.

Clause 17. DURATION AND TERMINATION

17.1 This agreement shall commence on the date of signature hereof and shall continue unless and until terminated by either party giving to the other not less than 30 days written notice to such effect.

17.2 Any termination in accordance with the provisions of Clause 17.1 above shall not affect the obligations of the parties to fulfill the terms of orders placed and accepted prior to the effective date of such termination.

17.3 If either party should enter into any liquidation, bankruptcy or receivership whether compulsorily or voluntarily or should enter into any Agreement with creditors compounding debts or should suffer the imposition of a receiver in respect of the whole or a material part of its assets or should otherwise become insolvent, then the other party may by notice in writing, forthwith terminate this Agreement.

17.4 Upon termination of this Agreement:

17.4.1 B Corp shall return at its own expense to A Corp any catalogues, sales literature, instruction books, technical pamphlets and advertising material relating to The Products which may have been supplied by A Corp.

17.4.2 B Corp shall immediately cease to trade as an agent of A Corp and shall cease to represent itself in such capacity.

17.4.3 Recognizing that the financial and other commitments to be made by the parties in order to operate this Agreement will be put at risk by a termination pursuant to Clause 17.1 above at any time, the parties agree that any termination by A Corp pursuant to the terms of Clause 17.1, other than a termination pursuant to the terms of Clause 17.3, and other than a termination for cause (which shall include but specifically not be limited to fraud, negligence, breach of the terms of this Agreement), shall entitle B Corp to receive, in addition to sums actually due pursuant to the terms of Clause 17.2 and 17.4.4 herein, an amount equal to the net commissions received by B Corp under this Agreement, during the twelve months immediately preceding the date of notification of such termination, such sum to be paid at the expiration of the 30 day notice period. In the event that termination is by reason of Clause 17.3 herein, or for cause as defined hereinabove, or if termination is at the request or by the notice of B Corp, B Corp shall be entitled only to the amount due to it pursuant to the terms of Clause 17.2 and 17.4.4 herein above. Since the exercise of such right to termination would not constitute any breach of this Agreement such amount as shall be payable as aforesaid shall not be deemed a penalty.

17.4.4   A Corp shall continue to pay commissions on those orders obtained prior to the date of termination as invoices are paid and widgets delivered.

17.4.5   Subsequent to termination of this Agreement by either party in any manner and for any reason whatsoever, neither party shall be prevented or restricted from doing business with any person, corporation, partnership or other business entity within the United States or elsewhere, specifically including but not limited to persons, corporations, partnerships and business entities who have previously purchased A Corp's products, whether through B Corp or otherwise; except that if A Corp terminates this Agreement under circumstances which entitle B Corp to the payment of compensation pursuant to the terms of paragraph 17.4.3 hereinabove, then A Corp agrees that it will not solicit orders from any customers who received the products, or who requested a quotation therefor from B Corp during the currency of this Agreement, for a period of two years from the date of such termination.

Clause 18. NOTICES

Any notice required to be given hereunder shall be sufficiently given if forwarded by any of the following methods: registered mail, cable, telegraph or telex to the registered office of A Corp or the principal office of B Corp as the case may be and shall be deemed to have been received and given at the time when in the ordinary course of transmission it should have been delivered or received at the address to which it was sent.

Clause 19. WAIVER

Failure by either party at any time to enforce any of the provisions of this Agreement shall not constitute a waiver by such party of such provision nor in any way affect the validity of this Agreement.

Clause 20. AMENDMENT

This Agreement may not be amended except by an instrument in writing signed by both parties and made subsequent to the date of this Agreement and which is expressly stated to amend this Agreement.

Clause 21. HEADINGS

The clause headings of this Agreement are for reference purposes only and shall not be deemed to affect the interpretation of any of the provisions of this Agreement.

Clause 22. LAW

This Agreement shall be subject to and interpreted in accordance with the Laws of _____.

IN WITNESS WHEREOF, the parties have caused this Agreement to be signed on their behalf by the hand of a duly authorized officer.

FOR A CORP

_____ (Title)

FOR B CORP

_____ (Title)

DISTRIBUTORSHIP AGREEMENT
(between foreign exporter and U.S. importer/distributor)

AGREEMENT made this _____ day of _____, 20__, by and between A Corp, a company organized under the laws of C Country with its principal place of business located at _____ (hereinafter called the "PRODUCER") and B Corp, located at S State (hereinafter called the "DISTRIBUTOR");

WITNESSETH:

WHEREAS, the PRODUCER is engaged in the design, manufacture and marketing of, among other things, widgets (the "Product"); under the brand name "Widgets."

WHEREAS, the DISTRIBUTOR maintains a marketing organization and markets widgets in the United States; and

WHEREAS, the PRODUCER and DISTRIBUTOR desire to cooperate for the purpose of marketing the product in the United States to civilians under the terms hereinafter set forth;

NOW THEREFORE, in consideration of the foregoing premises, the mutual covenants and agreements contained herein and other good and valuable consideration, the receipt, sufficiency and adequacy of which is hereby acknowledge, the parties hereto agree as follows:

SECTION I. APPOINTMENT

The PRODUCER hereby appoints the DISTRIBUTOR to be its exclusive Distributor of the Product to civilians in the Territories as defined below, and the DISTRIBUTOR hereby accepts that appointment and agrees to act as the exclusive Distributor for the PRODUCER. PRODUCER specifically reserves to itself the right to market the Product to all Local, State and Federal organizations and entities, and the term "civilian" shall not include any such organizations or entities.

A.   As used herein, Territories shall mean the States of _____

_____ .

B.   In addition to paragraph A, Section 1 above, Territories shall also mean all other states east of the Mississippi River at such time as the DISTRIBUTOR delivers to the PRODUCER a marketing plan acceptable to the PRODUCER. DISTRIBUTOR shall have ___ months from the date of this Agreement to deliver such plan.

C.   In addition to paragraphs A and B of Section 1 above, the DISTRIBUTOR shall be given the first option to include all States west of the Mississippi River in the above defined Territories, at such time as the DISTRIBUTOR delivers to the PRODUCER a business and marketing plan acceptable to the PRODUCER for all States west of the Mississippi River. The option shall expire if such a plan is not delivered within ___ months from the date of this Agreement.

SECTION II. SALES AND PROMOTION

A.   Energetically and faithfully use its best efforts to promote the sale of the Product to civilian customers and potential civilian customers throughout the Territories;

B.   Carry continuously and have readily available sufficient quantities of the Product to enable it to promptly meet current demands of all customers;

C.   Agree to price the Product at competitive levels, at wholesale and at retail, to sell the Product in accordance with the customs in the trade and will abstain from using selling methods or practices which, in the PRODUCER'S opinion, are harmful to the reputation of the Product or the PRODUCER;

D.   Employ such technically competent sales, commercial and service staff as may be reasonably necessary;

E.   Vigorously advertise and promote the Product within the Territories and bear all expense therefrom, which shall not be less than US$___ per year;

F.   Attend and participate annually in all significant trade shows and exhibitions, which includes, at the minimum, having a booth for demonstrations, promotions and advertising to all attendees of such shows or exhibitions. The booths should be staffed with technically qualified people. Such trade shows and exhibitions shall include, but is not limited to the following shows: _____ .

G.   Not undertake any obligations or promote/advertise the performance of the Product in excess of the limits specified by the PRODUCER.

H.   Be expressly permitted to make public announcements in the press of its appointment as the exclusive Distributor of the PRODUCER in the appropriate Territories.

I.   Pay for and send the appropriate personnel of the DISTRIBUTOR to the PRODUCER's manufacturing plant for necessary technical update or general orientation should the PRODUCER find it necessary.

J.   Not sell outside of the authorized Territories and if the Product is destined for outside the authorized Territories, the DISTRIBUTOR shall take all necessary and appropriate steps to stop such sales.

SECTION III.   TERM

This Agreement shall be for a term of three years from the date first written above and shall continue from year to year thereafter until either of the parties shall give ___ months written notice to the other prior that this Agreement shall terminate. Should the DISTRIBUTOR not purchase the minimum quantities set forth below, the PRODUCER may, at any time, terminate this Agreement upon ___ days written notice.

SECTION IV.   MINIMUM QUANTITIES

Throughout the term of this Agreement, the PRODUCER shall sell and the DISTRIBUTOR shall purchase from the PRODUCER (and from no other source) such minimum quantities of the Product at the minimum prices hereafter set out:

A.   In the first year of this Agreement, DISTRIBUTOR shall purchase at least US$_____ of the Product from the PRODUCER;

B.   In the first year of this Agreement, the DISTRIBUTOR shall purchase from the PRODUCER at least _____ pieces of the Product kits;

C.   In the second year of this Agreement and every year thereafter, the PRODUCER shall have the option of increasing the above minimum requirements for price and quantities; however, in no event shall any increase by over US$_____ per year, or _____ pieces per year.

SECTION V.   PAYMENT AND TERMS

A.   Payment shall be made by the DISTRIBUTOR to the PRODUCER (unless otherwise directed by PRODUCER) by irrevocable Letter of Credit in US dollars.

B.   The PRODUCER shall sell and the DISTRIBUTOR shall purchase the Products F.O.B. the manufacturing plant at the following prices for the first year:

After _____ months from the date of this Agreement, the PRODUCER shall have the option to raise or lower these prices by giving _____ days notice. However, in no event shall any price be raised by more than _____ percent (___%) per year of the above prices.

C.   Any duty, tax or other charge the PRODUCER may be required by any Federal, State, County, Municipal or other law, now in effect or hereafter enacted, to collect or pay with respect to the sale, delivery or use of the Product shall be added to the prices provided herein exclusive of Paragraph B above and be paid by the Distributor.

Distributor shall also maintain and pay for Product Liability Insurance of US_____ million dollars.

SECTION VI.   LEGAL COMPLIANCE

A.   The DISTRIBUTOR shall comply with all Local, State and Federal laws concerning the Product.

B.   The DISTRIBUTOR shall promptly inform the PRODUCER of all aspects of any new or revised legislation, regulation or orders affecting the use, sale or promotion of the Product in the United States of America.

SECTION VII.   TRADEMARKS, PATENTS, COPYRIGHT AND BRAND-NAMES

A.   Any and all trademarks, patents, copyrights and brand-names now in effect, created, applied for or received in the future, of the Product shall always be and remain the property of the PRODUCER.

B.   The DISTRIBUTOR shall not under any circumstances acquire any rights whatsoever in any trademark, patent, copyright, brand-name or other proprietary right of the PRODUCER.

SECTION VIII.   NONCOMPETITION

A.   The PRODUCER shall, at its discretion, repair or replace any Product at its own expense found by the DISTRIBUTOR to be defective, provided that:

(1)   In the case of visible and apparent defects, immediate written notice is given by the DISTRIBUTOR to the PRODUCER of such defects and the defective Products are returned to the PRODUCER within _____ weeks of the date of their shipment by the PRODUCER;

(2)   In the case of functional or non-apparent defects, written notice is given by the DISTRIBUTOR to the PRODUCER of such defects and the defective Products are returned to the PRODUCER within _____ months of the date of their shipment by the PRODUCER;

B.   The PRODUCER shall pay fifty percent (50%) of the round-trip cost for all validated warranty claims.

C.   The above limited warranty is subject to:

(1)   The Product not being used for any purpose other than the normal purpose that it was manufactured for;

(2)   The observance by the user of all operating instructions and recommendations provided by the PRODUCER; and

(3)   The DISTRIBUTOR's cooperation in and with any investigation by the PRODUCER or its representative with respect to said defects, including but not limited to any reports of the circumstances surrounding the defect.

SECTION IX.   CONFIDENTIALITY

A.   The DISTRIBUTOR shall not, either directly or indirectly, in whole or in part, except as required in the marketing of the Product or by written consent of an authorized representative of the PRODUCER, use or disclose to any person, firm, corporation or other entity, any information of a proprietary nature ("trade secrets") owned by the PRODUCER or any of its affiliated companies, including, but not limited to, records, customer lists, data, formulae, documents, drawings, specifications, inventions, processes, methods and intangible rights.

B.   Any information regarding the Product which, during the term of this Agreement is divulged by either party to the other is confidential and shall be protected from disclosure.

C.   The prohibited use or disclosure, as used herein, shall be for the term of the Agreement and at any time within five (5) years after the termination of this Agreement.

SECTION X.   ASSIGNMENT

The obligations and duties of the DISTRIBUTOR hereunder are personal and shall not be subcontracted or assigned to any third party without the prior written consent of the PRODUCER.

SECTION XI.   TERMINATION AND GOODWILL

A.   In the event that the DISTRIBUTOR shall default in the performance of any of its obligations hereunder, or shall fail to comply with any provision of this Agreement on its part to be performed, and if such default or failure shall continue for _____ days after written notice hereof from the PRODUCER, the PRODUCER may terminate this Agreement and the rights granted to the DISTRIBUTOR hereunder upon written notice to the DISTRIBUTOR, and neither waivers by the PRODUCER nor limitations of time may be asserted as a defense by the DISTRIBUTOR for any such failure or default. Such right of termination shall be in addition to any other rights and remedies of the PRODUCER at law or in equity.

B.   Upon expiration, termination or cancellation of this Agreement pursuant to the provisions of Section III, Section XI, or for any other reason, with or without cause, the PRODUCER will not be liable for, and the DISTRIBUTOR will not be entitled to, any compensation of any kind for goodwill or any other tangible or intangible elements of damages or costs, nor shall the PRODUCER be liable to the DISTRIBUTOR for any special or consequential damages of any kind or nature whatsoever.

C.   Upon the expiration of the term of this Agreement or any renewal thereof, the Products in the DISTRIBUTOR'S inventory may be sold, with the PRODUCER'S trademarks or brandnames thereon, only for one year after such expiration, subject to all the terms, covenants and conditions of this Agreement (other than the right of renewal), as though this Agreement had not expired. Any of the Products in the DISTRIB-UTOR'S inventory upon the termination or cancellation of this Agreement for any reason other than the natural expiration of its term, as set forth in Section III hereof, shall remain the property of the DISTRIBUTOR and may be sold only upon the removal of the PRODUCER'S owned trademarks and brandnames from the Products.

SECTION XII.   RELATIONSHIP OF PARTIES

Nothing in this Agreement shall constitute or be deemed to constitute a partnership between the parties hereto. It is understood and agreed that the DISTRIBUTOR is an independent contractor and is not, nor ever will be, an agent or an employee of the PRODUCER. The DISTRIBUTOR shall not have the right, power or authority, express or implied, to bind, assume or create any obligation or liability on behalf of the PRODUCER.

SECTION XIII.   CAPTIONS

The captions in this Agreement are inserted solely for ease of reference and are not deemed to form a part of, or in any way to modify, the text or meaning hereof.

SECTION XIV.   NOTICE

Any notice required to be given shall be deemed to be validly served if sent by prepaid registered or certified airmail to the address(es) stated below or to such other address as may be designated by either party in writing. Said notice shall be effective when posted by either party to said address(es), postage prepaid.

A.   PRODUCER: (address).

B.   DISTRIBUTOR: (address).

SECTION XV. DIVISIBILITY

The provisions of this Agreement contain a number of separate and divisible covenants. Each such covenant shall be construed as a separate covenant and shall be separately enforceable. If a court of competent jurisdiction shall determine that any part of any paragraph or any part of any separate covenant herein contained, is so restrictive as to be deemed void, the remaining part or parts, or the other such separate covenants, shall be considered valid and enforceable, notwithstanding the voidance of such covenant or part of a separate covenant. If certain covenants of this Agreement hereof are so broad as to be unenforceable, it is the desire of the parties hereto that such provisions be read as narrowly as necessary in order to make such provisions enforceable.

SECTION XVI. GOVERNING LAW

This Agreement shall be deemed to have been made in, and the relationship between the parties hereto shall be governed by, the laws of the State of _____, United States of America.

SECTION XVII. PRIOR AGREEMENTS

This Agreement contains a complete statement of arrangements among and between the parties hereto with respect to its subject matter, supersedes all existing agreements among them concerning the subject matter hereof and cannot be changed or terminated except in writing signed by all parties to this Agreement.

IN WITNESS WHEREOF, the parties hereto have executed this Agreement in duplicate by their duly authorized representatives and affixed their corporate seals (if any) the day and year first above written.

SEAL   PRODUCER:

                                    By: _____
                                    Title:

SEAL   DISTRIBUTOR:

                                    By: _____
                                    Title:

U.S. Export Assistance Center Directory

U.S. Department of Commerce, International Trade Administration, U.S. and Foreign Commercial Service (As of August 2001)

Alabama

Birmingham—George Norton, Director
950 22nd Street North, Room 707, ZIP: 35203
Phone: (205) 731-1331
Fax: (205) 731-0076

Alaska

Anchorage—Chuck Becker, Director
550 West 7th Ave., Suite 1770, ZIP: 99501
Phone: (907) 271-6237
Fax: (907) 271-6242

Arizona

Phoenix—Frank Woods, Director
2901 N. Central Ave., Suite 970, ZIP: 85012
Phone: (602) 640-2513
Fax: (602) 640-2518

Tucson—Eric Nielsen, Manager
166 West Alameda, ZIP: 85701
Phone: (520) 670-5540
Fax: (520) 791-5413

Arkansas

Little Rock—Lon J. Hardin, Director
425 W. Capitol Ave., Suite 700, ZIP: 72201
Phone: (501) 324-5794
Fax: (501) 324-7380

California

Cabazon—Cynthia Torres, Actg Int'l
  Trade Specialist
84-245 Indio Springs Drive
Indio, ZIP 92203-3499
Phone: 760-342-4455
Fax: 760-342-3535

Fresno—Eduardo Torres, Manager
390-B Fir Avenue, Clovis, ZIP: 93611
Phone: (559) 325-1619
Fax: (559) 325-1647

Inland Empire—Fred Latuperissa,
  Manager
2940 Inland Empire Blvd, Suite 121,
Ontario, ZIP: 91764
Phone: (909) 466-4134
Fax: (909) 466-4140

Los Angeles (Downtown)
Rachid Sayouty, Director
350 S. Figueroa St., Suite 509, ZIP:
  90071
Phone: (213) 894-8784
Fax: (213) 894-8789

Los Angeles (West)—JulieAnne
  Hennessy, Director
11150 Olympic Blvd., Suite 975, ZIP:
  90064
Phone: (310) 235-7104
Fax: (310) 235-7220

Monterey—Mark A. Weaver, Director
411 Pacific St., Suite 316A, ZIP:
  93940
Phone: (831) 641-9850
Fax: (831) 641-9849

North Bay—Elizabeth Krauth,
  Manager
4040 Civic Center Dr., Suite 200,
San Rafael, ZIP: 94903
Phone: (415) 492-4546/4548
Fax: (415) 492-4549

Oakland—Rod Hirsch, Manager
530 Water Street, Suite 740, ZIP:
  94607
Phone: (510) 273-7350
Fax: (510) 273-7352

Newport Beach (Orange County)
Richard Swanson, Director
Paul Tambakis, CS Director, Southern
  California and Arizona
3300 Irvine Ave, #305, ZIP: 92660
Phone: (949) 660-1688
Fax: (949) 660-1338

Ventura County—Gerald Vaughn,
  Manager
5700 Ralston Street, Suite 310,
  Ventura, ZIP: 93003
Phone: (805) 676-1573
Fax: (805) 676-1892

Sacramento—Dale Wright, Manager
917 7th Street, 2nd Floor, ZIP: 95814
Phone: (916) 498-5155
Fax: (916) 498-5923

San Diego—Matt Andersen, Director
6363 Greenwich Drive, Suite 230,
  ZIP: 92122
Phone: (619) 557-5395
Fax: (619) 557-6176

San Francisco—Stephan Crawford,
  Director
250 Montgomery St., 14th Floor,
  ZIP:94104
Phone: (415)705-2300
Fax: (415) 705-2297

San Jose (Silicon Valley) USEAC
Cluster—Greg Mignano, Director
Silicon Valley—Joanne Vliet,
Manager
125 South Market Street, Suite 1001,
ZIP: 95113
Phone: (408) 271-7300
Fax: (408) 271-7307

Colorado

Denver (Rocky Mountain)—Stephen
Craven, Director
World Trade Center
1625 Broadway, Suite 680, Denver,
ZIP: 80202
Phone: (303) 844-6001
Fax: (303) 844-5651

Connecticut

Middletown—Carl Jacobsen, Director
213 Court Street, Suite 903 ZIP:
06457-3346
Phone: (860) 638-6950
Fax: (860) 638-6970

Delaware

Served by the Philadelphia EAC

District of Columbia

Served by the Northern Virginia
Export Assistance Center

Florida

Clearwater—George Martinez,
Manager
1130 Cleveland Street, ZIP: 33755
Phone: (727) 893-3738
Fax: (727) 449-2889

Ft. Lauderdale—John McCartney,
Director
200 E. Las Olas Blvd., Suite 1600,
ZIP: 33301
Phone: (954) 356-6640
Fax: (954) 356-6644

Miami—Michael McGee, Director
BuyUSA
777 North West 72nd Ave
Mail Box: 3L2, ZIP 33126-3009
Phone: (305) 526-7425 ext. 22
Fax: (305) 526-7434

Orlando—Philip A. Ouzts, Manager
200 E. Robinson Street, Suite 1270,
ZIP: 32801
Phone: (407) 648-6235
Fax: (407) 648-6756

Tallahassee—Michael Higgins,
Manager
The Atrium Building
325 John Knox Rd., Suite 201, ZIP:
32303
Phone: (850) 942-9635
Fax: (850) 922-9595

Georgia

Atlanta—Samuel P. Troy, Director
285 Peachtree Center Ave. NE, #900
ZIP: 30303-1229
Phone: (404) 657-1900
Fax: (404) 657-1970

Savannah—Barbara Myrick, Manager
6001 Chatham Center Dr., Suite 100,
ZIP: 31405
Phone: (912) 652-4204
Fax: (912) 652-4241

Hawaii/Pacific Islands

Honolulu—Robert Murphy, Director
1001 Bishop St., Pacific Tower
Suite 1140, ZIP: 96813
Phone: (808) 522-8040
Fax: (808) 522-8045

Idaho

Boise—James Hellwig, Manager
700 West State Street, 2nd Floor, ZIP:
83720
Phone: (208) 334-3857
Fax: (208) 334-2783

Illinois

Chicago—Mary N. Joyce, Director
55 West Monroe Street, Suite 2440,
ZIP: 60603
Phone: (312) 353-8045
Fax: (312) 353-8120

Highland Park—Robin F. Mugford,
Manager
610 Central Avenue, Suite 150, ZIP:
60035
Phone: (847) 681-8010
Fax: (847) 681-8012

Peoria—David Genovese, Manager
922 N. Glenwood Ave., Jobst Hall,
Room 141, ZIP: 61606
Phone: (309) 671-7815
Fax: (309) 671-7818

Rockford—Director (Vacant)
515 N. Court St., ZIP: 61103
Phone: (815) 987-8123
Fax: (815) 963-7943

Indiana

Indianapolis—Mark Cooper, Director
11405 N. Pennsylvania Street, Suite
106, Carmel, ZIP: 46032
Phone: (317) 582-2300
Fax: (317) 582-2301

Iowa

Des Moines—Allen Patch, Director
Partnership Building
700 Locust Street, Suite 100, ZIP:
50309
Phone: (515) 288-8614
Fax: (515) 288-1437

Kansas

Wichita—George D. Lavid, Manager
209 East William, Suite 300, ZIP:
67202-4012
Phone: (316) 263-4067
Fax: (316) 263-8306

Kentucky

Lexington—Sara Melton, Manager
4th Floor, Lexington Central Library
140 E. Main Street, ZIP: 40507
Phone: (859) 225-7001
Fax: (859) 225-6501

Louisville—John Autin, Director
601 W. Broadway, Room 634B, ZIP:
40202
Phone: (502) 582-5066
Fax: (502) 582-6573

Somerset—Sandra Munsey, Manager
2292 S. Highway 27, Suite 240, ZIP:
42501
Phone: (606) 677-6160
Fax: (606) 677-6161

Louisiana

New Orleans (Delta)—Donald Van
  De Werken, Director
365 Canal St., #1170, ZIP: 70130
Phone: (504) 589-6546
Fax: (504) 589-2337

Shreveport—Patricia Holt, Manager
7100 West Park Drive, ZIP: 71129
Phone: (318) 676-3064
Fax: (318) 676-3063

Maine

Portland—Jeffrey Porter, Manager
c/o Maine International Trade Center
511 Congress Street, ZIP: 04101
Phone: (207) 541-7400
Fax: (207) 541-7420

Maryland

Baltimore—Thomas Cox, Director
World Trade Center
401 E. Pratt Street, Suite 2432, ZIP:
  21202
Phone: (410) 962-4539
Fax: (410) 962-4529

Massachusetts

Boston—Frank J. O'Connor, Director
World Trade Center
164 Northern Ave., Suite 307, ZIP:
  02210
Phone: (617) 424-5990
Fax: (617) 424-5992

Michigan

Detroit—Neil Hesse, Director
211 W. Fort Street, Suite 2220, ZIP:
  48226
Phone: (313) 226-3650
Fax: (313) 226-3657

Grand Rapids—Thomas Maguire,
  Manager
301 W. Fulton St., Suite 718-S, ZIP:
  49504
Phone: (616) 458-3564
Fax: (616) 458-3872

Pontiac—Richard Corson, Manager
250 Elizabeth Lake Rd., Suite 1300
  West, ZIP: 48341
Phone: (248) 975-9600
Fax: (248) 975-9606

Ypsilanti—Paul Litton, Manager
c/o Eastern Michigan University
300 W. Michigan Avenue, Suite 311
  Owen, ZIP: 48197
Phone: (734) 487-0259
Fax: (734) 485-2396

Minnesota

Minneapolis—Ronald E. Kramer,
  Director
45 South 7th Street, Suite 2240, ZIP:
  55402
Phone: (612) 348-1638
Fax: (612) 348-1650

Mississippi

Mississippi—Harrison Ford, Manager
704 East Main St., Raymond, ZIP:
  39154
Phone: (601) 857-0128
Fax: (601) 857-0026

Missouri

St. Louis—Randall J. LaBounty,
Director
8182 Maryland Avenue, Suite 303,
ZIP: 63105
Phone: (314) 425-3302
Fax: (314) 425-3381

Kansas City—David McNeill, Director
2345 Grand, Suite 650, ZIP: 64108
Phone: (816) 410-9201
Fax: (816) 410-9208

Montana

Missoula—Mark Peters, Director
c/o Montana World Trade Center
Gallagher Business Building, Suite
257, ZIP: 59812
Phone: (406) 542-6656
Fax: (406) 243-5259

Nebraska

Omaha—Meredith Bond, Manager
11135 "O" Street, ZIP: 68137
Phone: (402) 221-3664
Fax: (402) 221-3668

Nevada

Las Vegas—William E. Cline,
Manager
400 Las Vegas Blvd. South
Las Vegas, ZIP: 89101
Phone: (702) 229-1157
Fax: (702) 385-3128

Reno—Jere Dabbs, Manager
1755 East Plumb Lane, Suite 152,
ZIP: 89502
Phone: (775) 784-5203
Fax: (775) 784-5343

New Hampshire

Portsmouth—Susan Berry, Manager
17 New Hampshire Avenue, ZIP:
03801-2838
Phone: (603) 334-6074
Fax: (603) 334-6110

New Jersey

Newark—William Spitler, Director
One Gateway Center, 9th Floor, ZIP:
07102
Phone: (973) 645-4682
Fax: (973) 645-4783

Trenton—Rod Stuart, Director
3131 Princeton Pike, Bldg. 4, Ste.
105, ZIP: 08648-2319
Phone: (609) 989-2100
Fax: (609) 989-2395

New Mexico

Santa Fe—Sandra Necessary, Manager
c/o New Mexico Dept. of Economic
Development
1100 St. Francis Drive, ZIP: 87503
Phone: (505) 827-0350
Fax: (505) 827-0263

New York

Buffalo—James Mariano, Director
111 West Huron Street, Rm. 1304,
ZIP: 14202
Phone: (716) 551-4191
Fax: (716) 551-5290

Harlem—K.L. Fredericks, Manager
163 W. 125th St., Suite 904, ZIP:
10027
Phone: (212) 860-6200
Fax: (212) 860-6203

Long Island—George Soteros,
  Manager
1550 Franklin Avenue, Room 207,
  Mineola, ZIP: 11501
Phone: (516) 739-1765
Fax: (516) 739-3310

New York—William Spitler, Director
Formerly in the World Trade Center.
  New address not available as of
  publication date.

Rochester—Charles Ranado, Manager
400 Andrews Street, Suite 710, ZIP:
  14604
Phone: (716) 263-6480
Fax: (716) 325-6505

Westchester—Joan Kanlian, Director
707 Westchester Ave., Suite 209,
  White Plains, ZIP: 10604
Phone: (914) 682-6712
Fax: (914) 682-6698

North Carolina

Charlotte (Carolinas)—Roger Fortner,
  Director
521 E. Morehead St., Suite 435, ZIP:
  28202
Phone: (704) 333-4886
Fax: (704) 332-2681

Greensboro—Debbie Strader, Acting
  Director
400 West Market Street, Suite 102,
  ZIP: 27401
Phone: (336) 333-5345
Fax: (336) 333-5158

Raleigh—Debbie Strader, Director
Triangle Export Assistance Center
5 West Hargett Street, Suite 600, ZIP:
  27601
Phone: (919) 715-7373, Ext. 612
Fax: (919) 715-7777

North Dakota

Served by the Minneapolis EAC

Ohio

Akron—Sue Strumbel, Manager
One Cascade Plaza, 8th Floor, ZIP:
  44308
Phone: (330) 376-5550
Fax: (330) 375-5612

Cincinnati—Dao Le, Director
36 East 7th Street, Suite 2650, ZIP:
  45202
Phone: (513) 684-2944
Fax: (513) 684-3227

Cleveland—Michael Miller, Director
600 Superior Avenue, East, Suite 700,
  ZIP: 44114
Phone: (216) 522-4750
Fax: (216) 522-2235

Columbus—Manager (Vacant)
Two Nationwide Plaza, Suite 1400,
  ZIP: 43215
Phone: (614) 365-9510
Fax: (614) 365-9598

Toledo—Robert Abrahams, Director
300 Madison Avenue, ZIP: 43604
Phone: (419) 241-0683
Fax: (419) 241-0684

Oklahoma

Oklahoma City—Ronald L. Wilson,
  Director
301 Northwest 63rd Street, Suite 330,
  ZIP: 73116
Phone: (405) 608-5302
Fax: (405) 608-4211

Tulsa—Jim Williams, Manager
700 N. Greenwood Avenue, Suite
  1400, ZIP: 74106
Phone: (918) 581-7650
Fax: (918) 581-6263

Oregon

Eugene—John O'Connell, Director
1401 Willamette St., ZIP: 97401
Phone: (541) 242-2384, FAX (541)
  465-8833

Portland—Scott Goddin, Director
One World Trade Center
121 S.W. Salmon Street, Suite 242,
  ZIP: 97204
Phone: (503) 326-3001
Fax: (503) 326-6351

Pennsylvania

Harrisburg—Deborah Doherty,
  Manager
One Commerce Square
228 Walnut St, #850, P.O. Box 11698,
  ZIP: 17108-1698
Phone: (717) 221-4510
Fax: (717) 221-4505

Philadelphia—Edward Burton,
  Director
The Curtis Center, Suite 580 West,
Independence Square West, ZIP:
  19106
Phone: (215) 597-6101
Fax: (215) 597-6123

Pittsburgh—Keith Kirkham, Director
2002 Federal Bldg., 1000 Liberty Ave.,
  ZIP: 15222
Phone: (412) 395-5050
Fax: (412) 395-4875

Puerto Rico

San Juan (Hato Rey)—Vacant,
  Director
525 F.D. Roosevelt Ave, Suite 905,
  ZIP: 00918
Phone: (787) 766-5555
Fax: (787) 766-5692

Rhode Island

Providence—Keith Yatsuhashi,
  Manager
One West Exchange Street, ZIP:
  02903
Phone: (401) 528-5104
Fax: (401) 528-5067

South Carolina

Charleston—Phil Minard, Manager
5300 International Blvd., Suite 201-C,
North Charleston, ZIP: 29418
Phone: (843) 760-3794
Fax: (843) 760-3798

Columbia—Ann Watts, Director
1835 Assembly Street, Suite 172, ZIP:
  29201
Phone: (803) 765-5345
Fax: (803) 253-3614

Greenville (Upstate)—Denis
  Csizmadia, Manager
555 N. Pleasantburg Drive
Bldg. 1, Suite 109, ZIP: 29607
Phone: (864) 271-1976
Fax: (864) 271-4171

South Dakota

Sioux Falls—Cinnamon King,
  Manager
Augustana College, 2001 S. Summit
  Avenue,
Madsen Center, Room 122,
  ZIP: 57197
Phone: (605) 330-4264
Fax: (605) 330-4266

Tennessee

Knoxville—George Frank, Manager
601 West Summit Hill Drive
Suite 300, ZIP: 37902-2011
Phone: (865) 545-4637
Fax: (865) 545-4435

Memphis—Ree Russell, Manager
Buckman Hall, 650 E. Parkway South,
  Suite 348, ZIP: 38104
Phone: (901) 323-1543
Fax: (901) 320-9128

Nashville—Dean Peterson, Director
211 Commerce Street, 3rd Floor, Suite
  100, ZIP: 37201
Phone: (615) 259-6060
Fax: (615) 259-6064

Texas

Austin—Karen Parker, Manager
1700 Congress, 2nd Floor, ZIP: 78701
P.O. Box 12728, ZIP: 78711
Phone: (512) 916-5939
Fax: (512) 916-5940

Fort Worth—Vavie Sellschopp,
  Manager
711 Houston Street, ZIP: 76102
Phone: (817) 212-2673
Fax: (817) 978-0178

Houston—James D. Cook, Director
500 Dallas, Suite 1160, ZIP: 77002
Phone: (713) 718-3062
Fax: (713) 718-3060

Arlington—Daniel Swart, Director
2000 East Lamar Blvd., Suite 430,
  ZIP: 76006
Phone: (817) 277-1313
Fax: (817) 299-9601

San Antonio—Daniel G. Rodriguez,
  Manager
203 South St. Mary's Street, Suite
  360, ZIP: 78205
Phone: (210) 228-9878, FAX (210)
  228-9874

Utah

Salt Lake City—Stanley Rees,
  Director
324 S. State Street, Suite 221, ZIP:
  84111
Phone: (801) 524-5116
Fax: (801) 524-5886

Vermont

Montpelier—Susan Murray, Manager
National Life Building, 6th Floor, ZIP:
   05620-0501
Phone: (802) 828-4508
Fax: (802) 828-3258

Virginia

Northern Virginia—Greg Sizemore,
   Director
1401 Wilson Boulevard, Suite 1225,
   Arlington, ZIP: 22209
Phone: (703) 524-2885
Fax: (703) 524-2649

Richmond—Carol Kim, Manager
400 N 8th St., #540, ZIP: 23240-0026
P.O. Box 10026, ZIP: 23240
Phone: (804) 771-2246
Fax: (804) 771-2390

Washington

Seattle—David Spann, Director
2601 Fourth Ave, Suite 320, ZIP:
   98121
Phone: (206) 553-5615
Fax: (206) 553-7253

Snohomish County—Richard Henry,
   Director
c/o Office of the County Executive
3000 Rockefeller Ave., Everett, ZIP:
   98201
Phone: (425) 388-3052
Fax: (425) 388-3434

Spokane—Janet Daubel, Director
Spokane Regional Chamber of
   Commerce
801 W. Riverside Ave, Suite 400, ZIP:
   99201
Phone: (509) 353-2625
Fax: (509) 353-2449

Tacoma—Bob Deane, Director
950 Pacific Avenue, Suite 410, ZIP:
   98402
Phone: (253) 593-6736
Fax: (253) 383-4676

West Virginia

Charleston—Harvey Timberlake,
   Director
405 Capitol Street, Suite 807, ZIP:
   25301
Phone: (304) 347-5123
Fax: (304) 347-5408

Wheeling—David Kotler, Director
Wheeling Jesuit University/NTTC
316 Washington Ave., ZIP: 26003
Phone: (304) 243-5493
Fax: (304) 243-5494

Wisconsin

Milwaukee—Paul D. Churchill,
   Director
517 E. Wisconsin Avenue, Room 596,
   ZIP: 53202
Phone: (414) 297-3473
Fax: (414) 297-3470

Wyoming

Served by the Denver Export
   Assistance Center

REGIONAL—ADMINISTRATIVE OFFICES:

Eastern Region

Thomas McGinty, Regional Director
WTC, Suite 2450, 401 E. Pratt St.,
  Baltimore, MD 21202
Phone: (410) 962-2805
Fax: (410) 962-2799

Mideastern Region

James Kennedy, Regional Director
36 E. 7th St., Suite 2025, Cincinnati,
  OH 45202
Phone: (513) 684-2947
Fax: (513) 684-3200

Midwestern Region

Sandra Gerley, Regional Director
8182 Maryland Ave, Suite 1011
  St. Louis, MO 63105
Phone: (314) 425-3300
Fax: (314) 425-3375

Western Region

Mary Delmege, Regional Director
250 Montgomery St., 14th Floor, San
  Francisco, CA 94104
Phone: (415) 705-2300/2310
Fax: (415) 705-2299

E-Commerce Task Force (ECTF)
Sylvia Burns, Acting Director
Mailing: 14th and Constitution Ave.,
  NW, Room 3810
Washington, DC 20230
Location: 1300 Pennsylvania Ave.,
  NW
USA Trade Center, Mezzanine Level
Washington, DC 20004
Phone: (202) 482-6463
Fax: (202) 482-5495

BUYUSA—Miami
Michael McGee, Director
777 North West 72nd Ave.
Mail Box: 3L2
Miami, FL 33126-3009
Phone: (305) 526-7430
Fax: (305) 526-7434

Product-Specific Customs Information

To get information about regulations on importing specific products, you can do the following:

- Look on the Customs web site for duties, rulings (especially New York rulings) and other information about your product. These are at www.customs.gov/impoexpo/impoexpo.htm.

- Contact Customs at the port through which you want to bring in the merchandise. The ports are listed on the Customs web site.

- As a last resort, if you still have unanswered questions, contact a U.S. Customs National Import Specialist in New York. The following is a list of the product assignments and telephone numbers as of June 2001. Specialists' names are not given because they change frequently. They can be contacted by phone at (646) 733-3000 or fax (646) 733-3250.

Commodities

- Automobiles, motorcycles, special purpose vehicles, bicycles, and parts for all above
- Valves, pumps, fans, gears, transmissions, and bearings
- Heavy industrial machinery
- Furnaces, refrigeration, filtering and purifying apparatus, molds, weighing machinery, textile and dry cleaning machinery, and machine tools
- Navigational, surveying, drafting and drawing, X-ray, other radiation, measuring and testing instruments and apparatus, counters, medical

apparatus, regulating and controlling apparatus, and tariff number (HTS) 9014-9033 except medical

- Agricultural machinery, engines, tractors, railroad and rail equipment, vessels, aircraft, excavating machinery, mechanical appliances for projecting, dispersing or spraying liquids or powders; machinery, and plant or laboratory equipment for treating materials through a change in temperature

- Consumer electronics, televisions, radios, tape/CD player/recorders, cellular telephones, transmitters/receivers, and software

- Telecommunications equipment, electronic components, resisters, rectifiers, capacitors, semiconductor components, transformers, and tubes

- Data processing machinery, office machines, copiers, and computers

- Electrical articles, conduits, relays, structures, batteries, and magnets

- Small household appliances, stoves, locks, hinges and hardware, metal decorative articles, metal containers, electric motors, metal kitchen and cookware, key chains, cutlery, articles of iron and steel, and other metal articles

- Cameras, optical equipment, watches, and clocks

- Iron and steel of Chapter 72/pipe and tube fittings, chain, wire rope, cable and cloth of Chapter 73

- Fasteners (bolts and screws), springs, needles, nonferrous metals, precious metals, coins, and hand tools

- Plastic and rubber monofilaments, rods, profile shapes, sheet, tubes, pipes, hoses, containers, builders' ware and miscellaneous articles except household, and writing instruments

- Artificial flowers, Christmas decorations, tires, clasps, buttons, plastic household articles, zippers, and buckles

- Games, stuffed animals, inflatable articles, balls, sports equipment, firearms, and ammunition

- Models, dolls, toys and stress balls, and puzzles

- Glass, stone, abrasives, nonmetallic minerals, ores, and ash and residue

- Ceramic products, musical instruments, electric lamps, and lighting fittings

- Fruits, vegetables, and edible preparations

- Wood products, cork products, and manufactures of plaiting materials
- Tobacco, plants, grains, spices, nuts, animal feeds, live animals, meat, fish, dairy products (cheese), products of animal origin, and smokers' articles (lighters, pipes)
- Beer, distilled spirits, juices, oils, sugar, confectionery, cocoa, coffee, tea, beverages, oil-bearing seeds, seaweed, and other algae
- Furniture, antiques, sculptures, works of art, drawings, jewelry, combs, barrettes, brushes, and mops
- Paper products, printed matter, paper pulp, and labels
- Glue, pigments, waxes, gelatin, fertilizers, paint, varnish, film, inorganic chemicals, surface active agents, soap
- Synthetic polymers in primary forms, natural and synthetic rubber in primary forms, petroleum and motor oil, explosives, candles, graphites, starches, dextrins, and ethyl alcohol
- Drugs, bandages, pharmaceutical plants, vegetable saps and extracts, diagnostic and laboratory reagents, enzymes, and pesticides
- Organic chemical compounds, dye, and miscellaneous chemical products (including mixtures)
- Luggage, handbags, flat goods, travel bags, and cases
- Footwear and footwear parts
- Blankets; bed, table, toilet, and kitchen linen; textile furnishings, wall hangings, curtains, drapes, mattresses, quilts, comforters, pillows, cushions, wigs, floor coverings, rugs, carpeting, and linoleum
- Wadding, felt, nonwoven coated/filled fabric, machine belts, technical-use fabric, fish nets and netting, and trimmings
- Fibers, yarns, rope, cordage, narrow woven fabrics and ribbons, packing bags, tents, sleeping bags, and miscellaneous textile articles (except apparel and furnishings)
- Woven, lace, net, knitted, pile, tufted, and embroidered fabrics
- Leather, down, plastic, fur, and beaded wearing apparel, belt NSPF, leather/fur articles, scarves, ties, visors, handkerchiefs, hosiery, wigs, disposable apparel, feathers, umbrellas, uniforms, headwear, diapers, and Bible book covers
- Underwear (except T-shirts), body support garments, and gloves
- Men's and boys' woven (8-20) , all swimwear except children's below size 7

- Men's/women's/boys' woven outerwear, coated garments, and tracksuits
- All children's apparel, sizes newborn to girls' 16 and boys' 7 (except underwear for boys/girls 2T and above)
- Women's knit coats, capes, suits, ensembles, sweaters, dresses, vests, and tracksuits
- Women's woven apparel excluding bottoms, woven sleepwear
- Other women's knitwear, women's woven bottoms excluding tops, knit sleepwear

Index

Figures are indicated in *italics*.

About the Author

Kenneth D. Weiss is the owner of Plans and Solutions Inc., for planning and problem solving in business, marketing, and international trade. He has lived and worked in Africa, Asia, and Latin America and has wide experience as a practitioner, consultant, and trainer in importing and exporting. He works in English, Spanish, and French. His formal education includes degrees in business from the University of Minnesota and Stanford and doctoral studies at Pace University in New York.